SWEDISH AND GERMAN LIBERALISM

Swedish and German Liberalism

From Factions to Parties 1860–1920

Martin Åberg

NORDIC ACADEMIC PRESS

In memory of my father

Nordic Academic Press
P.O. Box 1206
S-221 05 Lund, Sweden
info@nordicacademicpress.com
www.nordicacademicpress.com

© Nordic Academic Press and Martin Åberg 2011
Typesetting: Stilbildarna i Mölle, Frederic Täckström, www.sbmolle.com
Cover: Maria Jörgel Andersson
Cover image: The 1896 People's Assembly, Stockholm. Mauritz Hellberg's
collection, Folkrörelsernas arkiv för Värmland, Arkivcentrum Karlstad.
Print: ScandBook, Falun 2011
ISBN: 978-91-85509-54-6

Contents

Preface

From one point of view, political parties are an integral part of democracy as we know it today; likewise, for instance, the left–right cleavage is considered as the 'normal' scale along which parties are supposed to orientate themselves. From a historical point of view, however, the very idea of organizing interests in the form of 'parties', as well as clear-cut conceptions of 'left' and 'right', are novel phenomena. We only have to turn back to the early twentieth century to find that the concept of the modern mass party was met with great caution. To contemporary society, 'party' may well have been a necessary solution to the emerging problem of mass politics and political association. This does not mean that the idea was embraced willingly.

Political movements such as socialism, liberalism, and conservatism managed the idea of political association differently. The main argument of this book is that liberals in particular were divided over the idea of party; this because of the individualistic traits embedded in liberal ideology. In terms of organization the result was often what I have labelled 'organization by proxy'. Indeed, this pattern seems not to have been restricted to Sweden specifically but was most likely typical for European liberal movements more generally. This book, then, is about modern liberalism: how it failed the transition to hierarchically organized mass parties, and the consequences in a longer perspective. More specifically my focus is on Sweden and Germany.

Generous funding for my research and for the publication of the results has been received from the Swedish Research Council, grants no. 2006-1054 and 2010-6154. Archivists and librarians in Sweden and Germany have most kindly given their help and assistance during the process. I would like to thank the staff at the National Archives in Stockholm, the Regional Archive in Värmland, the

Landesarchiv Schleswig-Holstein, and the Schleswig-Holsteinische Landesbibliothek, Kiel.

It is also with deeply-felt gratitude I thank Tomas Nilsson, Peter Olausson, and Martin Stolare for reading my texts and making valuable suggestions. At an early stage of my research I also had the opportunity to discuss my ideas with Robert Bohn, Universität Flensburg. Also, parts of the analysis – later published in Swedish – were presented at a workshop on liberal party organization in Karlstad in the spring of 2009; I would like to thank in particular Ingrid Åberg for valuable comments. Finally, Gerhard Fellsman has kindly scrutinized my translations from German to English.

Martin Åberg
Henån/Karlstad

Introduction

> It is self-evident that the proposed changes in the electoral procedure will by no means be able to prevent malpractice grounded in lack of knowledge about the electoral procedure as such, or in improper forms of campaigning. The latter, in particular, is illustrated by the recent and disloyal attempts to claim the party label of rival factions as one's own. Should, however, the freedom allowed for by the current procedure continue to be abused in the future, and should political morale likewise fail to correct such abuse, we are left with no other course than to introduce rules of public candidacy and publicly ratified candidacy lists. (Albert Petersson, parliamentarian. Motion to parliament for reform of the election laws in the aftermath of the Swedish 1911 general election.)[1]

Political modernization carries with it a number of common features, regardless of its outcome and timetable. As Inglehart (1997: 315) has pointed out, these include a shift in the power relationships of society. Institutions and organizations embedded in pre-industrial traditions and culture give way to new types of institutions and modes of social action. They tie in closely with the state and derive their legitimacy from strictly legal forms of rationality. Simultaneously, new types of association come to the fore as intermediaries between the individual citizen and the state. The political party is among the most important of these.

However, changes of this kind do not necessarily alone result in democratization. Neither is the juxtaposition of 'tradition' and 'rationality' always an obvious property of political modernization if considered from an empirical point of view. If looked at more closely, this process reveals substantial differences depending on the socioeconomic context. As Barrington Moore (1967) pointed out, the rise of both fascism and communism during the twentieth

9

century bear grim witness to this fact, as does, indeed, more recent developments in the successor states of the Soviet Union. Put simply, the problem identified by Moore and others involves the modes by which constitutional reform and electoral democracy, on the one hand, and grass roots mobilization and democratization of societal values and norm systems, on the other hand, relate to each other.

Included in this issue are questions about the extent to which 'history matters': does successful democratization require a gradual and specific sequence of social, economic and political changes across time? Is it the case that new institutions and new types of organizational structures, such as party systems, need to fall into place in a particular order, and must they occur simultaneously with other types of changes, such as industrialization and the spread of literacy? Although 'sequentialist' arguments, i.e. the assumption that there exists a universal and linear path to democracy, have been challenged, analysts nevertheless tend to agree that time is of the essence, since time allows for democratic institutions and practices to mature and stabilize (Carothers 2007; Berman 2007). In the case of election campaigns, this is illustrated by my introductory example. Whether changes must necessarily follow upon each other in a particular sequence is, however, a different matter. For instance, a focus on countries such as Britain – a 'standard model' of democratization – might, perhaps, be misleading from that perspective. Although British political philosophy exercised great influence on the paths subsequently taken in the Western hemisphere, a comparative approach to countries on the Continent, or Scandinavia in the nineteenth and early twentieth centuries, enables us to better appreciate the great variation and complexity in modes of political modernization and its organizational framework.

The problem – an outline

Viewed from one perspective, conventional wisdom would hold that Swedish democratization was favoured by certain ancient and deeply rooted egalitarian traditions in society; these somehow thrusting the political system down a path stretching towards 'classic' Western-type, liberal democracy (for a recent review, see Andrén 2007: 34–41).

Viewed from another perspective, though, such traditions did not immediately transform into a flawless and smoothly working democratic system, once formal institutions started to allow for it. Indeed, the pitfalls and complications implied by linear interpretations of political modernization can be illustrated in several ways. A case such as Germany is likewise difficult to interpret. The 'Sonderweg hypothesis', an obvious analogy to the sequentialist conception of democratization, has been thoroughly criticized since the 1980s. As a result it has become less credible as an explanation for the German historical pattern and the turn taken towards totalitarianism (see, for instance, Raulet 2001; Gross 2004: 15–17; Clark 2006: xiii–xvi). The manner in which new organizational practices, and most notably political parties, were introduced in modernizing societies of this kind does, however, offer valuable insights into the complicated relation between institutional change and grass roots democratization.

One of the most prominent features of political association in the late nineteenth century was the gradual replacement of 'elite parties' by 'mass parties'. However, to contemporary society itself there was nothing self-evident about this shift. For example, research has pointed out that the Swedish 1911 elections were peculiar due to the fact that they took place shortly after a reform that more than doubled the size of the electorate, i.e. the extension of suffrage to all male adults in 1909 (women won the right to vote only as late as 1918–21).[2] Consequently, the prospect of winning vast numbers of new supporters and votes was apparent to the competing parties, but, importantly, the situation also harboured confusion since mass politics was a relatively speaking new phenomenon in social life (Stolare 2003: 212). The very idea of parties had yet to become widely accepted. Much the same can be said about the development of political parties in Germany or, indeed, many other countries as well, and Sweden was no exception. Hence the topic of this book is about 'the idea of party' in a historical context.

In hindsight it is obvious that parties, and in particular mass parties, were finally accepted as a legitimate means of organizing political interests and channelling grass-roots activism: democratization and political participation became, if not unthinkable, in the expression of Aldrich considered to be 'unworkable' without parties mediating between the individual citizen and government (1995: 3; see also, for instance, Sartori 1976). The reasons for this were fairly straightforward and reflected the mounting difficulties involved with managing politics once more inclusive rules for suffrage had been introduced. Still, these circumstances beg the important question of which *alternative* organizational strategies, although perhaps eventually proven obsolete, redundant, and unsuccessful, were put to the test in the face of the challenges brought about by mass politics. In particular the latter is a relevant topic of inquiry since some political movements, such as most notably liberalism, mobilized support and voters quite successfully right up to the beginning of the twentieth century, but on the foundations of organizations that were neither typical elite parties of the traditional kind, nor typical mass parties. In the following chapters I will forward the hypothesis that liberals, for certain reasons, usually favoured organization *by proxy*. In one sense these proxies were 'secondary organizations', but still at the same time not, compared to trade unions and ancillary social organizations, such as recreational and educational societies in the case of the German and Swedish social democratic parties. Rather, liberal parties were normally a part of large, but loosely-knit networks of non-affiliated associations often lacking any formal ties between them. They evolved into a peculiar breed of hybrid organizations in which traits typical to both elite and mass parties were mixed together (chapter 1). The following, therefore, is to no small extent the history of what might have been. It is the history of a partly lost and forgotten trait of democratization, as much as an account of how modern standards of political association slowly fell into place. Considering the complexities of the problem, however, some limitation of scope is necessary, both for practical reasons as well as for analytical purposes.

Scope and rationale of the study

From one point of view, parties emerged as the obvious and natural means of organizing interests and voters in modernizing political systems. Yet, parties and the kind of new political rationality they embodied were often met with considerable suspicion from all ideological camps in contemporary society. Furthermore, right up to the verge of the twentieth century, liberals in particular regularly opted for alternative strategies in order to manage popular and voter mobilization; this because of ideas on citizenship and political association that were typical for liberalism as an ideology (chapters 1 and 2). Circumstances such as these are not sufficiently explained by standard organizational models of party formation: in other words, I cannot agree with the influential remark made by Maurice Duverger that the ideas and doctrines of parties are a subordinate factor, once the organizational structures have developed (Duverger (1967) [1954]: xiv–xv).[3] Rather, the process must be understood with respect to the relationship between ideology and organizational practice. More precisely I will devote my attention to the organizational behaviour of liberal movements in Sweden and Germany. The focus will be on the 1860–1920 period, although analyzing the historical background conditions of the idea of party will necessarily involve peering back, in certain respects, well into the eighteenth century.[4]

Liberalism as such represents an intriguing organizational problem; suffice it here to say that the tension between individual action and collective behaviour inherent in all organizations was brought to an extreme in the case of liberalism, ultimately because of ideological factors. Although successful from the outset, in the long run liberalism somehow 'failed', in both Sweden and Germany, in part because neither movement made the last, critical transition, to that of tightly-knit, mass-based party. In the first case liberalism lost momentum somewhere between the appearance of nineteenth-century middle-class radicalism, and the gradually more successful grass-roots organization of voters into the Social Democratic Party by the beginning of the next century. Emerging class-based political cleavages, weak middle classes, and the introduction of universal suffrage were part of the picture (Therborn 1989; Stråth 1990b). However, these factors do not provide the entire explanation. In the second case liberalism not only lost ground to socialism. It also became, in the apt expression of Sheehan, more and more 'illiberal', and ended up, somewhat over-simplified, as a pawn of bourgeois and state-centred authoritarian politics (Sheehan 1978; see also Gall 1975).

Firstly, though, these interpretations of liberalism are not entirely justified in light of more recent research.[5] In some parts of both countries liberalism succeeded in retaining vital traits. Still without support from a centralized, mass organization, it remained able to consolidate enough popular support to secure a prominent and occasionally dominant position in public life and politics for an extended period. Organization by proxy was arguably an important part of this pattern. Yet, historical explanation is never contingent on one, single factor. Political association does not occur in a vacuum. Therefore the study of alternative modes of organization logically extends into an analysis of the relationship between organization and liberal ideology on the local level. From that perspective I will stress the contribution of socioeconomic and cultural peculiarities in the local environment to specific modes of organizational behaviour.

Secondly, circumstances such as these favour a comparative approach, since this allows for gauging more precisely *how* uniquely different such alternative organizational strategies really were, and precisely *how* singular different paths of political modernization actually were when scrutinized more closely. Sweden and Germany, countries that epitomize extremely different outcomes of political modernization are suitable for contrasting against each other from that point of view. An in-depth analysis of liberal party formation processes in two entire countries, during a period which encompasses more than one century, is not feasible for practical reasons, though. Furthermore, neither is the choice of countries as the actual units of analysis obvious. Rather, I execute a study of regions, whereas the national level is considered in terms of historical, ideological, and institutional context.

It could be argued that a focus on regions rather than countries imposes limits on how far the results of empirical study can be extended. From one point of view that is, of course, true. At the same time a state-centred perspective, too, tends to be biased when considering the period in question. By the mid-nineteenth century the European nation-states were not wholly consolidated and, not least in such cases as Italy or Germany, still in the process of emerging in terms of political communities. Similarly the parties first to emerge were, generally speaking, local in origin and make-up. Also, modern means of nationwide mass communication were still developing and, for instance, the nomination of candidates and electoral mobilization, i.e. two of the most important tasks of modern political parties, were coordinated on the local and regional rather than the national level. Party systems formation and political practice were different due to regional factors, even in cases where the institutional conditions were otherwise the same (Lipset & Rokkan 1967; Daalder 2001). Parties were therefore not homogeneous bodies with respect to organization or programme. Arguably, this was the case in Sweden at least until the end of the century. A similar pattern, only far more extreme, was typical in Germany, too, because of its long history of political and cultural fragmentation (the federalist traits of the German state are the perhaps best illustration of this feature; see, for instance, Koselleck 2000).

For these reasons I have selected two regions for the purpose of my study. These are the province of Värmland in western central Sweden and the Prussian, formerly Danish, province of Schleswig-Holstein (Map 1). Thus we are dealing not only with two very different countries but also two very different regions. To begin with, however, the modest level of urbanization in large parts of Northern Europe, as well as the relatively speaking late advent of industrialization, must be considered. Together with institutional factors, such as constitution and the design of the electoral system, these particularities played an important part in shaping emerging party systems. This was the case not least in regard to liberalism. True – similarly to the situation in other countries, Swedish liberalism first emerged, in the early nineteenth century, as part of post-1789 urban, middle-class radicalism. Yet, by the turn of the twentieth century, it actually drew most of its support from voters in rural constituencies (chapter 1).

Hence it should be stressed that liberalism in Sweden to a great extent developed under conditions which differed from those more commonly associated with the formation of liberalism, viz. urban and industrialized environments. All other historical, cultural, and institutional differences between Värmland and Schleswig-Holstein set aside, this is an important feature that the regions have in common. Värmland and Schleswig-Holstein differ from each other in almost every possible respect except one: they both have a historical

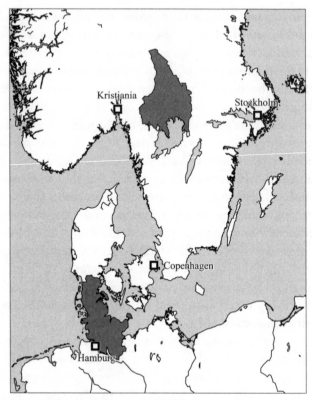

Map 1. The two regions, shaded black.

tradition of above-average strong liberal movements, but movements which unfolded in a rural rather than an urban–industrial setting.

Regions that are extremely *dissimilar* are therefore analyzed in search of a plausible explanation for one *common* feature.[6] Put more succinctly, the common feature in question (i.e. the 'dependent variable') is successful political mobilization, as indicated by high levels of liberal voting turnout in the 1860–1920 period. There should, hypothetically speaking, be at least one common quality (or 'independent variable') that helps explain the electoral successes of liberalism in both of my two otherwise different regions.[7] Presumably ideology may explain negative attitudes to party in both Swedish and German contexts on a more general level. Yet other dimensions must, however, also be explored. Therefore, if we assume that organizational efficacy is, if not decisive, at least incremental to a mobilization of voters, organizational practice and, thus, the regional perspective are brought into focus.[9]

The main question pursued in the following chapters is therefore formulated in the following manner: *how did liberals go about managing political association in Värmland and Schleswig-Holstein respectively?* Answering this question requires a closer historical and qualitative reading of three related issues. Firstly, what was the ideological and institutional context of Swedish and German liberalism? Did Värmland and Schleswig-Holstein somehow differ in comparison to the national level in this respect? Secondly, which were the main features of liberal organizational practice on the regional level? Does evidence render support to the hypothesis of organization by means of proxy? Finally, which additional factors beyond purely organizational ones might help explain the success of liberalism in Värmland and Schleswig-Holstein? What of the importance of the overwhelmingly rural character of both regions in relation to civic and political association?

CHAPTER I

Parties –
the roots of suspicion

The idea of party

The structure and role of parties depend not only on the type of political system or constitutional factors. The design of these organizations is also contingent on historical peculiarities and culture, including competing notions and ideas about the most appropriate manner in which to organize political action. A range of functionalist, organizational, and sociological typologies are possible, as Gunther & Diamond (2001) point out; typologies that, one might add, often neglect the relationship between ideology and party formation. The same authors also warn against the use of 'excessively deductive' models and 'reductionist argumentation' (2001: 6) when approaching the problem. (Duverger's classic distinction between 'cadre parties' and 'mass parties' is presented as a case in point, since social class – i.e. the circumstance that cadre parties were often linked to the middle and upper strata of society, and mass parties to the working class – was reduced by Duverger to a purely organizational factor; ibid.) Indeed, any assessment of real-world parties confirms the immense difficulties involved in defining precisely what a 'political party' is, particularly in a nineteenth-century context.

In our case there was a striking contrast between the liberals and, most notably, the social democrats, both of whom originated as oppositional movements and as radical, anti-establishment alternatives. Eventually, though, only the social democrats clearly opted for a centralized, mass party solution for coping with the grass-roots level, whereas liberal parties during the same period fit better (but far from always) with Gunther & Diamond's description (2001) of elite parties (see also Daalder 2001). True, originally liberal parties were often local and elitist both in composition and, in particular, leadership, but this was not always the case and conditions tended to change across time. Indeed, the notion of 'elitist' is often misleading if their membership structure by the end of the century is considered, not least in regard to Sweden (chapter 2).

The main argument of this book is that liberal parties made frequent use of non-party organizations in order to mobilize support (see later in this chapter). By this I refer to organization using a wide range of intermediate, voluntary organizations typical to nineteenth-century civil society. This strategy resembled the rationale of mass parties more than the pattern characteristic of elite parties, except for one important difference. Liberal support organizations were 'proxies' rather than 'secondary organizations' proper, since they were not normally affiliated with the party organization in any formal sense. They often emerged before the actual formation of parties themselves, and they operated as independent bodies with agendas and goals that were usually 'non-political'. In certain respects, though, their interests would, from time to time, converge with those of the liberals. In part as a consequence of this organizational structure, liberal parties also lacked another feature typical of mass parties; more specifically, highly formalized and centralized bureaucratic structures. Arguably, this pattern holds for both Sweden and Germany during the period. Gradually more inclusive rules for political participation, or variations in external pressure, viz. the often noted circumstance that the German social democrats faced harsher conditions than their Swedish comrades, in particular under Bismarck's Anti-Socialist Laws, 1878–90, does not provide sufficient explanation for the difference between liberal and socialist political association.[1]

For the above reasons, then, the principal *functions* performed by parties and not *typologies* are a more suitable point of departure for studying liberal organizational behaviour. These functions include (1) nomination of candidates, and (2) electoral mobilization, presumably by force of (3) interest aggregation and (4) issue structuring, on the basis of which a party might eventually (5) form and sustain a government (Gunther & Diamond 2001).

Usually these functions are grounded, albeit however loosely, in some kind of ideological concern or political programme, such as in the case of liberal and socialist parties. As result, parties also serve the purpose of (6) societal representation and (7) social integration (Gunther & Diamond 2001). Not all of these criteria are necessarily always met by every party, and least not during the formative phases of party systems. In addition, political practice and emerging modes of organization did differ between different regions, as I have pointed out. For instance, Offerman's analysis (1988) of the left-liberal movements in Cologne and Berlin in the 1860s reveals an interesting variation between the cities with respect to the attitudes towards mass organization as well as parliamentarianism as a principle.

Bearing this in mind, not only electoral mobilization but particularly functions such as societal representation and integration become extremely important from the point of view of democratization. It may not always be self-evident to the individuals themselves, but by nominating candidates for office and by mobilizing voters with the aim of forming a government, parties 'enable citizens to participate effectively in the political process and, if successful in that task, to feel that they have a vested interest in its perpetuation' (Gunther & Diamond 2001: 8). Parties thereby become a mediating arena in which the democratic system has the opportunity to consolidate itself and, among the array of competing practices typical to modernizing political systems, become instituted as 'the only game in town', to follow Linz & Stepan (1996: 5). Still, the demise of the Weimar Republic and the subsequent path taken by Germany illustrates how difficult the long-term outcomes of this process are to predict (cf. Suval 1985).

Although parties were eventually accepted in democratizing societies, accepting is not necessarily the same as embracing them. The political party was more often met with suspicion until well into the twentieth century. Criticism of the 'political morale' of parties was voiced regardless of national setting and ideological orientation. It could, as in my introductory example from the Swedish 1911 general election emanate from a formerly conservative minister of justice, concerned by the lack of 'fair play' in the political game.[2] It could also be voiced by local liberals, such as Emil Rylander from northern Värmland, when running, somewhat hesitantly, for a seat in the 1917 election; in his case concern was raised in regard to the tension between personal conviction and practical necessity implied by formal affiliation to the party.[3] And it could, indeed, be articulated with respect to the growing bureaucracy and alledged democratic deficit of organized socialism, as in Robert Michels' famous (1911) account of the German Social Democratic Party ('Sozialdemokratische Partei Deutschlands', SPD).

Examples such as these are in no sense unique in the history of democracy, since a political system in transition and its key actors may, at least theoretically, choose between any number of organizational strategies to manage mass politics. The mere variety of functions performed by parties suggests that the formation of 'typical' mass parties was but one of several hypothetical solutions. Obviously, too, the problem of party system formation involves the issue of gradual change and adjustment versus institutional incentives. Importantly, however, whatever the merits of 'sequentialist' and 'non-sequentialist' arguments alike, they do not wholly explain the transition from traditional, community based forms of association and elite parties, and the channelling of social action into new types of organizations, such as the modern political party. For example, the coming together of a fully-fledged, clearly left-right orientated, mass party system was closely related to the franchise in Sweden. In Germany the reform of the election laws in the late 1860s did not achieve the same effects on a systemic level. A different analytical approach is therefore called for.

Ultimately, the problem of how the modern political party emerged is one of *social cooperation*, and a problem which involved ideological considerations from those involved, as well as practical, organizational tasks. To begin with, it is easy to demonstrate a long tradition of philosophical arguments raised against the very idea of party; arguments the pros and cons of which filtered down into the political ideologies of conservatives, liberals, and socialists alike around Europe. A few examples will suffice in order to illustrate my point. David Hume, for instance, the great Enlightenment advocate of voluntary cooperation, voiced considerable suspicion towards political parties in his famous essays. According to Hume's view, parties – or 'factions', as he knew them – 'subvert government, render laws impotent, and beget the fiercest animosities among men of the same nation, who ought to give assistance and protection to each other' (Hume 1904 [1741–42]: 55).[4]

Similar arguments, although framed by different historical considerations to those of Hume, were, as indicated, also widespread in nineteenth-century Sweden and Germany. For one thing, the very meaning of 'party' as well as the implications of 'membership' remained uncertain. Partisanship and factionalism were abhorred, although the latter often arose precisely because of the lack of organizational stability and transparency. In relation to the German states, it has been noted how early liberals – in this particular case Hamburg liberals in the late 1840s – held a sceptical view of party and the formal organization of political interests. Following Breuilly, parties were considered 'sectional' and 'divisive' (Breuilly 1994: 223). Likewise, fear of factional strife, real or imagined, was to haunt the Schleswig-Holstein liberals, too, from the very first all-German elections in 1871 onwards.[5]

Considerations such as these necessitate, as a first step of my analysis, a focus on arguments on the idea of party from a historical, ideological, and institutional (particularly constitutional) perspective. Doing so involves dissecting the contradictory but nevertheless close relationship that has, historically speaking, existed between the idea of party and the problem of social cooperation, including the rise of new modes of civic association from the Enlightenment onwards. One relevant topic of debate from that perspective was, of course, Adam Ferguson's 1767 essay on 'civil society': could political parties actually be considered a part of civil society in the new, post-1789 political landscape? Or did parties belong to another realm?

Clearly, for instance, notions such as 'civil society' and 'party' implied one kind of political rationality in British usage, but evoked another frame of mind in regard to voluntary association and, importantly, citizenship in the Swedish or German context. For instance, as Jürgen Kocka (2005: 36) has pointed out, the positive connotations of 'civil society' lasted longer in Britain and France compared with the German states, where the 'semantic change from "Zivilgesellschaft" or "Bürgergesellschaft" to "Bürgerliche Gesellschaft"' implied a 'basic devaluation of the concept', following Hegel's and Marx' inclusion of the market in it.[6] Consequently, establishing a fundamental difference between organizations in a historical perspective in terms of 'civil', or 'civic association', and 'political association' respectively is a notoriously difficult and most likely impossible task. I will use the terms 'civic' and 'political association' and consider them, in principle, as subsets of 'civil society' when voluntary association is referred to more commonly in the following, but it is possible to address the problem in more detail only in connection to specific cases.[7] Although sharing certain philosophical and ideological traits rooted in a more common, European intellectual tradition, Sweden and Germany illustrate ample variation in the manner of how the 'idea of party' was eventually managed. Clarifying the logic of this problem also includes providing the historical background and rationale of my comparison of Värmland and Schleswig-Holstein. This comparison constitutes the link between my concern for political modernization and the second step of my inquiry, viz. patterns of liberal organizational practice and behaviour at the regional level.

Interestingly, it would seem that it was liberals, rather than conservatives or socialists, who had most difficulties in adapting to the idea of party. At this point we confront something of a paradox. The evolution of political parties was an integral part of democratization, although parties were simultaneously met with suspicion. Yet, even if attitudes among nineteenth-century liberals capture this ambiguity very nicely, it should also be noted that among the major ideological camps of the time, liberals were also among the earliest to attempt nationwide organization and national election campaigns. This was the case in Sweden, where radical liberals in Stockholm – in vain it should be added – rallied for all-out mobilization as early (relatively speaking) as the 1869 general elections (Esaiasson 1990:70–71). Also in Germany organizational issues emerged as a main problem among the liberals when the 1848–49 Frankfurt Parliament assembled. Later on, the liberal leadership in both countries did not, despite the resistance put up against the idea of centralized parties, lack strong proponents of formal organization along strict lines. These included (in Sweden) Karl Staaff,[8] prime minister in 1905 and 1911–14, and (in Germany) parliamentarians in the 1870s such as Max von Forckenbeck or Franz Schenk von Stauffenberg, to mention only a few (Sheehan 1978: 128–29).

These circumstances capture something of the essence of the controversies surrounding 'the idea of party'. For instance, as late as the early 1930s, and following a decade of severe factionalizing among the Swedish liberals over whether or not to support the prohibition of alcohol, local representatives in Värmland still spoke in favour of creating as loosely a knit organizational framework as possible, when the prospect of a reunited party eventually opened up.[9] Although it may have been wise to favour a cautious strategy, given the delicate task of reuniting a party split right down to the core, opinions such as these were also due to the historical underpinnings of liberalism. Somewhat oversimplified, early conservatives could lean back on the corporatist traditions of pre-revolutionary Europe. And although conservative elite parties later proved that they were not alien to the idea of indirect action via various proxy organizations if the situation called for it, they lacked the ideological arguments for institutionalizing this as a standard. As for the socialists, they were, by force of Marxist ideology, in a sense naturally 'predestined', or inclined to move, eventually, towards collective agency on a massscale. (At least that would seem to be the case with reformist, social democratic parties. Most notably, the manner in which the Russian Bolsheviks decided to organize did, of course, represent a different solution, also in part because of doctrine.) The options facing nineteenth-century liberalism were equally complicated. Liberalism in the nineteenth century was certainly complex in nature and outlook, and reveals great variation once we start to compare countries. Nevertheless, on a general level, the 'creed of individualism' inherent in liberalism (Smith 1988: 20) is, together with its Enlightenment extensions, most likely one of the main reasons why liberal parties in many countries share a tradition of weak organization.

By way of conclusion I will concentrate on two tasks in the remainder of this chapter. Firstly, in searching for an explanation for liberal organizational behaviour it is, for reasons already indicated, necessary to embark upon a more elaborate discussion of the theoretical relationship between the 'idea of party' as a problem of social cooperation and the ideological tenets of liberalism. Secondly, I will outline my research design in more detail, most notably with respect to my comparative approach to organizational practice, and the choice of Värmland and Schleswig-Holstein as regions suitable for comparison.

The rest of this book is divided into four main chapters. Chapter 2 provides an analysis of contemporary ideas on the nature and use of political parties in a historical, ideological, and institutional context. The issue of citizenship became of critical importance from that perspective. My focus will be Sweden/Värmland and Germany/Schleswig-Holstein during the period following the French Revolution. Regional specificities *vis à vis* the respective national frameworks will be dealt with. In this chapter I will also posit early examples of organizational behaviour in relation to the formation of modern liberalism. I will forward the hypothesis that mobilization of public support and voters, i.e. high levels of liberal voting turnout during the 1860–1920 period (tasks which loosely organized factions and elite parties were, indeed, ill-fit to manage), was contingent on political association by means of proxy. At the same time, though, the risk of faction among the liberals also increased, since this kind of organizational structure made it more difficult, for instance, to execute issue structuring and interest aggregation in a coherent manner. A case in point is the close relationship between Swedish liberalism and organized temperance, the latter movement providing important, organizational support to the liberals. Yet, as previously noted, the rise of teetotalism and controversies about prohibition also resulted in factional strife and, finally, contributed to the split of the party. Based on ideas of citizenship that originated in the civil society discourse of post-1789 Europe, the strategy of mobilizing by means of proxy was therefore flawed, since it made the organizational behaviour path dependent in a manner which hampered the formation of tightly-knit mass party structures. As the 'social issues' represented by bourgeois civil society became more and more politicized, and as the competition over mass support with other political movements, such as most notably the social democrats, grew fiercer, liberal parties became marginalized.

In chapters 3 and 4, I will analyse how the tension between ideology and mass politics was managed when liberals actually went ahead with the task of political association in Värmland and Schleswig-Holstein. Particular attention will be paid to electioneering in the two regions, for analytical as well as practical reasons. The nomination of candidates and electoral mobilization are among the two most important tasks for political organizations competing for office, and early liberal factions and parties were mostly quite inactive during the periods between general elections. Also, it is during election campaigns that we perhaps are most easily able to approach the important issue of how parties managed 'societal representation' and 'social integration', viz. a critical aspect of grass-roots democratization. This feature, therefore, also brings forward the problem of liberal ideology in relation to socioeconomic and cultural factors in the local environment.

Some further clarification, though, is still required. As I pointed out in the introduction, organizational efficacy presumably has effects on electoral mobilization. Firstly, however, the outcomes of elections may also produce effects on organization. Secondly, rather than juxtaposing 'ideology' and 'organization' in search of explanations for this relationship, these two factors should be considered together in the life of real-world parties. The analysis in chapter 3 and 4 will address organizational behaviour in three related dimensions (cf. Panebianco 1988: 239–61, in particular 243–47). More specifically these dimensions include a focus on various (1) external challenges (including, most notably, electoral defeat) which, in turn, may provoke changes in the (2) internal conditions of parties, including the rise of competing factions and, eventually, changes in the composition of leadership. Such changes may result (3) in adjustments in organizational structure, such as mergers of factions or attempts to centralize organization.

In the same way as the functions identified by Gunther & Diamond (2001) are applicable to the study of party organization at regional as well as state level, so the above-mentioned dimensions apply to the former level as well, particularly with respect to the initial stages of party systems formation. Again: one important feature of party systems formation in nineteenth- and early twentieth-century Europe was precisely the integration of regional political interests on the national level (Lipset & Rokkan 1967). Organization of centralized parties and concerted aggregation of interests were – in both Sweden and Germany – to a great extent a matter of competition between regionally entrenched factions, each one with their specific social base, make-up, and outlook. Also, changes in local leadership and, in effect, organizational structure, had implications for electoral mobilization strategies on the regional level even within the framework of centrally adopted structures. This was indeed the case in Schleswig-Holstein, where highly autonomous party structures became typical for the region after 1871 (chapters 2 and 4). Importantly, too, all of these dimensions involved discussions that ranged beyond those of purely organizational problems. In fact they involved and were sometimes ultimately embedded in ideological conflict, reflecting the historical and socioeconomic peculiarities of the region. Competition between various factions over programme issues therefore illustrates the complex relationship between ideology and organization. Not only a smart organization but also ideology as filtered by organizational structures does, indeed, help bring voters to the ballot box.

In chapter 3, the framework of my narrative will be the development of Swedish liberalism from the introduction of a modern, bicameral parliament in 1866 up to the introduction of universal suffrage in 1921. An epilogue necessary to include in this case, though, is a concluding assessment of the liberal movement given its split on the issue of prohibition in 1922–23, and the reappearance of a unified party in 1934. In chapter 4, I will likewise follow liberalism in Schleswig-Holstein, from the incorporation of the region as a province of royal Prussia in 1867, via the formation of a unified Germany, and up to the 1912 elections. Analogous to the Swedish case, certain concluding remarks which extend beyond the First World War are necessary. These include the introduction and demise of the Weimar Republic, and the sharp turn of the regional electorate in favour of, first, right-wing parties and, later, the Nazis. Chapter 5, finally, is a comparative assessment of my two regions. Here I will relate my hypothesis on liberal organizational strategies to the paths taken by Swedish and German liberalism in a longer perspective.

Political association as social cooperation

It was in late eighteenth-century America that the world's first modern party system began to evolve. Consequently, it is also to that context we owe one of the first, more complex considerations as to the nature of parties. It is a well-known fact that the founding fathers of the Republic, men like Benjamin Franklin, Alexander Hamilton, and Thomas Jefferson, were hesitant about the matter of parties. Parties were ultimately something negative, but – alas – also a necessary evil in public life (Goodman 1967; Aldrich 1995). Somewhat less negative views were put into print a few decades later (1835–40), by Alexis de Tocqueville, in his reflections on American society and politics. Tocqueville identified a close and mutual relationship between civic and political association, although at the same time he also separated them, somehow making them both part of civil society and yet not: 'Civil associations … facilitate political association; but, on the other hand, political association singularly strengthens and improves associations for civil purposes' (Tocqueville 2003 [1840]: 12; see also Putnam 2000). Whereas Tocqueville did warn against 'unstrained liberty of political association' (2003 [1840]: 16) because of the perils of self-interest, his views on the topic were still less emphatically put than those of David Hume a century earlier.

There were perfectly good reasons for this difference. The US political system was far more inclusive than was the case in either Britain or any other European state at the time of Hume. 'Politics' for Hume primarily involved matters of state (cf. Viroli 1992). By force of tradition politics were at the same time overtly elitist, corrupted by self-interest, and not a concern of voluntary association. In contrast, Americans faced the practical problems and needs involved in political association and coordination of mass politics earlier, and in a different manner to Europe. Considering this difference in historical background, Schattschneider's dictum (1942: 1), that 'democracy is unthinkable save in terms of parties', or Aldrich's paraphrase (1995: 3) that 'democracy is *unworkable* save in terms of parties', are not surprising from an American point of view. In Europe, however, the relationship between democratization and parties turned out to be more confusing. Put simply, the 'sequence' by which mass politics, party systems, and democratic institutions fell into place differed and was, in important respects, reversed compared to the US. At this point, though, the problem also becomes more complicated to assess.

Contemporary liberals in Sweden and Germany liked to stress that the defining quality of the movement which they were spearheading was that is was – more than anything else – an 'ideological community', or 'Bewegung', brought about by individuals, rather than a strictly formalized organization. It is this property of liberalism that comes to the fore if, for example, we consider early, urban middle-class radicalism in Sweden. The very same feature is also present in the German context, if we try to gauge the importance contemporary liberals attached to the large but diverse middle class, or the 'Mittelstand', including the role of the 'Bildungsbürgertum' as a steward of the Enlightenment notion of a modern, public sphere (Langewiesche 2000 [1988]; Gross 2004). Although these ideas proved to be unrealistic, not least in regard to the possibilities of managing interest aggregation, social representation, and integration, they became a lasting legacy of liberal thinking. Examples of this are, firstly, Rönblom's work (1929) in part scholarly account, in part political statement on the Swedish Liberal Party around 1900: in his view the party was a broad coalition of ideas and, precisely because of this, a party with far-reaching extensions that brought social classes together rather than pitting them against each other (1929: 96–97). The other example is the German national liberal Eduard Lasker's description in 1876 of his movement as a 'great political community', filled with 'a variety of opinions', but still characterized by 'great unity' (quoted in Sheehan 1978: 128).

Such a broader understanding of liberalism is at the same time not without merit from an analytical point of view. Ambiguous as liberalism certainly was, this still was a trait typical to all great ideologies of the nineteenth century. Liberalism, socialism, and conservatism alike must be considered as a set of tentatively formulated responses to the no less amorphous problem of modernity itself, just as much as mere divided opinions on the concrete, day-to-day issues of government. The major issues at stake involved nothing less than transforming more widely dispersed ideas and beliefs on the nature of man and society into doctrines that could be used for moulding the social and cultural fabric of modern life. This kind of sociological perspective on liberalism has also been applied to more recent analyses of German liberalism (Gross 2004: 22–23). Yet, all this does not of course imply that nineteenth-century liberalism lacked distinguishable features. In the search for defining elements, it could be argued that precisely the problem of self-interest and – in crucial respects yet another Enlightenment legacy – that of *individualism*, economic and political, formed the core of emerging liberalism.

On the one hand, all of the critical issues of liberalism, such as the call for 'freedom for economic enterprise', for 'constitutional reform', for 'enlargement and the protection of civil liberties', as well as its anti-clericalism, were ultimately related to the 'creed of individualism' (Smith 1988: 17–20). This celebration of individual achievement and action was congruent with the kind of small-scale, local level civic association that became typical to both Swedish and German liberalism during the first decades of the nineteenth century. At the same time, though, the visceral relationship between liberal ideology and community, and the difficulties involved in coordinating what were only loosely integrated organizational networks, simultaneously guaranteed that any of the above-mentioned issues became subject to a range of different and competing interpretations whenever ideas were put to the test in real life. This feature, too, is vividly illustrated by liberalism, and not least in Germany during the 'Vormärz'. In short, it became characteristic of many nineteenth-century liberals that one and the same person could take different, and occasionally 'illiberal' or outright conservative positions on related issues, thus acting in a manner signalling a lack of any coherent ideological conviction at all. In the words of Galston (2003 [1989]: 123), liberal individualism emerged from a 'divided' conception of the self, in the sense that 'individuality is not only shaped but also threatened by the community'. Then, again, the exact nature and limits of community were also unclear. Liberalism could signal one set of more or less specific attitudes in urban, industrial environments, and yet another in rural regions, with a different economic and social make-up, such as Värmland, or Schleswig-Holstein (chapters 3–4). Therefore, if the tension between competing ideas, and between ideas and 'political necessity', or 'realpolitik', explains a lot of these contradictions, the nature of the conflict would always differ depending on the actual situation and context.

Individualism and the call for liberty would automatically seem to imply a certain, sometimes considerable, amount of criticism and mistrust regarding the state and its power, but this was not always the case, neither in Sweden nor in Germany. For instance, once the notion of economic individualism had made inroads in Swedish parliamentary debate, liberal attitudes towards state intervention in certain sectors of the economy proved surprisingly pragmatic in the long run. A fitting illustration of the latter is how the issue of railway construction was managed in the 1850s, i.e. a large, costly, and strategically important project in which state-ownership proved necessary (Oredsson 1969; Ohlsson 1994). Another example pertains to political individualism and state–citizen relations in Germany. In this case we should consider the alliance struck between the right-wing liberals (from 1867 formalized as the National Liberal Party), and the Prussian state during the second half of the 1860s. Following the failed 1848 reform movement and, later, the outcome of the Prusso-Austrian war in 1866, the Prussian liberals were driven closer to Bismarck's programme of creating a unified Germany by 'revolution from above'. As Sheehan put it, 'Bismarck, the man whom they had vilified as a hopeless reactionary, suddenly emerged as one of Europe's most creative statesmen' (Sheehan 1978: 123). Whereas this turn for all practical purposes meant that the idea of building a nation-state solely on the basis of grass-roots activism finally had to be abandoned, it was nevertheless accepted and even embraced by many liberals, including in Schleswig-Holstein, where autonomist sentiments otherwise remained strong (chapter 2).[10]

The issue of nationhood at the same time points to an obvious difference between Swedish and German liberalism; a difference which was to produce effects on both ideology and political practice in the latter case. Put simply, unlike the case in Sweden, liberals in the German states faced a situation in which they were forced to manage somehow both the 'classic' liberal dilemmas of civic liberty and constitutional reform as well as the overwhelming problem of how to create a unified nation. Failing to accomplish this task by mobilization from below, and with the middle classes in the vanguard of the only viable option left to many liberals was alignment with the state and the traditional Prussian elite. Also, another typical trait of German liberalism was the nature of anti-clericalism and anti-Catholicism, something which in effect opened the way for yet another area of close cooperation with the emerging state apparatus of the Second Empire (Gross 2004). Tensions such as these signalled a degradation of democratic conceptions of citizenship. Indeed, this is reflected in the remark made by the famous liberal constitutional lawyer Hugo Preuss, during the First World War that the German people had led their history in a 'serene state of political innocence' (Preuss 1916: 7–8).[11]

Such apparent differences notwithstanding, however, one feature which Swedish and German liberalism undoubtedly had in common was the problem of self-interest and individualism, whether economic or political, in relation to certain formalized expressions of community, i.e. party. Indeed, 'individualism', 'community' or, to mention yet another critical concept, 'freedom', are abstract categories. In that sense there were no simple solutions to resolve the tension between individualism and collective agency, whether in the shape of the 'state', the 'nation', or – as in our case – in the guise of political parties. Managing individualism in relation to society, to be sure, is a major concern of all major political ideologies. The problem of liberalism, at least from an organizational point of view, was that individualistic beliefs formed the core element, ideologically speaking, of the movement in addition to being a social issue potentially subject to political management.

What, then, constitutes a plausible theoretical point of departure for analyzing liberal organizational behaviour? To begin with, we must scrutinize the relationship between the two types of association identified by Tocqueville, namely political association and civic association. As I have suggested, it is in the manner of how these problems were approached in contemporary society that we find clues to both the ideological as well as the practical dimension of the 'idea of party'. In essence I argue that political association, including parties, is subject to the same basic logic and faces the same basic challenges as most other types of social cooperation.

Yet, as indicated, Tocqueville and many other thinkers of the time drew a not always clear but nevertheless distinguishable line of demarcation between voluntary social cooperation, including civic association, and political association. Somehow these expressions of human endeavour seemed to represent distinct modes of agency. Let us again consider David Hume.

From one point of view, the emergence of political parties embodied one of the many possible solutions to Hume's problem of social cooperation. Viewed from a slightly different perspective, however, it was precisely the tension between (political) interests, or self-interest, and cooperation that made the picture complicated. Hume was very specific about the limits of self-interest:

> When every individual person labours a-part, and only for himself, his force is too small to execute any considerable work; his labour being employ'd in supplying all his different necessities, he never attains a perfection in any particular art; and as his force and success are not at all times equal, the least failure in either of these particulars must be attended with inevitable ruin and misery. Society provides a remedy for these *three* inconveniences: by the partition of employment, our ability encreases: and by mutual succour we are less expos'd to fortune and accidents. 'Tis by this additional force, ability, and security, that society becomes advantageous (Hume 1960 [1739–40]: 485).

It is easy to see how formal organization in terms of party, according to this view, promotes the kind of collective 'force' and 'ability' that facilitate, for instance, interest aggregation and electoral mobilization. Importantly, too, Hume also identified a close relationship between, on the one hand, social practice and, on the other hand, laws, rules, and customs or, in one word, institutions (Hume 1960 [1739–40]: 492). Only under the protection of the rule of law would social cooperation thrive.

Underpinning the notion of social cooperation was the assumption that it provided a remedy for the ills of excessive self-interest; as was Ferguson's notion of a civil society (Kettler 1977). Yet, considering that political parties in Europe traditionally emerged on the basis of competition between various parliamentary factions, and were often closely associated with the ambitions of established regional elites and individual wielders of power, it was hardly surprising that Hume and his contemporaries held the idea of party in low esteem. This is reflected in Aldrich's statement that political parties were ultimately the creation of 'the politicians, the ambitious office seeker and officeholder'. Thus party became a means of obtaining a multitude of goals, ranging simply from the 'desire to have a long and successful career in political office', to the ambition of achieving various policy ends (Aldrich 1995: 4). All differences between the US and Europe set aside, this pattern illustrates what seems to have been a more or less general rule by the turn of the nineteenth century. Two factors, however, changed the working conditions of politics and simultaneously spelled the demise of traditional elite parties. One circumstance was the emergence of modern political ideologies and critical reflection on the concept of citizenship, following the French Revolution, whereas the other factor was the gradual rise of mass politics.

In brief, the first circumstance provided political parties with incentive and motives beyond those of mere self-interest, while the other provided the necessary external pressure needed to provoke experiments with new modes of organizational behaviour. Hence, the future would have seemed secure for the establishment of the political party as an appropriate solution to the social and political problems posed by a new era. A critical factor both from the point of view of principle as well as organization, however, was ideology. To begin with, voluntary cooperation as understood by Hume and, indeed, in more recent times most notably by Ostrom (1990), rests on what could best be labelled economic calculations of the likely net profit to be gained from cooperation. This is the essence of the prisoner's dilemma game and other game theory models: if, among other things, mechanisms securing commitment, monitoring, and accountability, are properly institutionalised (Ostrom 1990: 185–86), we arrive at the kind of conditions where social cooperation based on mutual trust becomes possible, and where the individual actor is provided with the 'additional force, ability, and security' needed for prosperity (Hume 1960 [1739–40]: 485).

Mechanisms to harness excessive self-interest, then, are possible – even among citizens within the framework of a political party. Obviously such arrangements, or rules of the game, may be a direct property of organizational structures, analogous to Panebianco's model of parties (1988). But if we take 'trust' to be the operative word, there are also other ways of restraining self-interest. Let us only consider the role played by parties in terms of societal representation and social integration. Representation and integration do not only require proper organization and leadership; they also imply shared beliefs and convictions. Ideology, therefore, may under certain conditions serve as a strong incentive for the creation of mutual trust and social cooperation (but it may, of course, also function as a source of conflict).

Therefore, whereas I do concur with Aldrich that elites and ambitious politicians (i.e. to some extent self-interest) had a lot to do with the creation of political parties, ideology must also be made part of the picture. Similarly, it is possible to argue that commitment to political ideologies – liberalism, socialism, conservatism, etc. – is, at least in part, about calculating possible future dividends in a way roughly similar to game theory. Yet, precisely at this point two contingencies also become obvious. First of all I would argue that notions such as, for instance, 'civil liberty' or a 'communist society' represent rather less tangible objectives compared to the future profits made possible by solving irrigation problems or forming fishing cooperatives, as in the cases presented by Ostrom (1990). Political ideologies, and not least liberalism and socialism in the nineteenth century, were to a great extent about commitment to different, however vaguely defined, visions of society, as much as more immediate, material considerations of the kind envisaged by Hume, or Ostrom. Secondly, the task faced by nineteenth-century liberals of creating new forms of political association on the basis of commitment to an ideology, would also have had to include finding theoretical arguments in favour of practical solutions to organization. This, as I will demonstrate in the following chapters, proved to be difficult, considering the emphasis put on the role of the individual and enlightened citizen, rather than on collective agency.

Arguably, the problem of inventing proper organizational mechanisms for the restraining of self-interest gradually became more difficult to manage, once the first steps towards universal suffrage had been taken, and the problems of mass politics became increasingly apparent. As I have stressed, voluntary association, political association included, is not only about commitment to a common good, but also about building trust. Organizations do not, as a rule, work, or in any event operate only poorly, if those involved do not trust the organization as such, or one another. Apart from the ideological dimension, this issue also involves what could be termed a problem of scale, analogous to what Dolšak & Ostrom (2003: 23) point out is the case with so-called common-pool resources of high complexity. Put simply: size matters, and social trust is normally more easily generated in relatively small, homogeneous, and locally contingent environments, involving limited numbers of individual agents (e.g. Ostrom 1990: 189; other examples are presented in Åberg & Sandberg 2003: 121, 127). Although 'anomalies exist' in the pattern, one successful case mentioned by Ostrom included only 100 members, whereas other types of association presented included multi-layered, agricultural federations based on local units ranging in size from 20 to 75 members (1990: 188–189, quote at 188).

Certain implications follow from this, if we take stock of liberal organizational strategies from a historical perspective. If we hold face-to-face interaction to be instrumental in the formation of trust, it is easy to see how the idea of social cooperation – based on the union of small numbers of dedicated citizens, and (before universal suffrage) would-be citizens – can fit with the liberal celebration of the individual and of individual achievement. This is particularly true if we look more closely at the evolution of liberal movements during the first half of the nineteenth century (chapter 2). However, small-scale forms of association are not necessarily easy, or perhaps at all possible, to transform into political association on a mass basis – the kind of scenario which emerged by the end of the nineteenth century. Later I will demonstrate how contemporary liberals had few, if any, organizational antecedents that could be used as blueprints for organizing mass parties. Rather, the blueprints for electoral mobilization and election campaigning were drawn on the

Figure 1. The party systems in Sweden and Germany: their main roots according to Duverger.

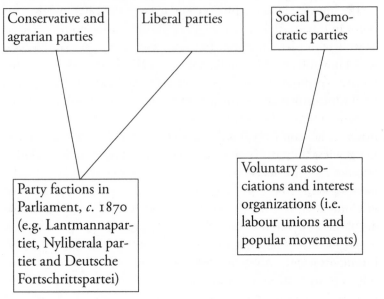

basis of other prototypes, resulting in a mixed and loosely integrated organizational structure.

The only type of parties hitherto known in Sweden and Germany in the late nineteenth century were those entrenched in the interests of traditional elites and intra-parliamentary factions, i.e. elite parties. The basic difference between the two modes of political association which I have outlined was formalized by Maurice Duverger (1967 [1954]) in his classification of party lineages (although he spoke of them in terms of cadre parties and mass parties). Thus, Duverger made a distinction between parties that had intra-parliamentarian origins, and those parties that had evolved from various extra-parliamentarian interest groups. According to this model, such parties would include, for instance, the Swedish 'Lantmannapartiet' (which appeared in 1867 and mainly represented agrarian interests) in the former category, but also the short-lived liberal faction 'Nyliberalerna' (1868–71), or the left-liberal 'Deutsche Fortschrittspartei' (German Progressive Party) established in 1861. Most notably the Swedish and German Social Democratic parties, however, belonged in the latter group (Figure 1).

The lineages inspired by Duverger's model, though, were at no point in time as clear-cut as Figure 1 indicates. Rather, in Sweden as well as in Germany and, indeed, most other countries, it is a well-known fact that early liberalism also owed a lot to the, albeit poorly coordinated, activities of relatively small local and regional level educational and temperance societies, workers' associations, welfare organizations and similar types of associations (see, for instance, Jansson 1985; Bernstein 1986; Breuilly 1994; Hurd 2000; Langewiesche 2000 [1988]; Gross 2004). Later on the Swedish popular movements (in particular nonconformist religious movements and organized teetotalism, such as the International Order of Good Templars and, in particular, the Blue Ribbon, ('Blå bandet')[12] became important arenas for the liberals; this in line with my hypothesis of political association by proxy (see also Back 1967; Lundkvist 1977). Also, the press played an extremely important role in promoting and spreading liberal ideas to a wider audience, in Värmland most notably *Karlstads-tidningen*, and particularly so under the editorship of Mauritz Hellberg from 1890 onwards (chapter 3). Liberalism in the German states, and in Prussia and its provinces, shared the same dual quality of originating *both* on the basis of intra-parliamentarian factions *and* from the activities of local-level organizations, including various 'Bürgervereine' (chapter 4). And, as in Sweden, newspapers such as the *Kieler Zeitung* represented one of the most powerful tools for disseminating ideas and mobilizing voters (although, in contrast to Sweden, the press – viz. the socialist and left-liberal press – was under close surveillance by the official authorities).[13] Thus, properly modified, the branching of party lineages should rather resemble Figure 2, if we consider liberal parties.

Although the extent and nature of linkages between the first generations of voluntary and civic associations and, in the case of Sweden, the popular movements have been a topic of dispute (most recently Abelius 2007), it is at the same time obvious that in particular the former kind of organizations were ideologically close to early liberal ideas of the individual as an enlightened citizen and

Figure 2. The party systems in Sweden and Germany revisited.

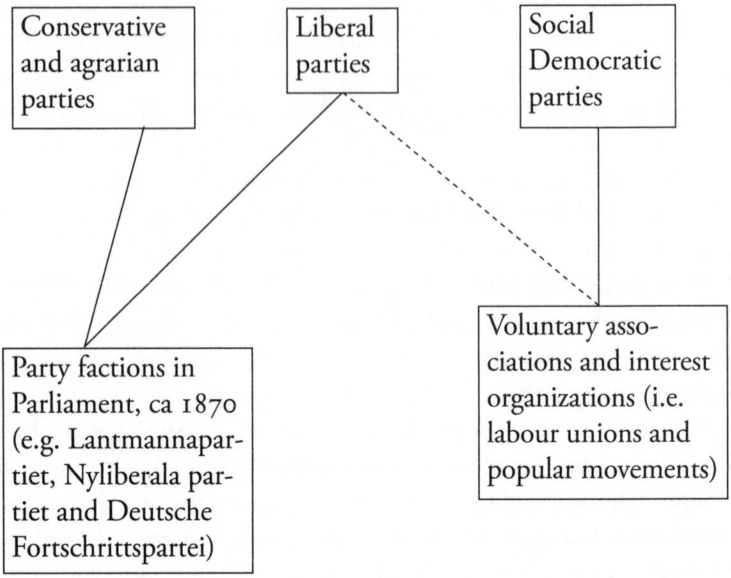

| Conservative and agrarian parties | Liberal parties | Social Democratic parties |

Party factions in Parliament, ca 1870 (e.g. Lantmannapartiet, Nyliberala partiet and Deutsche Fortschrittspartei)

Voluntary associations and interest organizations (i.e. labour unions and popular movements)

active participant in the civil society. These associations represented social cooperation stemming from close, face-to-face interaction. Indeed, the historian, philosopher, poet and composer Erik Gustaf Geijer, born and bred in Värmland, argued that the rise of associations represented nothing less than the spirit of a new era in social life (Geijer 1845: 35–36); however, on other occasions he was also careful to stress that the family, historically speaking, represented the oldest and most fundamental type of social organization (Geijer 1844: 4). It is certainly difficult to imagine a kind of association any more small-scale than the latter. Geijer was perhaps not a 'typical' liberal of his time (but, on the other hand, so were very few liberals, due to the diverse make-up of their ideological convictions; on Geijer specifically, see Petterson 1992: 246–58), yet his basic views on the foundations of social cooperation were not in any sense unique among liberals during the first half of the nineteenth century. At the same time, however, the social and political development during the crucial years of the 1840s – not least in Germany – made it abundantly clear that any attempt to transform society according to the liberal creed would also have to rest firmly on mass support and mass organization.

The geographical setting –
Värmland and Schleswig-Holstein

It is hard to find two regions that are as different as Värmland and Schleswig-Holstein, both from a historical point of view and with respect to their institutional setting. Värmland, to begin with, is located in western central Sweden, and borders the neighbouring country of Norway. It is a border region, but not in the sense of a contested, multi-ethnic border region that has been shifted between states throughout history. Excepting that the proximity to Norway was of some importance to the political climate in Värmland (Norway modernized more rapidly than Sweden in certain respects; see chapter 2), the geographic variable was of no direct importance to political association. This was certainly not the case with Schleswig-Holstein. Unlike Värmland, this mixed German–Danish region does, indeed, carry the tradition of being contested. In brief, it was the ancient political and diplomatic peculiarities of the region that induced Lord Palmerston to make his famous remark on the difficulty of how to decide the legal status of Schleswig-Holstein.[14] These circumstances filtered back into organized political life long after the region had been incorporated as a Prussian province in 1867 on the North German Confederation. Matters of national identity, then, complicated political life. For instance, the Danish minority entered the parliamentary elections with their own candidates, much in the same manner as the Poles in the eastern borderlands of Prussia organized separately in the parliamentary (*Reichstag*) elections (Suval 1985).

Patriotism and the issue of nationhood, to be sure, provided the outer perimeter of liberalism in both Sweden and Germany, but whereas modern nationalism in Sweden developed within clearly defined borders, and was based upon ethnic and linguistic homogeneity, the German nation-state was still little more than an idea around 1850. At the same time the break-up from Denmark, and the relationship with Berlin and Prussia, posed a problem of some concern in Schleswig-Holstein. In particular the prominent role played by the military in Prussian society, and the implementation of three-year conscription, were met with criticism. Yet, to many prominent leaders in the region, including the left-liberal professor Albert Hänel in Kiel, the future of Schleswig-Holstein and Prussia was, for better or worse, fused. In addition, the liberal parties in the region – national liberals and left-liberals alike – should also be considered as more right-wing compared to their national counterparts (Schultz Hansen 2003: 459–60; Ibs 2006: 138, 144, 146).

Notwithstanding contrasts such as those indicated, Värmland and Schleswig-Holstein do appear similar in one key dimension: the relative strength of the liberal movement in these two rural regions during the latter part of the nineteenth century and the beginning of the twentieth century. Let us first return to Sweden and the 1911 general election. On the national level the social democrats more than doubled their number of seats in parliament, primarily at the expense of the conservatives. the liberals, at the same time, defended their previous results from the 1908 elections. In Värmland, however, they fared better than this (although Värmland was not an extreme case of liberal voting in the same manner as, most notably, the northern province of Västerbotten).[15] Whereas the liberal turnout on a national level was 40.2 per cent in 1911, it reached 46.1 per cent in the Värmland constituencies (Table 1). Since the social democrats simultaneously gained votes, it was the conservatives who lost support in this case, too.

Table 1. Liberal votes in the 1911 and 1921 general elections: national and regional level results (per cent of votes cast).

Election year	1911	1921
Värmland	46.1	29.5
National average	40.2	18.7

Source: *SOS. Allmänna val. Riksdagsmannavalen 1911* and *1921*.

Although the period from 1911 to 1921, and the introduction of universal suffrage, marked a period of expansion for the social democrats and a gradual decline for the liberals, the latter were successful in defending their position on the regional level. As late as the 1921 elections, 29.5 per cent of the votes cast in Värmland were in favour of the liberals, compared to a national average of 18.7 per cent (Table 1). Despite the region turning more and more 'red', i.e. social democratic, Värmland remained relatively speaking more 'liberal' in contrast to many other parts of the country. This was the case even after the split of the Liberal Party in 1923 and, as a result, the general weakening of Swedish liberalism as a political movement (chapter 3). Liberals on the local and regional level were somehow, relatively speaking, skilful in sustaining their electoral basis and, indirectly, successful at integrating and representing large social strata in society during a critical period of political modernization.

A similar pattern is typical in the case of Schleswig-Holstein, although the German liberals, while organizing earlier compared to in Sweden, were also divided into more parties, which occasionally merged and cooperated. For example, in the 1884 general elections, the Schleswig-Holstein liberals (national liberals and left-liberal factions together) received a total of 62.1 per cent of the votes in the region compared to a 36.9 per cent national average (Table 2; in particular the left-liberals fared well, in contrast to the national level results). In the 1890–1912 period, during which the Social Democratic Party gradually consolidated itself as the largest political party in Germany, liberalism still managed to hold its ground in the region, despite split-ups and setbacks (Ibs 2006: 152–53). In the 1912 elections the liberal parties in Schleswig-Holstein received a total of 43.2 per cent of all votes, compared to a national average of 25.9 per cent (Table 2). After the First World War and the introduction of the Weimar Republic, however, the situation shifted, only more rapidly and in a different direction compared to Värmland.

Table 2. Liberal votes in the 1884 and 1912 general elections: national and regional level results (per cent of votes cast).

Election year	1884	1912
Schleswig-Holstein	62.1	43.2
National average	36.9	25.9

Sources: Sheehan, 1978, Table 14.5, 214; *Beiträge zur historischen Statistik Schleswig-Holsteins*, 1967, Table V 1 b, 73; *Sozialgeschichtliche Arbeitsbuch, II*, 1978, Table 9 b, 177–78. Note: national level data for 1884, as reproduced by Sheehan, includes votes cast for the National Liberals (Nationalliberale Partei), the Freisinnige Partei, and the Volkspartei (the latter two were both left-liberal parties). For Schleswig-Holstein the data includes the National Liberals and factions under the joint-label 'Deutschfreisinnige partei'. The data for 1912 – national and regional levels – includes votes cast for the National Liberals, and the 'Fortschrittliche Volkspartei' (left-liberals).

In the 1919 elections to the new, national assembly the liberals received 27.2 per cent of the votes, but in subsequent elections the situation polarized between the socialist and communist left and the extreme right. With this the liberals rapidly lost support (Tilton 1975; Wulf 2003). In fact, many among those who had traditionally voted liberal eventually turned to the Nazis in the early 1930s. According to Tilton, this was due to the 1920s agricultural crisis and the inability of the Republic to provide relief to the farmers, but also 'the lack of organization' among the liberals forms part of his explanation (Tilton 1975: 29–33, 135–37, quote at 137). Indeed, in the July 1932 elections, the Nazi votes cast in Schleswig-Holstein reached 52.7 per cent,[16] an ill-boding result. Political modernization therefore ended with diametrically opposed results if we compare Värmland and Schleswig-Holstein in a longer perspective. In that sense these two regions epitomize the outcome of political modernization on the national level with respect to the development in Sweden and Germany during the late nineteenth and early twentieth centuries.

At the same time it should be stressed that neither Värmland nor Schleswig-Holstein were 'typical' host regions of liberal movements. Liberal regions in the sense that, for instance, Max Weber would have argued, according to his principle of ideal types, would preferably be urbanized and heavily industrialized in the manner typical to the Rhineland, or, in Britain, major industrial centres, such as Manchester. Indeed, considering Germany, Suval (1985) identified a pattern according to which liberal parties were strongest in modernized and, more precisely, 'Protestant, industrialized areas', whereas their strength declined 'with the strength of urbanization' (Suval 1985: 121). Judging from electoral behaviour, these were similar environments, he argues, to those of 'American progressivism', or 'voting habits in the mid-Victorian English industrial towns' (ibid.). Persuasive as this conclusion sounds, it is not, however, entirely free of pitfalls. This is because – similarly to the 'Sonderweg hypothesis', or sequentialism – it rests on the assumption that there, indeed, exists a historical standard, or a 'normal' path of political organization, association, and modernization. The emergence of liberalism, as of all political ideologies and political movements, was more complicated.

As I have pointed out, Sweden as a whole urbanized at a later stage, and at a slower pace, than countries such as Britain and Germany. This created a different framework for political movements. Even so, Värmland was by most standards more rural compared to several parts of the country. Geographically speaking a large region (19,979 km²), it was not densely populated. There were only 260,000 inhabitants in 1910, which made it a small region in comparison to most German counterparts, including Schleswig-Holstein (15,658 km²), which at the same time mustered a population of about 1.6 million (equivalent to almost a third of the entire population of Sweden at that time).[17] Towns were few and small, and the only real city in the province was the regional capital of Karlstad. In 1910 roughly a quarter of all people in Sweden lived in cities and towns, but only about one-tenth of the population in Värmland.[18] Consequently, the liberal electorate, too, was overwhelmingly rural. In the 1921 general elections, 86.6 per cent of all liberal votes were cast in rural constituencies (compared to an average of 76.3 per cent for the country as a whole).[19]

Economic, demographic, and social conditions differed if we compare the western, eastern, and northern parts of Värmland, yet some general features should be stressed. The province had a strong tradition of mining and iron processing, industries which – similarly to what had become typical to Swedish industrialization

– were located in the countryside, rather than in urbanized areas. This sector, however, was in serious decline by the second half of the nineteenth century. Presumably as an effect of economic crisis, Värmland was also tapped of human resources by mass emigration to North America after 1860.[20] And by the end of the First World War there were still only 65 industrial workers per 1,000 inhabitants in the province, compared to a national average of 69.[21] Small-scale family farming formed the core of the regional economy and, particularly so in northern Värmland, with forestry as an ancillary industry: In 1890, six out of seven rural constituencies in the province were dominated by small farmers (Carlsson 1953: 19–20). This situation remained stable well into the twentieth century. By 1945 between 50.8 and 88.6 per cent of the population in the northern districts of the province were still employed in agriculture (Nilsson 1950: 162).

At the same time, political radicalism in the shape, above all, of liberalism started to make strong inroads in the region during the last decades of the nineteenth century. This mixture of decline and modernization, and the social and cultural tensions involved, was noted, *inter alia*, by the Church. In 1899, Claes Herman Rundgren, bishop of the diocese, remarked that much that had once been good in the province had now faded away.[22] The Church represented, among other things, traditional value systems, established dogma, and respect for religious and secular authority, but the erosion of the established social order was blamed not only on secularization and political radicalism. The advance of nonconformist religious movements and other popular movements also played an important role in these processes.

Obvious, but nevertheless important to point out, a main reason why liberalism and the Church were at loggerheads with each other related precisely to the issue of individualism; because since life and, indirectly, individuality ultimately was of God's making, there was a fundamental difference in perspective on existential issues between the Church and liberalism that reached all the way back to the Enlightenment. We should also note the emphasis Rundgren put on the 'good of tradition'. He thereby struck a particular chord concerning the nature of historical change to which we will return. Declining or not, remarks such as Rundgren's and others (chapters

2–3) indicate a region looking backwards into history as well as forward to the future.

Liberalism in Schleswig-Holstein similarly originated from the basis of a rural social structure in the mid-nineteenth century. Traditionally, the region was divided into three parts – the west, characterized by independent and relatively well-to-do farmers (in particular Dithmarschen, Eiderstedt, and North Friesia); mid-Schleswig-Holstein, with its small and middle-sized farming; and the east, with a mixture of well-to-to farmers and, above all, large manors ('Güter'). At the time of the incorporation with Prussia in 1867, circa 70.0 per cent of the working population was employed in agriculture (Ibs 2006: 129–30). Industrialization and urbanization transformed the region during the following decades, thus creating a new class of industrial workers in cities and towns such as Kiel, Flensburg, Neumünster, Altona, and Wandsbek, the latter two on the outskirts of Hamburg. Nevertheless, Schleswig-Holstein still in 1907 belonged to a cluster of north-western German regions which ranked below the national average in terms of industrial employment.[23] Roughly one-third of the working population of the region was employed in agriculture, forestry, and fishing in 1907, although conditions varied significantly between overwhelmingly agrarian districts such as Hadersleben, Tondern, or Segeberg, and industrial enclaves such as Altona.[24] Similarly to Värmland, finally, Schleswig-Holstein also experienced emigration during the latter part of the nineteenth century; in part for political reasons (following the incorporation with Prussia), and in part because of economic pressure (Lorenzen-Schmidt 2003; see also Grant 2005).[25]

In terms of urbanization, 39.5 per cent of the population in Schleswig-Holstein lived in cities by 1890, but this was still less compared to the more heavily industrialized regions in central and western Germany. For instance, in Saxony 45.6 per cent of the population was urban by the same time,[26] and by 1910 a majority of people in Schleswig-Holstein, viz. 53.4 per cent, still lived in communities with 5,000 inhabitants or less.[27] In these rural areas, in districts such as Segeberg, liberalism, although contested, stood strong. As late as the 1912 elections, the mandates in seven out of the ten constituencies in Schleswig-Holstein were still held by liberal deputies, all of them left-liberal (Schultz Hansen 2003: 464). Generally speaking, the division between areas of different geographic and economic make-up was more obvious compared to Värmland, and it became more marked as time passed. However, following Tilton (1975: 135), 'one could still speak of Schleswig-Holstein as an *Agrarland* without serious inaccuracy', considering the situation by the early 1930s. Similarly to Värmland, the pattern therefore reveals both modernization and, if not decline, so in any event lingering traditionalism. This basic similarity between Värmland and Schleswig-Holstein – i.e. a relatively speaking strong liberal tradition in a predominantly rural and traditional setting – constitutes the point of departure for my comparison of the two regions. Political modernization, however, was also a process that unfolded against a background of profound changes in the respective national arenas. First of all we should therefore approach the 'idea of party' and how this problem was considered in the Swedish and German historical contexts.

CHAPTER 2

Partisanship rising

Beginnings

Liberalism in Sweden and Prussia both originated in the same ideas that toppled *l'ancien regime* in France. It was fuelled by the same kind of challenges that were raised against monarchies all over Europe during the subsequent wars. The effects did, however, differ greatly if we compare the countries. In the case of Sweden the result was not only lost territory and border adjustments. Other outcomes included the introduction of a constitutional monarchy – albeit on the basis of the traditional, corporate bodies of the Estates – and a mode of liberalism that, although diffuse, started to play a role in political life.[1] In a similar manner the reformed Prussian state machinery of Frederick William III, which emerged after the defeats at Jena and Auerstedt in 1806, helped to trigger the 'Vormärz' and radical liberalism as a political force. At the same time, though, absolutism prevailed and the corporate institutions of pre-revolutionary Prussia retained a stronger position compared to Sweden. Despite promises made, Prussia remained without either constitution or parliament (except provincial 'Landtage'). Differences such as these proved decisive to the patterning of liberalism in both our two regions.

In Sweden, radicalism framed the introduction of constitutional monarchy in 1809, but it was not until the 1820s that the concept of 'liberalism' became more widely used in public debate. If not the sweet smell of far-reaching reform (because there was none to be had at this stage), a certain amount of optimism nevertheless scented the air, somehow signalling that opportunities were at hand. This change of mood was present in Värmland, too. Henrik Lilljebjörn, former captain of the light infantry, reminisced about his native region some fifty-odd years later. He remembered how 'the freer form of rule made society brighten up in matters great and small – What was good by tradition had not yet faded, whereas change and novelties sprouted vigorously' (Lilljebjörn 1912 [1867–1874]: 3–4).[2] The catalyst of political modernization in Northern Europe was the upheavals brought about by the Napoleonic Wars. Following the Treaty of Tilsit in 1807, Tsar Alexander had invaded Finland in February the following year. Finland, which represented more than a third of the pre-war territory of the Swedish state, was permanently lost when the peace treaty with Russia was finally negotiated in September 1809. At that stage King Gustav IV Adolf, by many in governing circles considered the principal architect of the disaster, had already been forced to abdicate in March 1809. He was succeeded by his uncle in June, at the same time as a new constitution was adopted, one main feature of which was the division of legislative power between the Estates and the monarch.

The loss of Finland did not, however, mean that the country succumbed to national paralysis. Traumatic as the defeat was, it also resulted in a sharpening of focus in domestic debates on social, economic, and political reform. The 1809 peace treaty was a final conformation of the fact that Sweden was no longer a great power, but it also coincided with a long period of dynamic changes. Since the mid-eighteenth century the country had experienced a rapid growth of population and development of the agricultural sector, but also increasing social stratification among the rural population (Gadd 2000). In Värmland the first decades of the nineteenth century were also the heyday of the regional iron industry. As modern nationalism simultaneously began to emerge, a concern for the 'national interest' was regularly used as a fitting motive by the many reform societies and civic associations that now formed. These societies played a part in replacing, at least to some extent, old and crumbling corporatist modes of social and political association (cf. Jansson 1985). A new public sphere began to emerge, and with it debates on citizenship gained momentum; in effect, some of these organizations performed functions of interest aggregation and issue structuring, but before the advent of political parties proper.

A different logic applies to the case of Swedish–Norwegian relations. Norway, following negotiations with Russia and Great Britain, had been ceded by Denmark, and forced into union with Sweden in the 1814 peace treaty of Kiel. Decades later, when nationalistic sentiments in Norway surged, and paved the way for the dissolution of the union (1905), the country served as a model for the Swedish left with respect to parliamentarism, the breakthrough of which occurred much earlier there, in the mid-1880s, but thirty years later in Sweden (Stråth 2005).[3]

In 1820, however, all this lay in the future. Once constitutionalism had prevailed, radicalism accepted the monarchy, but in combination with a strongly anti-bureaucratic element. Also, liberalism could still imply almost any form of political radicalism. As Kahan (1992: 145–49, quote at 146) has stressed, it would certainly be simplistic to depict nineteenth-century liberalism simply as 'the representative political movement of the ascendant middle classes'. For instance, both Värmland and Schleswig-Holstein illustrate that it had far greater reach than that. Yet, in terms of ideology the watershed in Sweden was without doubt the formation of a liberal middle-class movement in the 1830s. It was supported by urban intellectuals and merchants, but also by industrialists from the Swedish mining districts ('Bergslagen'), which included the eastern parts of Värmland.

Newspapers such as *Aftonbladet* (1830), but also *Göteborgs Handels- och Sjöfartstidning* (1832), played important roles in advancing ideas of extended political rights, parliamentarism, freedom of the press, and deregulation of the economy. Filtered through and, occasion- ally, put into practice on a small scale in various civic associations and reform societies, such commonly dispersed ideas were slowly moulded into liberal ideology. Importantly, the struggle for political rights, in combination with anti-bureaucratic motives, also opened up the way for cooperation with the peasantry, the fourth Estate, in the early 1840s; indeed, as early as 1834, Per Ericsson, a farmer from Nysäter in Värmland, had presented a motion in parliament (*Riksdag*) for the introduction of a single-chamber system, precisely on the grounds that the interests of the traditional Estates and the bureaucracy hampered reform (Christensen 1997: 148; for Ericsson, see also Olausson 2007). As Christensen (1997) stresses, though, the peasants were at this stage driven less by middle-class individu- alism, and more by arguments based on what they considered to be their ancient liberties, and by concern for their large share of tax contributions to the state. Differences such as these meant that the liberal–agrarian alignment rested on fragile ground. It did not survive the negotiations at the 1844–45 Riksdag.

At the heart of the problem were also divided views on the issue of political reform among the liberals themselves. The gradual deconstruction of corporatism opened up society for the modern individual as a political agent. Importantly, though, modern individualism had also to be qualified for the tasks and responsibilities involved with political freedom. In addition to this philosophical dimension, there were, as among the peasantry, numerous economic issues and other interests to be considered. It is possible to distinguish between radical, or left-liberal, and moderate lines of argument in the debates, although notions such as these are by no means mutually exclusive, nor do they signal an absolute difference in relation to conservative opinion. (For example, moderate and more restrictive proposals of political reform sometimes ran close to conservative views on the matter in the 1840s. At the same time not all conservatives were hostile to economic reform and, hence, found themselves closer to a liberal position in that respect. (Christensen 1997: 13–15)). In principle, however, 'economic individualism' meant putting self-interest, and the freedom for economic enterprise, in the forefront. At the same time the linchpin of 'political individualism', as in connection to issues of constitutional reform and civil liberties, was that the individual agent, proper grooming provided, was, indeed, capable of making rational decisions extending beyond the limits of mere self-interest (Andrén 2005: 25–31).

In the end, therefore, the problem reduced to the matter of precisely *how* inclusive a future reform of political representation would have to be. Where, indeed, was the line to be drawn between citizens and the rest of society? That the new middle classes were somehow the vanguard of reform was beyond dispute – but would extensive rules of suffrage make them or break them as the leaders of modernization (Christensen 1997: 8–9)? The peasantry and the growing agrarian proletariat represented a troublesome group from a perspective of social representation, but it was the same case with the slowly emerging working classes. Since differences in opinion on these matters involved diverging conceptions of citizenship, they also, as I will demonstrate later, implied different conceptions in regard to the role of voluntary association and collective action in political modernization.

The context of Prussian liberalism looked entirely different. From the moment the word 'liberalism' became firmly rooted in the political vocabulary (at the same time as in Sweden, in the 1820s), issues of constitutional reform were enmeshed with the problem of German identity and unification. Basically, those who aimed at transforming the German 'Volk' into a 'Nation' faced two options. One alternative meant following a strand of argument which, ever since Samuel Pufendorf's reading of Hobbes in the seventeenth century, had influenced political thinking heavily in Central Europe; i.e. that the state constituted the *primus motor* of progress. This argument led to the conclusion that the monarch was, in effect, the 'guarantor of the state's collective interest' (Clark 2006: 240).[4] In Prussia this idea found a particular and immensely influential expression through Hegel but, importantly, different to Pufendorf. By rejecting Pufendorf's conception of the state as a mere machine, an instrument, and by instilling it with a will and rationality of its own, the state thus defined became a *leitmotiv* in German political thinking and nation-building.

Another alternative was represented by the middle classes, according to which the middle strata of society, and especially the 'Bildungs-bürgertum', should play an essential role in educating but, at the same time, also restraining the masses. The task was to mould the latter into becoming responsible citizens. However, the Prussian state represented one of the leading elements from this perspective as well, as illustrated by the ideas first put forward in Immanuel Kant's famous 1784 essay, 'Beantwortung der Frage: Was ist Aufklärung'. An enlightened 'Öffentlichkeit', to be sure, was the key to modernity but, as Kant had also stressed, this public sphere was possible only under the rule of law; that is, under the authority of the state. Influential as this view remained, it was still difficult to reconcile it with the new, Hegelian conception of state.

Treading the path towards political modernization meant that liberals were somehow forced to strike a compromise between appearing as loyal 'Untertanen' (subjects) and, at the same time, of being enlightened 'Staatsbürger' (citizens). Because of the lingering uncertainty about the precise relationship between nation, state, and citizenship, this also meant that the moral and ethical responsibilities implied by political individualism remained blurred: did individual fulfilment belong to the realm of civil society, or was it, ultimately, possible only through the life of a purposive state? As this dilemma was never satisfactorily resolved, we also see one important factor which helps to explain the characteristic features of Prussian and German liberalism in the nineteenth century. However, at the same time as the role of Prussia proved decisive to German unification, the traits of Prussian liberalism became problematic when applied to conditions in Schleswig-Holstein.

An important part of the problem faced by liberalism was the regional and political fragmentation of the Germans lands. As in Sweden, the press, and certain publications such as the famous *Staatslexikon*,[5] played an important role in disseminating liberal ideas. Local-level voluntary association was a prominent feature as well. Yet, the geopolitical fragmentation of Germany swamped, or in any event, complicated communication and cooperation between liberals in different states and regions. Offermann's analysis (1988) of Cologne and Berlin has already been offered, in the previous chapter, as an example of how liberalism retained regional peculiarities on critical issues, including organization. Liberalism in Hamburg (Breuilly 1994; Hurd 2000), or in Schleswig-Holstein are other cases in point. Particularly the latter case amply illustrates the much more apparent regional cleavage in German political life compared to Sweden. Similarly to conditions in the eastern borderlands or, after 1871, the situation in Alsace-Lorraine, this particular case reveals the ethnic divisions that were also embedded in German political modernization. In the same way as, for instance, the Catholic Poles in Prussia were considered problematic from the point of view of Berlin, so too were the relations between the German and Danish populations in Schleswig-Holstein (see Baier 1980; Suval 1985; Wolff 2003; Åberg & Sandberg 2003; Gross 2004). In addition, Schleswig-Holstein had a disputed but nevertheless centuries-long tradition of relative autonomy, symbolized by the fact that the duchies had retained an administration separate from that of the kingdom of Denmark proper. This story, in turn, had a long and complicated background.

From the late fourteenth century onwards, the fates of the Duchy of Schleswig and the county of Holstein (from 1474 the Duchy of Holstein) had been intertwined. Entangled in a complicated web of competing dynastic claims, rooted in the feudal past of Europe, the region represented a problem both from the perspective of the Danish state as well as, increasingly, from the point of view of Prussia. After the 'Holy Roman Empire of the German Nation' had collapsed, Holstein entered the German Confederation in 1815 (together with Lauenburg, which, after the Prusso-Danish war, passed to Prussia and, from 1876, was included as part of the province of Schleswig-Holstein). At the same time Denmark claimed sovereignty over both Schleswig and Holstein. Emerging liberalism in the region played a critical role in these conflicts, whether its followers opted for or against a closer relation to Denmark.

As was the case in Prussia and Sweden, liberalism in Schleswig-Holstein started out as an urban middle-class movement. And as in Prussia, Denmark also, on the verge of the nineteenth century, represented a case of absolute monarchy. Despite limitations and censorship, new newspapers such as *Kieler Correspondenz-Blatt* (1830), and small, hitherto non-political local newspapers such as, for instance, *Eckenförder Wochenblatt* and *Itzehoer Wochenblatt*, became important to the formation of political radicalism. Later on the *Kieler Zeitung* (1864), established by banker Wilhelm Ahlmann, became the leading, liberal newspaper in the region. At the same time the peasantry held a weaker social and political position compared to Sweden. Only in 1805 had they been relieved from servitude (albeit two years earlier than their counterparts in Prussia, following the famous 'October Edict' of 1807). When consultative, provincial diets were introduced in 1831, the peasants in Schleswig-Holstein were represented, although the reform did not as such spell an end to absolutism. Also, similarly to what may be noticed in the case of Sweden, the peasants and their interests did not readily fit into any conventional left-right political spectrum. Considering the provincial diets of the 1830s, where intra-parliamentarian factions first started to appear, Schultz Hansen (2003:

432) simply remarks that the peasants 'held true to the King and Constitutional status quo, but with a critical eye to the bureaucracy'.[6]

From this point onwards, however, liberalism and nationalism started to mutually reinforce each other. This resulted in a polarization of Danish and German interests. A small group of autonomists acting in 1830, the 'Lornsenbewegung',[7] challenged the Danish monarchy by stressing the unique, but also German character of Schleswig-Holstein. This, in turn, triggered a Danish counter-movement which later was formalized as the so-called 'Ejder programme' of 1842. The programme won the support of the Danish national liberals, and came to serve as the official government policy on Schleswig-Holstein well into the 1860s. In essence it implied splitting the whole region, since the ambition to integrate Schleswig more closely with Denmark went hand-in-hand with separation from Holstein and Lauenburg. From the 1840s, too, the provincial diet became an arena for Danish–German strife. This shift was symbolized by the succession of leading radical liberal Peter Hiort Lorenzen, a merchant from Hadersleben, to the pro-Danish movement. At the same time the majority of radicals among the ethnic Germans in Schleswig-Holstein moved closer to a pro-German, national liberal position. In March 1848, the notion of a Danish 'helstat' ('Gesamtstaat'), that would also include Schleswig, was finally shattered when a provisional government for both duchies was declared in Rendsburg. War followed, including intervention by the German Confederation and Prussia (Bjørn 1998; Schultz Hansen 2003). The conflict spluttered on for the next twenty years and included, firstly, a final showdown between Danish and Prussian interests in 1864 and, secondly, the Austro-Prussian war in 1866 and the formation of the North German Confederation: Whereas Schleswig-Holstein had been put under joint Austrian-Prussian administration in 1864, the cross-cultural region of Schleswig-Holstein became a Prussian province in 1867.

The issue of how to manoeuvre in relation to Prussia remained of critical importance to how the Schleswig-Holstein liberals factionalized after 1867 (see later in this chapter). Autonomy from Denmark was certainly achieved, but it was replaced by Prussian supremacy. Indeed, neither before nor after 1848 did the latter option attract any widespread support in the region. Most importantly, the combination of separatist traditions and suspicion towards Prussia explains why liberalism in Schleswig-Holstein – unlike Värmland – long maintained autonomous party organizations in relation to the emerging Prussian and German party system. However, as events turned out, culminating with the proclamation of the German Empire in 1871, there was also political reality to consider. As Schultz Hansen (2003: 460) put it, the encounter between the old and sluggish administration of Schleswig-Holstein with the new, Prussian civil service initially resulted in somewhat of a 'clash of cultures'. Still, many leading politicians, including the left-liberal Albert Hänel, associated themselves with the Bismarckian project of unity by 'revolution from above.'

As leader of the 'Schleswig-Holsteinische Liberale Partei' (1867), which emanated from the 'Schleswig-Holsteinische Landespartei' (1863), Hänel played an important role in this process, which was reflected in, among other things, the subsequent changes of party label: in 1870 the name was changed to 'Liberale Partei Schleswig-Holsteins' (LPSH), signalling a careful but deliberate shift towards the Prussian Progressives. At the same time there were obvious differences between the left-liberals – and in particular the so-called Democratic and Particularistic factions, who left the party in 1868–70 – and the national liberals (Kiehl 1966; Schultz Hansen 2003). Whereas the national liberals were ready to trade off democratic reforms in favour of national unity and, as during the preparations for the 1874 elections, appealed to 'all those national-minded and true to Kaiser and Reich',[8] Hänel entered the post-1867 situation with a different agenda. He was neither discarding the need for extended political rights and social reform, nor rejecting the historically speaking unique position of Schleswig-Holstein. Hence the framework for liberal political association and campaigning had been set.

Sweden – liberalism on the verge of mass politics

The liberal–agrarian alignment of the early 1840s had rested on motives too diverse for making any long-term cooperation feasible. Yet the decade did turn out to be a progressive period. For instance, reforms in 1842 resulted in the introduction of elementary schools and, in 1846, the old guilds were abolished. Hence a chief impediment to the advancement of industry was removed. In addition, the first steps towards reformation of local self-government were taken. The many 'civil associations', to follow Tocqueville, that were formed in Sweden during the first decades of the nineteenth century played an important role in the public debates around issues such as these.

Associations and reform societies were enthusiastically introduced as the remedy for almost any social and economic ailment. There emerged associations for the improvement of the economy and agriculture, associations for religious, educational, and cultural purposes, associations for poor relief and temperance, and later on, in the 1850s and 1860s, workers' associations and rifle clubs. Similarly to Hegel's conception of the civil society, too, voluntary association in the Swedish context also included economic organizations of various kinds, such as companies and banks. Whether formed by state inititative, such as, for instance, the Swedish Temperance Society ('Svenska nykterhetssällskapet', 1837), or by private initiative, such as many local educational societies and workers' associations, they shared a concern for the improvement of the national standard within their respective fields. Self-interest played a role, but it was self-interest in the guise of national interest (Jansson 1985). As indicated, some of the organizations were close to being virtual 'political parties', in a manner in which the interests of the middle classes were mobilized, but without being recognized as such, not even by their own members. Considering both Tocqueville, as well as for instance Erik Gustaf Geijer, who was well aquainted with Tocquevilles's work, the very meaning of 'political', as well as of 'citizenship', remained a matter of dispute.

Civic life centred on the activities of these, usually rather small, associations, although their outward appearance would often indicate otherwise, such as in the case of the Temperance Society, in which the clergy played a leading role as organizers. By the mid-1840s the movement claimed to have collected 100,000 vows of temperance all over the country. In actual fact, as Jansson (1985) points out, the number of active members did not exceed 120 in the whole of the country by 1845. Part of the confusion regarding the numerical strength of early voluntary associations is explained simply by the uncertainty surrounding the notion of 'membership', similar to the confusion over 'politics', or 'citizenship'. Another prominent association, the Swedish Bible Society ('Svenska bibelsällskapet', 1815), also had a national scope of interest, but had only 55 permanent members. Many associations and reform societies during the first half of the nineteenth century were not only small but also overtly local in character and outlook, as had been the case with early civic association in the German states. The Friends of Destitute People ('Sällskapet De nödlidandes vänner'), a Stockholm poor-relief society, which had also formed in 1815, may be used as an illustration. It had 127 permanent members in 1816–17, which, indeed, was a small number, yet larger compared to the organization of the Swedish Bible Society (Jansson 1985: 130, 139, 143–54). Associations such as the Temperance Society and others therefore resemble the kind of closely-knit organizations that were at the core of Ostrom's analysis (1990) of the foundations of social cooperation, or the principles outlined by Hume. Of course, this does not mean that the associations of the early nineteenth century were always successful. On the contrary, internal conditions often included factional competition similar to what would later become typical of liberal and other political parties. At the same time, though, the very size of these associations, despite their internal weaknesses, suggests a potential for building organizational trust, and thus also a potential for mobilization, interest aggregation and close, face-to-face interaction around shared issues.

I would argue that early forms of civic association were of critical importance to the organization of middle-class radicalism, although the ideological underpinnings of the various movements and associations were more often than not diffuse, excepting a commonly shared utilitarian outlook towards the world (cf. Petterson 1992). Compared to political parties proper, and in particular mass parties, ideology and statutes could not yet substitute social trust as organizational cement. At the same time the elitist composition of such associations posed a problem, if we consider functions such as societal representation and social integration. More often than not the actual members were recruited from the upper echelons and middle strata of society. In combination with the lack of any clearly defined doctrine, this circumstance created problems from the point of view of social and political legitimacy. Many of the civic associations of the early nineteenth century were pipe dreams, which never left the universe of the educated elite, or the middle-class drawing-room.

Nevertheless, these expressions of civic association corresponded closely to the ideals of the modern and enlightened middle-class citizen. United by roughly similar education, outlook, and perspective, they used their organizations to carefully tread towards reform and social improvement. Many of the individual agents involved were extremely active in promoting what they considered to be the public good, but at the same time also ensured that their own interests were favoured. A case in point was the mining inspector in Värmland, Franz Adolf von Schéele, who not only started a mining elementary school in Filipstad in 1830, but also by 1823 had also initiated one of the first savingsbanks in Sweden, also in Filipstad (actually the second one to appear in the region, since a similar bank had been established in Karlstad the previous year). At the same time he was active in establishing regional mortgage and insurance societies – all of which were considered expressions of 'civic association' according to the terminology of the period – and all of which were initiatives that also promoted Schéele's own career as a public figure and entrepreneur (on Schéele, see Frostlund 2005). Simultaneously, however, middle-class radicalism failed to develop the grass-roots extensions typical to democratization. In a wider perspective, therefore, we get a mixed impression of Värmland with respect to early civic association. On the one hand Johan af Wingård, governor of the province in the 1820s, wrote appreciatively about the new 'spirit' of civic association, symbolized by the introduction of a savingsbank in Karlstad, and from which, he was sure, society would prosper in the future (Jansson 1985: 23); his was a picture of a dynamic social advancement as well as economic growth. On the other hand, as we approach the mid-nineteenth century, it is at the same time clear that the mobilization of local society by means of middle-class civic association had failed.

Data from the official record does not suggest that organizational life, at least not before 1850, was exceptional in Värmland compared to other regions. For instance, the activities of the Temperance

Society were concentrated in the south and southwestern parts of the country, as well as in certain areas of the north, although the number of local branches in Värmland did increase dramatically in the late 1840s, from six in 1847 to 31 in 1848 (Båtefalk 2000: 319). Also, according to official estimates, only a modest number of so-called 'pious foundations', a label applying to both charitable institutions and self-help organizations of various kinds, appeared during the entire 1801–50 period. A total of 16 such societies were formed, compared, for instance, to 93 in the neighbouring province of Närke.[9] Voluntary association, and then on a mass scale, would eventually flourish in Värmland, but not during the first half of the nineteenth century. But the seeds had been sown. Moderately liberal opinions found early expression in *Nya Wermlands-Tidningen* (1836).[10] Gradually the newspaper turned conservative – its position in the debate on protectionism in the 1880s is a case in point (chapter 3) – but it was replaced by *Karlstads-tidningen* (1855)[11] as the main voice of liberalism in the region.

Importantly, in his reflections on civic association, governor Wingård anticipated professor Erik Gustaf Geijer's more analytical account, as laid down in his seminal 1844 lectures at Uppsala University. Geijer, with a chair in history, spoke out against the 'bankruptcy' of corporative institutions, and envisaged how, instead, voluntary associations would take the lead in the transformation of society (Geijer 1845: 35–36). In his analysis we find traits pertaining both to Ferguson's ideas about civil society and, in particular, to Tocqueville's analysis of civic and political association. Certainly these were ideas that were common currency at the time; for one thing, Geijer was also heavily influenced by German thinkers, and not least Hegel (Petterson 1992: 241–61). The main point, however, is that Geijer argued that the kind of civic-mindedness he saw vested in the associations found its foremost and final expression in form of the state. Citizenship and statehood were thus intimately connected, and the essence of the latter was ultimately political (Geijer 1845: 36). However, according to him, there were also grimmer future prospects to be considered. Into the political realm a new agent had recently entered – the people: the post-revolutionary situation in Europe and in Sweden had rendered the people a new and undeniably political role, but the call for emancipation and for extended civic liberties at the same time signalled a risk of outright anarchy, when cast under the spell of demagoguery (Geijer 1845: 122–23).

Although the historical background differed, the ambiguity of Geijer on politics resembled Tocqueville's assessment of civic and political association. These were two mutually connected and self-reinforcing processes, yet they still belonged to separate spheres and the latter had a dangerous and destructive potential (Tocqueville 2003 [1840]: 12). The fear expressed by Geijer and Tocqueville alike was, indeed, incorporated within early liberalism. Without condoning parties and factions, Geijer's interpretation of civic association and its political extensions portended a situation where interests, including class interests, the dread of many a nineteenth-century liberal, were about to crystallize and become politicized. New forms of political association, viz. the modern mass party, as opposed to the old coteries and factions of the aristocracy, were at hand. This volatile situation had somehow to be managed, something which pointed further to the critical issue of citizenship. Geijer himself had proposed to the 1840 Riksdag a model according to which women and the clergy, as well as professional teachers, should be excluded from political representation. His grounds were simply that these catgories were responsible for the crucial task of educating and fostering adolescent citizens in the family, in the religious community, and in the classroom (Geijer 1845: 37; he did afterwards concede that his proposal remained imperfect). Whether eccentric or not, Geijer's reasoning reflected a more widespread confusion regarding the relationship between politics and citizenship.

Ambiguities such as these were perhaps most clearly brought out in the matter of local self-government, the very cornerstone of Tocqueville's analysis of democracy. When local self-government was finally formalized and promulgated in Sweden in 1862, it was not as such considered a 'political' sphere, at least not in the same sense as we normally hold it to be (Norrlid 1970; Åberg 1997). Rather, politics remained a matter for parliament, whereas the local arena was supposedly the concern of motivated, knowledgeable, and unselfish individuals, not of partisanship. The manner in which the new legislation defined participation in self-government was, however, a confusing mixture of two basically different approaches to citizenship represented by economic and political individualism. On the one hand, the very idea of self-government rested on the assumption that unselfish individuals would converge on non-political decisions aimed at promoting a greater good for the community as a whole. On the other hand, the election laws made sure that only the wealthy and, therefore (implicitly), those proven as the most worthy, responsible, and conscientious members of the community should exercise the right to participate in the municipalities. One type of liberal individualism drove out the other.

As previously indicated, this flaw of middle-class liberalism had first become apperent when the extension of political representation became an issue of inconclusive parliamentary strife in the 1840s. In the 1850s political life entered a calmer phase, at the same time as issues of economic liberalism came to the fore. The problem of constitutional reform, though, was far from dead and buried. When the issue was finally resolved, in 1865–66, it turned out a success for a more cautious and conservative attitude on the matter, as had been the case when local self-government was introduced. Carefully designed by Minister of Justice Louis De Geer, the actual aim was, according to Nilsson (1969), to transfer as much as possible of the established interests of the old Estates to the new, bicameral parliament. Indeed, as a liberal of the moderate phalanx, De Geer was certainly no doctrinaire, and the reform did in effect mean that any ideas of using parliament as a tool for promoting urban middle-class interests had to be relinquished. Considering the socio-economic composition of the Swedish electorate, the limitations imposed by the reform punished the urban liberals almost to the same extent as they meant that the working class and the rural proletariat were excluded from political influence.

In a strictly formal sense, the reform did of course mean that political life broke with the ancient structure of the Estates, and with it the idea of corporate bodies as the foundation of parliamentary negotiations. At the same time new restrictions replaced old ones, analogous to the pattern typical of democratizing countries in Europe during this period. The franchise as well as the rules of eligibility were, as with local self -government, restricted by the election laws, and made contingent on the voter's degree of wealth and income. In particular this was the case concerning 'Första kammaren' (the First Chamber), the purpose of which was to secure stability and continuity in parliament. Its deputies were appointed by electoral colleges, viz. by the so -called 'Landstingen' (Provincial Councils) and, in the larger cities, by the City Councils ('Stadsfullmäktige'), and they were elected for terms of nine years. The First Chamber became home to a miniscule, landed elite resilient to anything that smacked of radicalism. To 'Andra kammaren' (the Second Chamber), the election laws were more open, but the right to vote still required ownership of property (which, again, usually meant ownership of land), or income. Candidates running for a seat were subject to the same economic requirements, and they had to be resident in their constituencies. Up to 1909 the deputies were elected in majority elections (by plurality, not absolute majority), usually in single-member constituencies (only large, urban constituencies had more than one deputy), and in direct *or* indirect elections: the crucial decision to choose between direct and indirect models of elections was left for the constituencies themselves to make (Jansson 1969). Hence, in a crucial dimension, the institutional conditions for party formation and elections did actually vary between different parts of the country.

In effect the make-up of the election laws, in combination with the socio-economic composition of the population, meant that the reform put the landed peasantry, rather than the urban middle classes, at the pinnacle of political power. Precisely in this respect, however, the new bicameral parliament at the same time meant that an important step towards political modernization had been taken, and it undoubtedly widened the extent of political participation in a manner unique among most other countries. Years later, in 1894, the poet Gustaf Fröding, son of a wealthy iron works owner in Värmland, lent a voice to this self-assured and confident peasantry. Written in (fake) dialect like much of Fröding's work, it presents us with a sharply drawn and at the same time ironic image of wealthy farmers, and their 'bushels of grain' as the true and undisputed masters of the country.[12] More now than ever before, it was among these groups that the liberals had to mobilize support in favour of their ideas – ideas that were still in many ways vague and inconsistent.

Neither were the election campaigns to the new parliament modelled on nationwide organizations, or outright political parties.
Campaigning remained local and personalized, as an effect of the
new electoral system: an electoral system based on single-member
constituencies and majoritarian elections is usually considered detrimental to the emergence of strong, centralized parties and coordinated election campaigns (Sartori 2001). Thus the nomination
of candidates, interest aggregation, and issue structuring were tasks
that were managed locally or, at best, regionally, rather than nationally under the aegis of organized parties. This feature was enhanced
further by the stipulation that candidates had to be recruited among
the residents of each constituency. As a result the system favoured
parochialism and the prevalence of local elite factions. It did not
facilitate the emergence of a nationwide party system.

When, therefore, radical liberals in Stockholm ('Nyliberalerna')
tried to launch a coordinated, nationwide campaign in the 1869
elections, the response was lukewarm. The strategy followed a two-
pronged approach. Since the liberal programme aimed at radical
social and political reform, including universal suffrage, the inten-
sion was to extend popular involvement in the election campaign.
A number of mass meetings were held throughout the country in
order to mobilize public support, but these met with any real success only locally, in the capital city itself (Esaiasson 1990: 70–71).
In Värmland, little debate was heard on the attempts to stir opinion. Although the appeal from Stockholm was published in the
press, more attention was paid to emigration from the province to
America, which had then started to gain impetus, and to the regional
economic situation, as was the case at one rally held in the district
of Nordmark in late August.[13] Indeed, Värmland was on the verge
of major social and economic transformations precisely because of
factors such as emigration, but also a drastic decline of the regional
iron industry, due to technological change and restructuring; and
these were not issues covered by the liberal programme.

Consequently, when the nuclei of modern political parties began
to emerge in the Second Chamber, they did so mainly on basis of
intra-parliamentarian factions based in the capital. The first, most
influential and longlasting of them were the agrarians, acting under

the name of 'Lantmannapartiet', founded in 1867. It was based mainly on the support of the farmers, but also of the landed proprietors. Ideologically speaking the party contained both conservative and liberal elements. In a wide sense it was still considered oppositional and, up to its split into two factions in 1888, exercised a major influence on domestic political life; the party was later reunited in 1895, but then with a more right-wing orientation (Thermænius 1933). Other 'parties' appeared as well. Among these were the 'Ministeriella' (which reformed in 1873 into a centre faction, and usually acted in support of the government), and the above-mentioned liberal faction 'Nyliberalerna'. The latter, however, only lasted between 1868–71. Among the early factions, only the 'Lantmannapartiet' came closest to resembling a political party proper, although it never created a formal, nationwide organization.

As for the liberals, when a national campaigning organization ('Frisinnande landsföreningen') was eventually created in 1902, one of its first measures was to try to sway local opinion in a number of constituencies in favour of direct elections to the Second Chamber. This was considered a way of wrestling power from the hands of local elites, and at the same time increasing the liberal turnout.[14] The Liberal Party as such – 'Liberala samlingspartiet' – had formed two years earlier. One of its main roots led back to another intra-parliamentarian group, the 'People's Party', which had come into being in the mid-1890s, but only with the formation of 'Frisinnade landsföreningen' did an actual party organization along the lines of mass mobilization appear. From the very outset, though, the relation between the Liberal Party and the 'landsföreningen' was fraught with complications. The Liberal Party consisted mainly of moderate liberals, whereas the national organization was considered more inclined to left-liberalism. This situation automatically created tensions (Johansson 1980). However, alongside emerging party structures other organizational tools were utilized as well.

Liberalism in Värmland
and the rise of popular movements

The manner in which the rules of political participation were extended piecemeal, first in 1865–66 and, later on, in the early twentieth century, corresponds well to what has long been a common interpretation of Swedish political modernization as a gradual and negotiated process, characterized by consensus rather than rapid change and conflict. According to conventional wisdom, the more horizontal nature of social power relationships in Sweden relative to most other countries, and the prominent role played by the peasantry, were an important part of this picture. Thus explained, the path taken towards a political culture of consensual bargaining was later successfully replicated by the labour movement and the social democrats once industrialization had paved the way for class-based divisions. Part of the same picture is also a weakly developed middle-class and a relatively speaking weak liberal movement (see, for instance, Therborn 1989 and 1994; Stråth 1990b). From this perspective, the reformation of parliament in the 1860s may well be interpreted as a confirmation of a particular set of social power relationships as much as a restructuring of them. From a longer perspective this interpretation does, however, tend to exaggerate the historical 'inevitability' of the 'Swedish model' (cf. Andrén 2007).

It should be noted that, in some respects, the Swedish pattern was far from unique. Rather, Sweden belonged to a group of countries, including Belgium, Spain, Austria, and Germany, in which regimes that were, at least formally, constitutional monarchies none the less facilitated modest moves towards parliamentarism and more inclusive rules of participation. (This monarchical path to democratization should be distinguished from the republican–presidential path typical to France, the US or, in the twentieth century, countries such as Finland and Czechoslovakia (Åberg & Sandberg 2003: 255–275)). To recognize such general commonalities does not necessitate embracing a squentialist reading of democratization; which, by the way, is illustrated by the immense differences that also existed between countries such as Sweden and Germany. Therefore, whereas those common properties of democratizing countries which undoubtedly existed must be accepted, exactly the same examples referred to, but to different ends, suggest great variation in terms of political modernization. Variation between countries, although governed by a similar type of regime, also challenges any assumptions of the inevibility of the Swedish path.

Another case in point is Duverger's classification of party lineages (1967 [1954]), according to whether parties have intra-parliamentarian or extra-parliamentarian roots (see the previous chapter). In its original form it is readily applicable to the 'Swedish model' interpretation: step-by-step reformation of the electoral system facilitated the reproduction of traditional elites in parliament and, up to a point, created conditions which were unfavourable to the formation of political mass movements. Indeed, against that background a group such as the 'Nyliberalerna' could only emerge as a mere parliamentarian group, since it lacked a wider socio-economic base. Only by the victory of class rethoric, and the rise of a clear-cut left–right spectrum, was the emergence of modern mass parties, such as most notably the social democrats, facilitated, and by this the introduction of universal suffrage. The formation not only of the Liberal Party, but also the Conservative Party (in 1904, see Stenlås 2002; Nilsson 2004), is often considered to be mainly a reaction to this process, and not as independent features of democratization and party systems formation. Yet, as I have pointed out, at least with respect to the liberals it is also possible to identify a number of important, extra-parliamentarian arenas, and an alternative mode of political association. In effect this pattern deviates from the pattern suggested by Duverger. It provides not only certain interesting parallels to early nineteenth-century association, but also renders support to the hypothesis of organization by means of proxy.

More to the point, the popular movements became extremely important to grass-roots mobilization in Sweden during the late nineteenth century. This was the case not only in regard to liberalism – especially considering certain nonconformist religious and organized temperance movements – but also with respect to socialism (most notably the temperance movement would soon enough host a tug of war between liberals and social democrats, see chapter 3). This feature illustrates both the importance of grass-roots activism on the local and regional level, at the same time as it highlights the role played by regional, liberal elites, since these groups were among the leadership of the popular movements. It indicates the importance of linkages between intra-parliamentarian factions *and* extra-parliamentarian organization.

In general terms, the political culture of nineteenth-century liberalism can, as Kahan (2003) has pointed out, be described as one of limited suffrage. Where Sweden was concerned, even after 1866 voices were still heard in favour of a step-by-step introduction of the franchise, rather than a single, all-out reform. To an increasing extent, however, Swedish liberals embraced the idea of universal suffrage (Vallinder 1984: 21), and they did so under the pressure of mounting demands voiced from all around the country. The contacts that were made with the popular movements, then, meant that liberalism was infused with a kind of radicalism that it had supposedly lost by the 1850s, and it led to a revitalization of liberal politics (but also to a renewed tension between moderate and more radical strands of liberalism, and between cities and the countryside, see chapter 3). Consequently, it would be wrong to depict Swedish liberalism as a mere tool of of bourgeois interests by the turn of the twentieth century. Well into the new century, liberals, including those in Värmland, considered themselves as representatives for a cross-class, left-wing option in politics.[15]

As far as the regional level is concerned, Värmland belonged to those parts of the country in which both nonconformism and organized temperance had developed strongly by the turn of the twentieth century (Lundkvist 1977: 72–74). Among other things we should note that areas with high levels of liberal voting turnout, and localities in which popular movements were firmly established, were often overlapping. For instance, in the Visnum, Väse, and Ölme districts in southeastern Värmland, the liberal candidate received a turnout ranging from 55.8 per cent (Ölme) to 73.2 per cent (Väse) in the 1911 elections.[16] At about the same time some 6 per cent of the overall population in Värmland were affiliated with a nonconformist church, whereas about 7.3 per cent were teetotallers, according to official records.[17] But these are average estimates. Roughly one-fifth of all registered nonconformists in the whole of Värmland, including baptists, methodists, and the Mission Covenant Church, and one-fifth of all registered members in various temperance organizations, were to be found precisely in the above districts by 1905. The latter included the IOGT (International Order of Good Templars), but also the Blue Ribbon, which was particularly closely associated with nonconformism.

Although the party records, admittedly, are scanty, they nevertheless suggest strong connections between liberalism, nonconformism, and teetotalism by the early twentieth century. By 1922 the local branch of 'Frisinnade landsföreningen' in Ölme reported 30 members. Of these, 16 were organized teetotallers and 14 were members of the Mission Covenant Church. A similar pattern was also typical for other local-level liberal associations. Thus another case in point, pertaining to the same area, were the liberals in Väse, at the same time as this particular association, although considerably smaller, also included a larger proportion of women among the members (5 of 16).[18]

Structures with similar historical roots to a varying extent evolved across the entire region. For instance, western Värmland also had an early and strong tradition of nonconformism, which was later boosted by the temperance movement and, at the same time, the populace's liberal political inclinations. The proximity to Norway – from which many of the early lay preachers travelled into Värmland – as well as connections southwards, to areas in western Sweden that had been touched by early religious revival, was one part of the explanation.[19] Another place of interest from our perspective is Munkfors, an industrial enclave in the central section of Värmland (Furuskog 1924), where, similarly to the Visnum, Väse, and Ölme districts, the popular movements played important parts in social life. Venues such as nonconformist chapels and, in particular, temperance lodges, gradually became used for political meetings throughout the region, both for campaigning as well as for appointing candidates to the parliamentary elections. It seems this practice developed first in the towns and cities, such as in Filipstad and Karlstad, during the 1887 elections.[20] It then spread across the countryside and became part of the campaigning process, for instance during the 1893, 1896, 1908, and 1911 elections.[21]

Map 2. Värmland's parliamentary constituencies by 1890.

Importantly, the very same *modus operandi*, i.e. using the venues of nonconformists and teetotallers as meeting spots, was replicated by 'Frisinnade landsföreningen', once a regional organization had evolved. In 1907 a regional office sprang to life ('Värmlands frisinnade länskommitté'). During the following years local branches also appeared, although a few of these, such as the one in Munkfors, actually preceded organization at the regional level; the Munkfors liberal association had started as early as 1904.[22] At the same time the party continued to draw heavily on established principles of political association, as laid down during the previous period. In connection with the 1917 general elections, 70 rallies were organized by the liberals in the northern constituency of the province. Even at this late stage, one-fourth of the campaign meetings were held either at IOGT lodges or in nonconformist chapels.[23]

The integration of grass-roots civic and political association also involved and, indeed, drew heavily on criss-crossing, inter-organizational ties on an individual level. The rank and file of the popular movements have traditionally been depicted as the 'salt of the earth'. In the case of local-level liberal organizations, data for Värmland suggests similarities in this respect, although strong and often dominating elements were recruited from the rural middle strata, viz. the farmers. Importantly, the latter also provided the province with many of its parliamentary deputies, such as Olof Andersson, who was at the same time a devoted member of the Mission Covenant Church in his constituency (chapter 3). Middle-class groups from the cities, small towns, and industrial hamlets scattered across the region played important parts in both spheres as well, in particular as activists, and campaign and administrative staff. Examples include supervisor Anders Henrik Göthberg in Munkfors, former sergeant major Carl Björling, son of a farmer and later ombudsman for the liberals in Värmland, and August Lindh, director of the Provincial Council. All of them had a background in either nonconformism or organized temperance, or, as in the case of Göthberg and Björling, both movements (*Svenska folkrörelser*, I, 1936: 248, 450, 691). Furthermore, elementary schoolteachers and journalists were important categories. Editor Mauritz Hellberg from Karlstad was the most prominent example from the 1890s onwards. Unlike Göthberg, Björling or Lindh, Hellberg was not personally affiliated with any of the above-mentioned popular movements, but nevertheless was a zealous civic activist and organizer. He represented a kind of urban and intellectual liberalism that was similar to that of Albert Hänel in Schleswig-Holstein, only much more radical in orientation.

Altogether, the case of Värmland indicates that the liberals, at least up to a point, were relatively successful at organizing grass roots support, and that this process was a bottom–up as much as a top–down process. This conclusion does, however, also raise a number of questions. Most importantly, it begs the question of why the liberals became so heavily involved with organizational proxies in the shape of the popular movements. In one sense the answer is obvious. As would later be the case with the social democrats, the members of the popular movements represented large and, before the introduction of universal suffrage, potentially influential groups of voters. Their extensive organizational network was simply too important to be neglected as a means by which to reach out to people and prospective voters, particularly so in the countryside. It should also be stressed that this development, from the 1890s onwards, coincided with the mobilization of the Swedish franchise movement. This, in turn, had been preceded by increased voter mobilization on the issue of protective duties in the 1880s – an issue which resulted in an emerging left-right polarization of political life (see chapter 3).

Moreover, the very idea of operating through voluntary civic organizations, rather than by outright organization in terms of a party, appealed as an appropriate solution to managing public opinion. Society certainly became more politicized by the end of the nineteenth century, yet 'partisanship' and 'party' in many ways remained tainted. In that respect the popular movements provided the liberals with a suitable set of officially 'non-political' proxies, similar to those of the civic associations of the early nineteenth century. Some among the liberal leadership, such as Hellberg, recognized the need for firm organization along party lines, yet seemed uncertain as to how to bring this about. All contingencies duly considered, organizing political interests on the basis of non-affiliated civic associations turned out to be a more natural way of going about business.

In this sense the popular movements could easily be interpreted as a logical extension of voluntary associations in the first part of the nineteenth century (Abelius 2007). To begin with, topographical data seems to suggest that such a pattern was present in some localities. By way of illustration, the above-mentioned Visnum, Väse, and Ölme districts were among those in Värmland which had been touched during the first wave of civic association in the 1840s; in all three areas the IOGT and Blue Ribbon lodges of the 1880s had precursors in terms of local branches established by the Swedish Temperance Society in 1847 (Mannström 1912: 233–35). Individual effort also occasionally connected the two waves of association. For instance, tailor and typographer Carl Forssell, a leading figure of the 1848 popular radicalism in Värmland (Forsell 2005), was also the man who first started *Karlstads-tidningen*, and laid the foundation for its subsequent leading position among the regional press. Finally, ideological affinities between the two waves of civic association have been proposed. One case in point is the relationship between temperance and teetotalism. In fact contemporary accounts, such as that by Mannström (1912), secretary of the Swedish Temperance Society, suggest a generic relation between the two movements. If scrutinized more closely, however, his account rather indicates an ambition among the old temperance advocates to adapt to the new ideas of prohibition proposed by the teetotallers. Indirectly, Mannström himself provided the best illustration of this by referring to an 1876 appeal signed by, among others, reverend Peter Wieselgren, originally one of the founding fathers of the Society. On the matter of drinking and its cause, alcohol – was it not, as laid down by Christ in the Sermon on the Mount, best simply to 'cut it off, and cast it from thee'? (quoted in Mannström 1912: 203–204).

Therefore, if we compare civic association before and after 1850 in greater detail, we face more differences and fewer similarities, but differences of a kind that were by no means self-evident to contemporary liberals themselves. Firstly, the *popular* movements, as opposed to civic association in the early nineteenth century, were also *mass* movements. This was the case, if not in respect to all of the local branches and separate associations themselves, then at least to the organizational framework which they gradually developed on the national level. Analogous to Ostrom's assessment (1990) of voluntary social cooperation, this feature also contained a two-edged problem of scale that was both different and more difficult to manage compared to that of the pre-1850 scenario. The problem of scale soon became appearent considering the many, and often conflicting interests represented by liberalism, by nonconformism, and by organized teetotalism respectively. On the one hand, performing concrete functions, such as societal representation and social integration (Gunther & Diamond 2001), is not feasible in organizations with a narrow social base, such as the case was with pre-1850 associations. On the other hand, conditions for generating mutual trust, with the aim of increasing organizational efficacy, also become more difficult once the overall organizational context is large, diffuse, and extends beyond that of known faces and shared acquaintancies. This became increasingly typical of the liberal popular movement networks. Any clear-cut agenda, with clearly defined issues and strategies, around which liberal proxy organizations could have united, was lacking from the late nineteenth century onwards.

Secondly, in part as a consequence of the latter situation, the two waves of Swedish civic organization depicted drew on different expressions of modern individualism, which pointed ultimately towards two conflicting conceptions of citizenship. Indeed, Mannström's attempt (1912) to harmonize temperance and teetotalism touches upon this problem. Up to a certain point both nonconformism and teetotalism did undoubtedly correspond to the liberal credo of individualism: nineteenth-century nonconformism emphasized the awakening of the individual and the personal relationship between the individual and God; this had also been the case with some of its precursors, such as various pietistic movements which in some Swedish regions, if not Värmland, had paved the way in the previous century.[24] This individualism was, however, interpreted primarily from the perspective of the community. Individual enterprise became highly appreciated, but as a means of serving the needs of the congregation (interestingly, this feature was noticed not least among early observers close to the liberal movement, such as Rönblom 1929: 27). Likewise, teetotallers often held abstinence to be the greatest of all individual liberties.[25] The important thing, though, was the capacity of the individual to submit himself/herself and his/her decisions to the better of the community in order to achieve this freedom. This perspective translated into a strong inclination towards monitoring the public demeanour of the members, and of their temperance vows.

This had far-reaching implications. Whereas liberalism never really succeeded in resolving the classic tension between 'economic individualism' and 'political individualism', the popular movements in a sense embraced 'political individualism' more coherently. In analogy to Tocqueville (2003 [1840]), one could also say that the ideological and organizational tenets of the popular movements served as a necessary restraining force in relation to (political) self-interest and its potential excesses. Precisely because of the difference in relation to mainstream, liberal conceptions of individualism and citizenship, though, organization by proxy also carried the seed of its own destruction when liberalism faced the demands posed by emerging mass politics. Yet the dilemma of Swedish liberalism was not unique. We need only to consider liberal political association and its historical roots in northern Germany and Schleswig-Holstein.

Schleswig-Holstein, Prussia, and the new Germany – region and nation

As in Sweden, Prussian liberals before 1850 usually organized themselves in clusters of social and cultural clubs, professional and educational associations, and 'Bürgervereine', in which political interests were more or less successfully cloaked as social and cultural issues. A flurry of civic and for all practical purposes political association during the 'Vormärz' preceded the formation of actual parties. Ususally local, and often small-scale, some relatively speaking large civic organizations were also established, such as the 'Königsberg Bürgergesellschaft', which allegedly had 1,000 members by the 1840s, or, if we extend the perspective beyond Prussia, the 'Bürgerliche Lesegesellschaft Harmonie', formed in Freiburg, Baden, in 1835 by Karl von Rotteck – one of the editors the *Staatslexikon*, i.e. the 'textbook' of early German liberalism: this particular society claimed to have 340 members by the time the Frankfurt Parliament was summoned in 1848 (Sheehan 1978: 23; Hartmann et al. 2001 [1992]). There were, of course, numerous cultural and choral societies named 'Harmonie' across the German states, many of them older than the one in Freiburg; yet the very choice of name is fitting, if we consider the propensity of middle-class liberalism to stress consensus, rather than social conflict. However, as was also the case with early Swedish civic association, some circumspection is warranted in regard to the number of active members in such organizations. Although the German 'Mittelstände' was numerically speaking much larger compared to in Sweden, the combination of a still narrow socio-economic base, and the simultaneous voicing of universal values, was confusing from the point of view of social representation.

A similar pattern to that of Prussia extends to Schleswig-Holstein under Danish reign. 'Bürgervereine' first appeared in the 1830s. Under liberal supervision they fulfilled a triple purpose of mobilization, interest aggregation, and issue structuring, which made them vaguely resemble parties. They took part in the struggle for extended public influence over local government; they organized campaigns in connection to the elections for the provincial diets; and they coordinated reform petitions. Associations of this kind formed in Flensburg (1835), as well as in Husum and Hadersleben (both in 1838) (Schultz Hansen 2003: 433). On the one hand, civic organizations such as these were, in the words of Sheehan (1978: 14), important as 'training grounds' for the early liberals. On the other hand, they had only limited reach at the grass-roots level, although associations in which middle-class liberals and the working class interacted to some extent did exist. One of these was the Flensburg Workers' Association ('Verein zur Förderung der Geselligkeit', 1857, later renamed 'Flensburger Arbeiter-Bauverein').

From the outset, the ambition of this association was to improve the cultural standing of the local working class, and to provide the workers and their families the opportunity to athletic exercise. As an effect of industrialization and urbanization, social issues, and most importantly housing, came to the fore, and in 1878 a workers' building society was created (*Festschrift* 1978: 30–32, 60–63; Heldt 1991: 144). Also, individuals appeared who, as in the case of Peter Christian Hansen, embodied the social accomplishments possible if only the liberal credo of individualism and entrepreneurial spirit was strictly abided by. Hansen had been born in a working-class family in Flensburg, in 1853, but later became a journalist for the *Kieler Zeitung*, and a secretary to the Chamber of Commerce in Kiel, only to advance, finally, to the position as social insurance commissioner to the Royal Provincial Government. Striving to improve the conditions of the Flensburg workers, he was heavily involved with the above-mentioned association. At an early stage Hansen had declared himself a national liberal. Typically for the time, he operated through a large, personal network, the natural habitat of many a nineteenth-century liberal, and was engaged in a number of different spheres and acitivties. For instance, he also participated in the German temperance movement as well as supporting the efforts of the Good Templars when this organization established itself in Schleswig-Holstein. Among his last efforts was to join in the creation of a German–Swedish society for Schleswig-Holstein, together with the Swedish seamen's chaplain at Kiel, C. G. Lagerfelt, in 1921 (*Festschrift* 1978: 45–58; Sievers 1979; Hansen 1982 [1928, manuscript]: 344). Yet, as for the workers' associations and other expressions of middle-class civic organization, the agendas of these organizations as a whole remained characteristically orientated towards the 'domestication' (metaphorically speaking) of the workers (Hurd 2000).

Apart from such general similarities to Värmland, voluntary association in Schleswig-Holstein followed a specific pattern. One circumstance that contributed was the harsher restrictions imposed on the press and public activities, both under Danish[26] and, in particular, under later Prussian rule. Pro-Danish and, above all, socialist campaigning were targeted. The *Amtsblatt*, the official government medium, posted decrees banning this and that publication in the newly acquired province. Before the Anti-Socialist Laws were lifted in 1890, censorship was enforced, particularly during election years.[27] To be sure, many leading liberals, such as Albert Hänel, were opposed to collaborating with the Danes, let alone with the social democrats. However, as far as Berlin was concerned the liberals were also among 'the usual suspects'.[28]

An important factor was that demands for civil liberties and political rights mixed with the ever-present problem of national identity. Basically this problem consisted of two components as far as Schleswig-Holstein was concerned – one ethnic dimension, and one regional dimension. Initially, mounting Danish–German tensions were of importance to political association in the region. For instance, 'Bürgervereine' emerged across the whole of Schleswig-Holstein during the first half of the nineteenth century, but it should be noted that all of the early examples previously mentioned in the above relate to northern Schleswig and, except Flensburg, pertain to localities today situated in Denmark (cf. Map 2.2); and that it was precisely in the northern parts of the region that the Danish movement mobilized, and entered the post-1867 general elections on the basis of separate lists. This geographical cleavage in terms of electoral behaviour by and large remained intact up to the First World War and the transfer of northern Schleswig to Denmark in 1920.

Ethnic conflict varied in intensity across time, though, as well as depending on locality. For instance, in the ethnically mixed environment of Flensburg, the Dane Gustav Johanssen became widely appreciated also among German voters (Kretzschmer 1955: 268). Generally speaking, however, tensions in the region gained momentum from the 1880s onwards, although they culminated only during the last years before the First World War. The growth of German nationalism was a crucial factor in this process, but nationalism in Schleswig-Holstein must also be considered in relation to simmering ideas of regional autonomy. In fact, rather than ethnicity, regionalism was decisive in the overall structuring of liberal political movements and parties in the province. Furthermore, to appreciate this situation correctly, the constitutional framework must also be included in the picture.

In the same manner as in Sweden, but unlike the US or Britain, German mass politics developed prior to parliamentarism, although formal, institutional arrangents allowed for it. In fact, the formation of all-German political institutions, as well as the emergence of modern political parties, were intertwined with each other, only in a more condensed manner and, in regard to party systems formation, at an earlier date than Sweden. Similarly to Sweden, too, the new German Reichstag that was assembled in 1871 left the deputies with only limited influence concerning the executive (see below): Constitutional reform and more extensive rules for political participation thus preceded the implementation of parliamentarism proper. At the same time it would, however, be wrong to consider the formation of party organizations in Schleswig-Holstein as a mere mirror image of the Prussian and, eventually, national German party system. The spirit of 1848 and the struggle for autonomy, or, as in some cases, even the idea of outright independence, were still very much alive in the province. These features had originally provided the ideological basis for Hänel's 'Schleswig-Holsteinischen Landespartei' in the 1860s, and in the years to follow they were echoed in a reluctance to merge formally with the 'Deutsche Fortschrittspartei' (the Progressive

Hamburg

Map 3. Schleswig-Holsteins parliamentary constituencies by 1876.

Party), which, in 1861, had been the first actual party to appear in the Prussian Landtag. The reason was simply that the Progressives had approved of Prussia's annexation of Schleswig-Holstein (Schultz Hansen 2003: 465–67).

The relationship with Prussia remained a critical issue at least up to the 1880s. Parallel with the emergence of a national liberal branch, as well as conservative factions in the region, the Schleswig-Holstein liberals split, mainly because of divided opinions on the status of the region: first the left wing left the party in 1868 on the grounds of a more radical federalistic agenda, based on the Swiss case, and in April 1870 the Augustenburg Particularists seceded (viz. those supporting the claims of the House of Augustenburg to Schleswig-Holstein. In effect this meant supporting the idea of turning the region into an independent state). The main body of the party, though, remained under the leadership of Albert Hänel. He sided with the 'Fortschrittspartei', consequently adding an 'F' to its name (LPSH/F), and continued to try to strike a balance between regionalism and German nationalism. Importantly, the dilemma was reflected in terms of party organization. The statutes of the Progressives had been formally accepted by the 'Liberale Partei Schleswig-Holsteins' in 1878, but at the same time this decision was not considered binding by the local leadership and the parties remained formally independent of each other. Also, on the basis of the collaboration of LPSH/F with the Progressives – and despite initial resistance from Eugen Richter, the leader of the Progressives in the Reichstag – Hänel managed a merger of the left-liberals with national liberal dissidents ('Liberale Vereinigung'). From 1884 these joined together, forming the 'Deutschfreisinnige Partei', but the alliance broke up again in 1893. Only in 1910 were the left-liberal factions united again, this time more firmly, and under the label of the 'Fortschrittlichen Volkspartei' (Kiehl 1966: 111; Schultz Hansen 2003: 465–67; Ibs 2006: 144–45, 149–53).

Hence the challenges posed by regionalism were reflected in the loosely integrated organization of the party (cf. Panebianco 1988). In turn there developed strands of radical liberalism suitable for everybody and nobody. How, then, were regionalism and national identity accommodated within one and the same conceptual and ideological framework? Firstly, during the last decades of the nineteenth century, regional modes of identification found particular expression through the notion of 'Heimat'. Established far earlier in the German language, it was only after 1815 and the gradual emergence of a new political landscape that 'Heimat' became inscribed with the meaning we now usually attach it to. It conceptualized a reaction to the rapid modernization of German society, and came to be used as an expression of profound attachment and deeply felt identification with one's native locality or region (Applegate 1990; cf. Jefferies 1992). With it a whole new genre of literature, the so-called 'Heimatkunst', developed. Often nostalgic and slightly sentimental in outlook, it was, in Schleswig-Holstein, represented by among others Gustav Frenssen and Theodor Storm. Being at the heart of the scholarship of concerned intellectuals, such as Max Weber, or

Ferdinand Tönnies, who had been born in the province as the son of a wealthy farmer in Oldenswort on the Eiderstedt peninsula, the enigma of German modernization was to remain unsolved. But from an ideological vantage point the construction of 'Heimat' turned out to be a useful tool with which the cultural clashes and identity issues caused by industrialization, emerging mass society, and nation-building, could be managed.[29]

Secondly, although Wilhelmine Germany lacked any equivalent to the myth-making, and even cult, which had been associated with the *persona* of Frederick II, the empire did undoubtedly strike a popular chord (Clark 2006: 587–96). Importantly, the notions of 'Heimat' and 'Nation' respectively were by no means exclusive in relation to each other within this federalistic context and its institutions. Rather, to the people in regions such as Schleswig-Holstein, 'Heimat' and 'Nation' helped reinforce each other. This alignment opened the way for cultural autonomy in a situation where, conversely, political and administrative autonomy could not be expected. At the same time it created a bond with the idea of the new Germany and its promise of splendour. Ferdinand Tönnies himself later admitted, when he recorded his youth and upbringing in 1935, that he, although cuffed by his father, had cried out: 'I want to join in!' at the news of the French declaration of war in 1870. At that time he was fifteen years old (quoted in Polley 1980: 203–204).[30]

Consequently, it would seem that the compromise between Schleswig-Holstein and Prussia/Germany, envisaged by the left-liberals, gradually became confirmed by a shift in political culture. However, a federalistic solution could still be criticized, from a particularist as well as a national liberal point of view. Hänel became one of the main targets in these attacks, since he was among the most staunch advocates of *détente* in the struggle between autonomism and the central authorities in Berlin. His was, according to the *Schleswiger Nachrichten* during the 1884 elections, a liberalism that was too lofty and simply 'not practical', but also something that was alien to the particular corner of the world that was Schleswig-Holstein. Defending national liberal policies, and promoting a truly 'German' mode of liberalism, the newspaper criticized Hänel's 'foreign' conception of the state – informed, among other things, by French stereotypes, as the newspaper saw it.[31] The critique did not only strike at what was considered Hänel's outlandish ideas (a critique which, possibly, also included a joke about the fact that Hänel had been born in Saxony and thus lacked proper roots in the soil of Schleswig-Holstein). It also hit at the heart of the dilemma of German liberalism, more specifically the difficulty of extending beyond the limits of highbrow urban, middle-class theorizing. The matter of citizenship and of the relationship between citizens and the state were at the heart of this problem.

Whereas federalism provided a favourable institutional environment for the amalgamation of regional and national identities, it did at the same time pose legal difficulties from the point of view of citizenship. As late as in 1867 and the emergence of the North German Confederation, there were no less than eight different systems for deciding a person's status in relation to 'Staatsangehörigkeit' in Prussia. Also, in German the notions used were 'Staatsbürgerschaft' and 'Staatsbürger', rather than 'Mitbürger', as opposed to 'citoyen', 'citizen', or, in Swedish, 'medborgare' (Andrén 2005: 55–60). In linguistic as well as ideological terms, this meant that greater stress was placed on vertical citizen–state relations. Only to a lesser extent were the extensions of citizenship into civil society recognized, various expressions of civic and political association included. The notion of being an 'Untertan', a subject, was more easily reconciled with political realities than the Enlightenment legacies of modern, political individualism. The lingering suspicion towards party and partisanship therefore had a particular meaning in German political philosophy and public discourse.

Political parties were certainly established at an earlier stage compared to Sweden, but feelings were still ambiguous as regards the kind of partisanship they represented. In this respect Albert Hänel, for example, was very precise. In an address to the voters in the Kiel-Rendsburg constituency in 1883,[32] he firmly declared himself an enemy of 'factional politics' and hoped for a merger between all the competing liberal parties (reprinted in Kiehl 1966, Appendix: 47). Although his statement primarily served as a preparation for the liberal alliance in the forthcoming 1884 elections, it also reflected a traditional, liberal uneasiness when faced with dangers of factional strife. Since, following Hegel, the state was an embodiment of historical progress, by its very definition, factionalism, and division in terms of partisanship were detrimental to the public good. Put simply, the 'reason of state' (cf. Viroli 1992) was always superior to the interests of parties. This particularly became the case once the state and the nation had been firmly allied after 1871. As Hänel stressed a decade later, in his 1892 inaugural speech as rector of the University of Kiel, the empire – *Das Kaisertum* – and the ancient idea of a federalistic state did, indeed, stand as the ultimate symbol of the fatherland, and, in line with the political and philosophical rhetoric of the time, as the fulfilment of a thousand years of historical development (Hänel 1892: 16). Anti-party sentiments, therefore, had fertile soil in which to grow.

Neither was the electoral system as such favourable to the formation of parties. Certainly the election laws were democratic enough. In the legislative work in which the parliament of the North German Confederation and, a few years later, the all-German Reichstag was grounded, the right to vote had been given to all male adults from 25 years of age (Diederich 1969). Direct elections were held in single-member constituencies. An absolute majority was required. In the event that no candidate received a majority, a second ballot ('Stichwahl') was held. Elections were held every third year up to 1888, and every fifth year from then on, but there were irregularities. At the same time, though, the demand for an absolute majority posed a problem most notably for the socialists. In constituencies where social democrats made it as far as the second ballot, they were often met by pre-planned countermeasures, not least from the conservatives and their support organizations. On occasion, such as with the Schleswig-Holstein 'Preussischer Landes-Kriegerverband' in connection to the 1912 campaign, these strategies were blatantly communicated to the official authorities well in advance of the elections.[33] In addition to the appearance of such organizations – formally independent but in actual fact operating under the auspices of the government – the system also opened up for unholy alliances between conservatives and liberals in order to prevent the election of social democratic deputies. Many voters would also opt for a liberal, rather than socialist candidate for purely pragmatic reasons (see, for instance, Beyer 1968). This made party alignments volatile, perhaps mostly so among the left-liberals, uneasily positioned between left and right as they were.

At the same time the system did not facilitate the formation and control of government policies through the elected parliament and its factions. In reality much of the actual power rested with the president of the parliament, i.e. the King of Prussia *cum* German Emperor, and with his chancellor. Although the Reichstag had legislative and budgetary powers, throughout his career Otto von Bismarck successfully manoeuvred to dismantle any attempts to implement rules of governmental responsibility. Finally, as in Sweden, the forms and possibilities of participation in local self-government were extremely limited in Prussia and its provinces due to the restrictive 'Dreiklassenwahlrecht'.[34]

Alltogether, and once again analogous to the case of Sweden, the design of the electoral system was rooted in a society and a political culture with lingering parochial features, and in which local elites constantly held the upper hand. Similarly, campaigning rested on individual performance and, in the words of Thompson (2000: 292), 'last-minute improvisation'. Yet, there were also differences. Individual performance, for one thing, implied different outcomes depending on the precise nature of the institutional setting. In contrast to Sweden, candidates running for a seat in the Reichstag were not required to be resident in their constituencies. As much as this feature had the potential to make election campaigns somewhat less localized compared to Sweden, it did however also lead to further alienation between parties and the voters, especially in rural areas. In the long run, Schultz Hansen argues, (2003: 473–74), it led to a widening of the urban–rural divide within liberalism in Schleswig-Holstein.

If we return to Duverger's model of party systems formation, then, the intra-parliamentarian roots of German parties, including those in Schleswig-Holstein, would seem more prominent compared to the case of Sweden. And by comparison, liberal parties in the German context did undoubtedly to greater extent retain traits of so-called 'Honoratiorenparteien', rather than mass parties (or, perhaps, at least in the case of Schleswig-Holstein left-liberalism, a 'professorial party', considering the number of academics on the leadership roster).[35] Yet, to make the picture complete, some important features must be added. In Sweden, early forms of middle-class civic and political association by and large belonged to the past as we approach the late nineteenth century. As a specific, small-scale form of – albeit elitist – expression of social cooperation, this kind of organization survived longer in Schleswig-Holstein. Similarly to the situation regarding Swedish popular movements, they continued to operate as proxies of political associations long after the establishing of political parties proper.

Local 'Bürgervereine', but also for instance workers' associations and women's organizations, were continuously used throughout the second half of the nineteenth century as instruments for mobilizing political opinion and the nomination of candidates. This was the case in the town of Schleswig in the 1871 elections, where the merchant Theodor Reinke, a national liberal from Altona, and his Particularist opponent, Count Baudissin, ran against each other for a seat.[36] During the same period new associations modelled on the old ones also formed, such as the 'Friedrichsberger Bürgerverein', which was established in the Friedrichsberg district of the town in 1883. Like the pre-1848 associations, it was devoted to promoting its members in matters of local and public interest, at the same time as it served as an arena for leisure and spiritual activities; similarly to pre-1848 associations, it was also a rather small organization, initially having 102 members.[37] Other situations involving proxies that operated parallel to regular party organizations pertain, for instance, to Bordesholm (1907 elections),[38] and to Itzehoe, the latter traditionally a left-liberal stronghold. There the local branches of the 'Alldeutscher Verband', the 'Reichsverband gegen die Sozialdemokratie', and the 'Evangelischer Bund' all served as electoral platforms, also in connection with the 1907 elections.[39]

In addition, it was often with some irregularity that the various 'Wählervereine', which formed as local level extensions of the parties, advertised their ideological label. This contributed further to blurring the distinction between party and proxies. Examples include Flensburg (1898 elections), and Steinburg (1907 elections).[40] Among left-liberals and national liberals alike, local branches and a nucleus of full-time appointed officials emerged, but only slowly, particularly so in the countryside, and largely by emulation of the Social Democratic Party. The administrative staff were kept to a minimum. Only by the beginning of the twentieth century did the left-liberals and the national liberals employ two party secretaries, stationed in Hamburg and in Schleswig-Holstein. 'As elsewhere, Schleswig-Holstein left-liberals had to compensate by relying on informal structures' (Thompson 2000: 284–92, quote at 286); and, one is tempted to add, by involving the help of organizational proxies. However, certain other traits in the regional environment also contributed to political mobilization and association in Schleswig-Holstein.

The dual roots of political individualism

Structures corresponding to those of the Swedish popular movements were lacking in Germany. The pattern of the German temperance movement is a striking example. Emerging in the north German states, which, like Scandinavia, had a strong tradition of producing and drinking spirits, it lost momentum after 1848, together with many other expressions of 'Vormärz' civic organization. Thirty-five years later it was succeeded by the 'Deutscher Verein gegen den Missbrauch geistiger Getränke' (DV, 1883). Contrary to the first wave of German temperance prior to 1848 or, as had become the case among Swedish teetotallers by the end of the century, the DV did not consider the issue of drinking connected to political reform. Rather, the efforts of the DV were directed more at collaboration with the state and the local authorities. It aimed at limiting the effects of drinking primarily by lobbying for administrative and legislative measures. In effect this meant rejecting electoral politics, and less stress was put on popular activism and voluntary association (Roberts 1984). In addition the IOGT struck root in the region in the 1880s; in fact Schleswig-Holstein and Hamburg both became strongholds of this movement. However, the IOGT did not, in any event not in Schleswig-Holstein, become a mass movement or a political platform in the same sense as in Sweden (chapter 4).

Finally, neither did organized nonconformism play a crucial part in the mobilization of liberalism. The number of nonconformists ('Freireligiöse') in Schleswig-Holstein was modest, amounting in fact to fewer than 5,000 people among a total population of over 1.6 million in 1910 (Lorenzen-Schmidt 2003: 415). This gave a proportion equivalent of 0.3 per cent of the total population, i.e. much less in comparison to the above-mentioned figures for Värmland. The concept of political association by proxy, therefore, prevailed among German liberals, but not on the basis of the kind of far-reaching organizational structures that developed in Sweden during the last decades of the nineteenth century. Viewed in a somewhat longer perspective, however, there was undoubtedly a feature of the local environment which, similarly to the popular movements in Värmland, stimulated modern individualism and individualistic political behaviour. And as in the Swedish case, it was individualism of a kind that was not primarily rooted in the enlightenment experience, nor bore the imprint of the dualism between 'economic' and 'political individualism'.

The legacy to which I am referring belonged to the realm of religious beliefs but, unlike German liberalism as a whole, it did not relate to the divide between Catholicism and Protestant anti-clericalism. (Not even as the 'Kulturkampf' unfolded in the 1870s, and pushed liberalism further into the arms of Bismarck, does this division readily apply to conditions in Schleswig-Holstein. Catholics made up only a small part of the population in the region, making them, as Schmidt (1985: 188) has it, a 'diaspora' more than a main group for political association. Instead, it should be emphasized that the north German states and Schleswig-Holstein had traditionally been at the centre of Pietist activity. Pietist revivalism first surfaced in Saxony and Prussia, in the seventeenth centrury, and then spread further north, both to Denmark and Sweden. Flensburg, Schleswig, Tondern, and Husum early on became important centres in the 1705–30 period; as was, during the next stage, the northernmost part of the region, and in particular the so-called Herrnhut colony at Christiansfeld, outside Hadersleben (Jakubowski-Tiessen & Lehmann 1984; on Flensburg specifically, see Hejselbjerg Paulsen 1955).

In essence, not only the personal relationship between man and

God was stressed by the Pietists, but – similarly to the gospel of the Enlightenment – also the ethic and moral responsibilities of the individual. However, whereas Pietism, in the case of Prussia, in part fused with the state (Clark 2006), this connection was less obvious in the case of other north German states and Schleswig-Holstein. Importantly, too, Jakubowski-Tiessen & Lehmann (1984) stress that, because of the multifaceted nature of Pietism, it played a part in promoting pluralism in society with respect to confessional matters. Neither was its influence limited to the burghers of the cities and towns. Many peasants and artisans were included, too (Jakubowski-Tiessen & Lehmann 1984: 315, 323). Importantly, the impact of Pietism was not limited to the seventeenth and eighteenth centuries. A new wave of Pietist awakening swept across the north German states in the early nineteenth century, and added an important dimension to emerging civic association, most notably, as pointed out by Roberts (1984), in connection with the formation of the early temperance movement.[41]

Parts of the Pietistic legacy found outlets through the Enlightenment, whereas in other instances impulses were channelled through the Lutheran Church. In the first case, a particularly emotional, or sentimental, strand of German literature was influenced by it ('empfindsame Aufklärung'), such as in the widespread works of Christian Fürchtegott Gellert. For instance, in the 1930s Ferdinand Tönnies recorded still having a copy of Gellert's *Moralische Vorlesungen* (1770) that had been handed down to him from his mother's side of the family (Polley 1980: 194). Regarding the principles of morality and character, Gellert's mixture of voluntarism and self-restraint were certainly not incompatible with the individual pursuit of happiness along the lines of liberalism; it was only that the final arbiter of right and wrong was neither the market, nor the community of citizens but, rather, God. Political individualism could find support in Gellert's first rule of virtue – self-reflection aiming at insight into one's own duties[42] – whereas economic individualism among men was accepted, but only insofar as it did not violate their 'responsibility towards God and fellow men'.[43]

In the second case the Pietistic legacy was transmitted to the so-called 'Innere Mission'/'Indre Mission'. Whereas at least the German variety of this movement, formed by Johan Hinrich Wichern, bore the hallmark of conservative Protestantism, at the same time it informed the work of the second wave of the German temperance movement, viz. the DV, in the late nineteenth century. Although religious awakening often led to an initial rejection of the material world, in the long run it could also provoke precisely the opposite effect (Weitling 1992). This is illustrated by the close relationship between nonconformism and liberalism in Sweden as well as, arguably, the case of Schleswig-Holstein. Indeed, this is most clearly demonstrated by the Danish in northern Schleswig, where, according to Weitling, the 'Indre Mission' became a catalyst of political activism, as Danish–German relations polarized in the years shortly before the First World War. By way of conclusion, the individualizing effects of religious revival allowed for a range of seemingly contradictory perspectives when applied to civic life: 'German, Danish, liberal, orthodox, religious, and confessional, as well as the tactics and purposes of other interests' (Weitling 1992: 19).[44]

Certain features of the regional, social environment therefore seem to have made people susceptible to liberalism in nineteenth-century Schleswig-Holstein and, perhaps, particularly so within the framework of a traditionally conservative, rural environment. This feature touches upon a problem which, since the studies conducted in exile in the 1940s by Rudolf Heberle, sociologist and son-in-law of Tönnies, has been pondered by analysts of liberalism in the region (see, for instance, Heberle 1944). On the one hand, Tilton (1975) argued that the rapid shift from liberalism to totalitarianism and Nazism in the 1920s and early 1930s could in part be explained by the traditionalism and conservatism of the farmers. On the other hand, Thompson (2000: 303) proposes the same logic of explanation, but in reverse. According to him, the success of left-liberalism in Schleswig-Holstein was largely due to its appeal to 'rural pride and independence'.

Under pressure from the social democrats among urban voters at the turn of the twentieth century, left-liberalism deliberately latched on to the socially conservative environments in the countryside, and thereby succeeded in reflecting a more deeply rooted trait of individualistic, political culture. 'Ironically', Thompson points out, 'a left liberal political tradition was itself part of the social conservatism of the Schleswig-Holstein countryside' (2000: 303). I do not dispute the fact that the farmers were conservative. In fact, the same was often the case in Sweden and Värmland. The same kind of conservative individualism and attachment to the land which, in the long run, could promote right-wing extremism was, indeed, at some point congenial to liberalism as well. Whether this strand of argument validates the 'Sonderweg hypothesis' with respect to Schleswig-Holstein is however a different matter.

Rural communities in transition

I will return to this issue at some length in chapter 4, but some contingencies are worth bringing up here, since they point in the direction of the problem of organization and, ultimately, election campaigning. Most importantly, the difference between Sweden and Germany was that the farmers in Schleswig-Holstein organized independently, outside the ranks of parties and the liberal movement, at an earlier stage than was the case in Värmland. By the turn of the twentieth century the farmers in Schleswig-Holstein certainly were not alien to the idea of voting for the liberals. But they preferred to organize separately, in professional and trade organizations, rather than on basis of outright parties (Schultz Hansen 2003: 473–74). We may also add Denmark to this comparison, in order to widen the perspective somewhat. In this case, contrary to both Sweden and Germany, the liberal movement was by and large defined in agrarian terms. The urban–rural cleavage, typical most notably of Swedish liberalism but also of liberalism in Schleswig-Holstein, was a less prominent feature in Denmark (cf. Thomas 1988). German civic and political association was simply 'compartmentalised' to a greater extent than in any of the two Scandinavian countries. With or without proxies, presumably this made mobilization and issue structuring, not to speak of societal representation and integration, a more difficult task in Schleswig-Holstein compared to Värmland. Yet, among these differences with respect to historical setting, ideological background conditions, and institutional framework, certain basic similarities in terms of liberal political association do at the same time appear, once we put the two regions side by side.

First of all, ideas on formal organization shared a common root in the ubiquitous hostility towards 'factionalism', and in the uncertainty with respect to the distinction between 'civic' and 'political association'. In the case of Prussia/Germany the importance attached to the state added further weight to the suspicion towards mass politics, factionalism, and, ultimately, political parties and partisanship. Secondly, notwithstanding the obvious differences in terms of organizational basis, there were, indeed, similarities precisely with respect to organization. In both Sweden/Värmland and Prussia/ Schleswig-Holstein, liberalism emerged on basis of small-scale urban, middle-class forms of civic association. Whereas this pattern was, in a sense, congenial to contemporary ideas celebrating the role of individual performance, it did at the same time prove ineffective as a means of social cooperation and mass organization although, appearently, for somewhat different reasons. In part this pattern of organizational behaviour was due to the unresolved tension between 'economic' and 'political individualism' which, particularly before 1850, prevented the formation of more inclusive conceptions of citizenship.

A third common feature which adds up to an explanation of what still turned out as the relative success of liberalism, and to our understanding of liberal political association, is to be found in the regional social, economic, and cultural environment of Värmland and Schleswig-Holstein. These regions illustrate how the sources of modern individualism were not restricted to urban and middle-class environments. In the case of Värmland the popular movements of the late nineteenth century, and most notably organized nonconformism and teetotalism, played an important part in advancing such ideas. This was particularly important in the countryside, which up to then was often untouched by modern forms of civic association. Similarly, such ideas were crucial also to the Pietist movement which, in waves, provoked changes in the social and cultural environment of Schleswig-Holstein. Although perhaps ultimately conservative in outlook, this was also a kind of individualism which could be appreciated among the farmers and rural population, and arguably it served as a link to urban liberalism. As the subsequent split of the Swedish liberal movement or the tensions of liberalism in Schleswig-Holstein illustrates, this urban–rural alliance however proved impossible to sustain in the long run.

CHAPTER 3

Värmland

Liberalism one step to the left

Citizen and society

Between 1870 and 1921 a total of twenty Second Chamber elections were held. By the end of the period universal suffrage had been introduced and the main elements of the Swedish party system and modern electioneering had fallen into place. Parts of the period are of lesser importance from our point of view. Regarding the election campaigns during the 1870s, these have justly been termed dull with respect to content as well as haphazard in management (Esaiasson 1990: 72–74). Neither did any regular party organizations come to the fore following the introduction of the new parliament. Somehow political life entered a stage of exhaustion once the bland outcomes of the 1865–66 reform became apparent. However, other elections, such as those held in the spring and autumn of 1887 and in 1893, 1896, 1911, and 1921, were the more important to the development of campaigning. These campaigns also illustrate the gradual shift from mobilization by means of proxy to organization by means of regular parties. Consequently, they have been chosen for the purposes of analysis.

The 1880s were not least important from the point of view of political association. The societal effects brought about by industrialization now became more tangible. Although Värmland lagged behind in terms of economic modernization, the period still remained one of critical transitions. It was a time of social and economic change, and of emerging grass-roots mobilization among an electorate struggling to embrace the positive effects of modernization and, at the same time, trying to preserve traditional ways of life. Whereas change for some posed a challenge to hallowed tradition and virtues, tradition could also be scolded for its attendant poverty and for its lack of justice and equality. Nowhere else were these contradictions more clearly put to words than in the works of Selma Lagerlöf and Gustaf Fröding. On the one hand, Lagerlöf, the first woman to become a Nobel laureate in literature, celebrated the refined, manorial culture of rural Värmland; something all but vanished by the late nineteenth century, since its economic foundations had altogether collapsed with the decline of regional iron-making. On the other hand, Fröding mocked the very same culture for the toil and back-breaking existence it imposed on the workers.[1] And while the clergy continued to criticize the decline of church attendance, the moral failings of people, and the increasing lack of ancestral attachment to the soil among the peasantry,[2] what was commonly known as the 'social issue' meanwhile moved to the forefront of political discourse. There it mixed with old demands for political reform. These two forces mutually reinforced each other in the years to follow.

Through a mix of pragmatism, deliberate redefinition of critical concepts such as 'citizenship', and genuine and radical concern for social issues, influential groups of Swedish liberals did move in the direction of progressivism from the mid-1880s onwards, (Rönblom 1929; Vallinder 1984; Hedin 2002; Lundberg 2007). At the same time yet more groups of moderate liberals had begun to move closer to the conservative camp (Christensen 2009: 277). Ideological divisions gradually became more clearly defined. Among the former groups this development, as well as the attempts to coordinate the liberal movement along stricter lines, reflected the emergence of a new kind of leadership, represented by people such as Ernst Beckman, Emilia Broomé, Georg Halfred von Koch, and the future chairman of the Liberal Party, Karl Staaff. Indeed, when local liberals in Karlstad tried to summarize the role of the party in municipal matters in 1918, the keynote speaker, Dr Hugo Severin, depicted it as a movement by the average man and for the average man. Its focus was the struggle for improved housing, and the fight against drinking, ignorance, and general coarseness.[3] As far as the liberals themselves were concerned, democratization and the struggle for improved social conditions were not to be left to the socialists to

96

single-handedly benefit from politically. Also, for many liberals by 1900, the idea of deliberately linking social reform to state intervention had become more palatable as a solution to the problems caused by modernization. Often described in terms of a gradual turn away from unhampered 'individualism' to 'collectivism', this shift could in fact also be justified precisely from the point of view of individualism.

Although emerging forms of voluntary social cooperation differed compared to those thirty or forty years earlier, political development by the end of the nineteenth century did not result in a rebuttal of individualism among influential liberals. If anything, the history of liberalism demonstrated the paramount role of individual agents in combating outdated social and political institutions. This was, for instance, stressed at a meeting of the Liberal Debating Society in Karlstad, in March 1918.[4] Duly considered contemporary events could also be described in terms of a victory for 'political individualism', viz. an acknowledgement of the capacity of the individual to make informed decisions with respect to the greater good of society. Consequently, this implied that the individual must now to a greater extent be prepared to accept binding decisions made on a collective, rather than solely individualistic basis, and, importantly, to accept the mediating role of the state between citizen and society. At the same time, however, the above meeting also emphasized that public duties on occasion had to take second place to duty 'to kin and, particularly, family'.[5] Corefamily values were, indeed, typical to the time, not least so among the middle classes. Yet the statement also illustrates – similarly to what had been the case with Erik Gustaf Geijer more than seventy years previously – how traditional conceptions of community continued to be a part of the liberal mindset.

To begin with, individualism and collectivism were not necessarily at loggerheads with each other, judged from a longer, historical perspective (Berggren & Trägårdh 2006: 9–11, 216–21). Interpreted from within the framework of the modern welfare state, Berggren and Trägårdh suggest that Geijer's ideas may be considered simply as one of the many roots to what eventually became a specifically Swedish way of maximizing individual liberty, but without endangering the fundamentals of society. This was so since, at the same time as Geijer had spoken about the relationship between community, voluntary association, citizenship, and the state, he also made individual liberty the core of his model. Notions such as these filtered back into a conception according to which human freedom and dignity were ultimately guaranteed *not* by mutual relations and dependence on peers, but independence from traditional forms of community. The key to obtaining this freedom was the state and its welfare institutions. At the same time, however, it is obvious that such an ideological framework differs from that of Hume's ideas on social cooperation. To Hume the basic dilemma seems ultimately not to have been that of the relationship between the individual and the state, but rather the conflict *within* the individual, between self-interest and altruism.

The conflict -ridden but also dynamic relation between individualism or, rather, different strands of individualism, and society was reflected in civic and political association on a grass-roots level by the late nineteenth century. As a confirmation of the dawning of a new society and new social identities, the popular movements had become firmly entrenched in many regions, such as Värmland. By gradually adopting progressivism, urban liberals, in principle, moved closer to nonconformism and teetotalism on the problem of individualism, although there were, of course, important exceptions to this pattern (see later in this chapter). For instance, in matters of faith, nonconformists – although stressing the personal relationship between the individual and God – still held the individual to be part of a greater community, that of the congregation; the secession from the state Church did not alter this fact. Similarly, as I have stressed, a more decisive turn from economic individualism in the direction of political individualism among liberals implied a greater emphasis on the collective dimension of citizenship, including traditional forms of community. To some extent a common ground for the understanding of the individual actor, and of his responsibilities as well as liberties, was laid.

Generally speaking, nonconformists were forerunners in creating a stronger sense of community by the help of egalitarian individualism and individual improvement, but a similar logic also applies in regard to teetotalism (Berggren & Trägårdh 2006: 212–15). In the latter case the weight of explicitly Christian motives differed between various types of teetotalist organizations. For instance, the IOGT was to become more and more secularized as time passed (Åberg 1975), but not the Blue Ribbon. Regardless of which, however, the temperance vows made by the individual members went hand in hand with accepting that the community represented by the lodges would monitor and police their behaviour with respect to alcohol. From the point of view of organization, established political factions were caught by surprise by this development of civic association and by what was for all purposes a new conception of partisanship.

Tariffs and party systems formation

By the late 1880s factionalism in parliament revolved around the transformation and subsequent break-up of the 'Lantmannapartiet'. The split was a direct effect of the controversies brought out in full by the 1887 elections on the issue of protective duties on, primarily, imported agricultural produce and particularly grain, but also manufactured products. Signalling a definite end to deregulation and ideas of free trade, political opinion at that point also revealed the first signs of polarization along a class-based, left–right axis: among those against protective duties were a majority of the urban deputies in the Second Chamber, defending what they identified as the consumer interests of the urban working-class populations, as well as the majority of family small-scale farmers from the northern and northwestern parts of the country, including Värmland (areas which, in any event, did not usually produce grain for sale on the market). By contrast, opinion in favour of tariffs was strongest in the eastern and southern parts of Sweden, among major grain producers and industrialists. And, as it happened, the conflict over duties also involved the issue of extended political rights, similarly to what had occurred in Germany in the late 1870s during the so-called 'Second Reichsgründung' (chapter 4); indeed, Germany, where protective duties had been introduced in 1879, was used as an example by both sides to prove their point. It is significant that the increased public interest in the election spurred a dramatic rise in turnout – from circa 25 per cent previously to closer to 50 per cent (Esaiasson 1990: 84).

Emerging class-based politics and increased participation at the same time forced the established factions in parliament, including the liberals, to consider the problem of societal representation and social integration as an integral part of electoral mobilization. As indicated, this was a situation for which they were quite unprepared. Full mass party organizations, let alone on the regional level, did not yet exist. What did come to the fore, rather, were two nationwide umbrella organizations, for and against protectionism duties respectively, but in neither case with any formal ties to the parliamentary factions of the parliament. Local associations, for and against protective duties, also formed. Although these lacked any clearly defined political affiliations, the pro-free trade camp was, as in Värmland, inclined to the left, whereas protectionists more often included conservatives.

What appeared was, in the terminology of Gunther and Diamond (2001: 12–16; see also Daalder 2001), a compromise between traditional elite party structures and the principles of mass parties. Factions with no actual organization, or in any event a very narrow organizational base, and mobilization by force of vertical networks and personal allegiance to faction leaders, were supplemented by attempts at mass-mobilization. Due to the lack of formal organization, public rallies, a massive usage of pamphlets, and campaigning in the press became main forces in creating and shaping political opinion (on the 1887 campaign and its organizational foundations in general, see Esaiasson 1990: 84–85). On the regional level, in particular two newspapers would from now on constantly be at the head of political debate. Whereas *Karlstads-tidningen*, at this stage under the editorship of Anders Jeurling, served as a platform for the pro-free trade election campaign, *Nya Wermlands-Tidningen* became an advocate of conservative interests. In addition to this, the appearance of political proxies added a qualitatively speaking new ingredient to the campaign compared to earlier elections. Local liberals took the first steps towards using nonconformism and organized temperance as political agents.

During the spring of 1887, free-traders and protectionists all over the country were rallying. For the first time, one and the same issue was discussed among voters across the country. Compared to earlier elections, campaigning became more detached from purely local interests. Tariffs had posed a troublesome issue since 1885, when protectionist interests had begun to consolidate in parliament. An intense but inconclusive debate followed and culminated in early 1887. In the First Chamber the issue fell through. Both sides in the Chamber agreed that duties were either to be introduced across the board, or not at all. The Second Chamber, however, was divided on the matter of tariffs on rye, with 111 deputies voting in favour and 101 against. Because of this situation, the king, Oscar II – himself positive towards free trade – decided to dissolve the Chamber and announce a re-election; in addition, regular elections were already scheduled for the autumn of the same year. Although opinion in Värmland as a whole was in favour of free trade (see, for instance, Rönblom 1929: 53), probably because of the large proportion of small-scale, family farming, both camps pushed their resources and arguments to the limit. From March onwards the newspapers filled with appeals enumerating the pros and cons of duties. For instance, *Nya Wermlands-Tidningen*, in an air of patriotism, criticized the free traders for reducing the whole matter to one of only duties on agricultural produce, when the issue, surely, concerned the entire national economy.[6] *Karlstads-tidningen*, for its part, used the same logic, only in reverse; i.e. that duties would harm the economic foundations of the country. Indirectly the newspaper also touched on the issue of political reform by concluding that the Swedish workers and peasantry were, indeed, enlightened and clear-sighted enough to understand and manage the problem laid before them in the election.[7]

The role of the popular movements in this process becomes obvious when contemporary press coverage of the election campaign is examined. Material pertaining to the various organizations as such is scant for this particular period (and, when available, the minutes of the proceedings do not indicate any discussions on the matter). That being said, *Karlstads-tidningen* reported, in early April, that 'several associations in Karlstad, such as the nonconformists, the Good Templars, and the members of the (non-socialist) workers' association' had met jointly to consider the forthcoming elections. According to the newspaper, they finally decided to support the liberal free trade candidate Gullbrand Elowson, a senior master from the secondary grammar school, for the constituency.[8] Other preparations were made at the chapel of the Mission Covenant Church and, in Filipstad, the local society against protective duties; in this case, too, at the local branch of the Mission Covenant Church.[9]

Another novelty of the campaign was that candidates running for a seat now were more closely scrutinized in respect of their actual opinion on the matter at stake. The 1887 elections, to be sure, were still not about regular and competing party programmes, but focused solely on the one, critical issue of protective duties. For this reason, too, the individual qualities and, for want for a better word, charisma of the respective candidates probably became somewhat less important than the position taken on tariffs. An individual's appearance and character were otherwise extremely important in a political landscape traditionally dominated by local elites, and in which the often small number of eligible voters were personally acquainted with the candidates. This was particularly the case in constituencies where direct rather than indirect elections were held and in which, as a rule, it was more important for the prospective deputy to attend regular meetings (Carlsson 1953: 35–39; Esaiasson 1990: 84; Gunther & Diamond 2001: 12–14).

Altogether this created a new situation for many of those who ran for a seat. The representation of Elowson in one of the local newspapers, *Filipstads Stads- och Bergslags Tidning*, gives a typical illustration of this. To begin with, a number of admirable features had been noted regarding Elowson's person. Apart from being a man of learning and letters he also had

> extensive experience from all walks of life ... a demeanour character-
> ized by calm and dignity whenever addressing an audience, as well
> as wit and wisdom; he expresses himself with great ease; he is a
> skilled negotiator and, last but not least, he is a just man of strong
> moral fibre.[10]

Whereas qualifications such as impeccable morals, a sense of fair play, and eloquence were hailed, these also, however, had to be supported by a thorough hands-on knowledge of the matter at hand, as well as the will and ability to argue and defend a specific course of political action. This, too, was a prominent feature of Elowson since he was, according to the newspaper, a warm and decided supporter of free trade.[11] At the same time Gullbrand Elowson's candidature typified the flimsiness of factional affiliations at this time. To begin with, it was not uncommon for candidates to run as independents; something they would continue to do until the turn of the century. Furthermore many, like Elofsson, were prone to shift allegiance. He won a pro-free trade seat by a great majority in the spring elections of 1887, but only a few years earlier, in connection with the 1881 elections, had actually drifted towards the conservatives in Karlstad, before later siding with the left-wing camp (Moberg 1983: 126). This kind of background added fuel to the traditional smearing of the opposition candidates by the newspapers.

Together with other free traders, Elowson was targeted by the conservative *Nya Wermlands-Tidningen*. In hindsight, some of the critical remarks seem, in fact, quite to the point, considering the situation. *Karlstads-tidningen*, when rejecting the attacks, considered it unfair of *Nya Wermlands-Tidningen* to allude to those of Elowson's qualities which, it presumed, would be viewed negatively by the 'different social classes making up the free trade party'.[12] On the one hand, it could be argued that *Nya Wermlands-Tidningen* played the card of class conflict. On the other hand, the criticism clearly struck at the heart of what was, without doubt, a dilemma of liberal politics, i.e. precisely the difficulties in forming durable, cross-class alliances among the electorate. In the opinion of *Nya Wermlands-Tidningen*, the workers had simply been duped by free trade propaganda.[13]

The spring elections turned out to be a great success for the pro-free trade alliance in Värmland, however. Of eleven deputies elected, all but two were free traders.[14] Part of the explanation was, as pointed out, that the issue of protective duties touched at the heart of everyday life. Another relevant aspect was that the problem of political representation and participation simmered more or less openly among the public during the campaign, and thus mobilized voters. Claiming to represent the rights of 'the people', therefore, rather than outright demands for 'democracy', became – as Lundberg (2007) has most recently demonstrated – a keynote of Swedish political modernization. Needless to say, the notion of 'the people' played an important part in German political discourse as well, but the important difference in Sweden was that this did not to the same extent as in Germany become infused with ethnic values and meanings (see, for instance, Stråth 1990a).[15] But, always malleable as a concept, 'the people' could also be used in conservative rhetoric. When contemplating the outcome of the spring elections, *Nya Wermlands-Tidningen* queried whether the election had really allowed the government to take on board the opinion of the 'the people' on the matter. The answer had to be 'No', considering the conditions and, according to the newspaper, the aggressive campaigning of the free traders.[16]

The regular elections in September followed a similar pattern, although the result – initially promising from a free trade point of view – eventually ended in an anticlimax. Certainly, it was not unusual that election results in some constituencies were contested and so, too, was the case this time. From a free trade perspective the single most alarming of these incidents occurred in Stockholm, but its repercussions affected the whole country. It was discovered that one of the free trade candidates in the capital, Olof Larsson, had failed to pay local taxes and hence was not formally eligible to run for election. In its ruling the Supreme Court decided that all ballots including Larsson's name and candidature would be declared invalid. In disappointment, *Karlstads-tidningen* concluded that, despite the Swedish people having so clearly shown their disapproval of protective duties, the election result would now be overthrown simply because of the negligence of a single citizen.[17] Thus no fewer than twenty-two free trade deputies from Stockholm were replaced by protectionist candidates. Thus, too, the majority in parliament swung in favour of tariffs which, early in 1888, were introduced on a number of agricultural products and manufactured goods.

Nevertheless, the outcome must be seen as successful for the free traders as far as campaigning and mobilization of grass roots opinion are concerned. To begin with, an important step had been taken towards the 'politicization of politics', albeit without actual parties to aggregate and structure opinion among the voters. Effects on the established, intra-parliamentarian factions as a result of these changes were even more tangible. As pointed out, one of the outcomes was the split of the agrarians and the 'Lantmannapartiet' into two factions, one protectionist and the other pro-free trade ('Nya lantmannapartiet' and 'Gamla lantmannapartiet'). Among the urban deputies, free traders similarly joined together to form a centre faction. Important to note is that the free trade faction of the 'Lantmannapartiet' and the left wing of the centre faction both contained elements which, together with the 'Folkpartiet' (People's Party, 1895), were later to be joined in the Liberal Party. At the same time, however, the latter feature also indicated what would become a recurring dilemma of the liberal movement.

Although the People's Party had originally been formed with the aim of reconciling urban and rural interests, the organizational roots of Swedish liberalism still meant that a cleavage between cities and the countryside was integrated with its electoral basis from the very outset. Ultimately this problem was part of the strategy chosen by the liberals in the 1880s. Although they had successfully managed to mobilize opinion when protective duties hit the political agenda, they had done so without any help of a coordinated, organizational framework. Considering the diverse, urban–rural composition of the liberal electorate, organization by means of proxy would therefore prove itself flawed in the long run. Confusion and, occasionally, dispute in connection with the nomination meetings would become a permanent ingredient during the following elections. At the same time, though, it is difficult to speak of these controversies in terms of clear-cut factional competition since, analogous to Panebianco's model (1988), this definition necessarily implies a formal organizational arena and a formally defined institutional framework.

The Swedish party system was therefore still in the making, although the 1887 elections did send important signals to the body politic. While these elections by no means meant the introduction of parliamentarism, small steps had indeed been taken in this direction. The alignment of protective duties – including the social extensions of the issue – with the matter of suffrage demonstrated that programmes and doctrines were about to emerge at the expense of campaigning on single issues. Politics to an increasing extent became embedded in ideology; and importantly, this also implied a shift, however modest, away from the more general, utilitarian outlook of liberalism that had originally made it attractive to many farmers. In addition, precisely because of this, it became more and more apparent that government in the future would become contingent on the composition of parliament. Public opinion did not fail to make a point of this. And there were models to relate to. The breakthrough of parliamentarism in Norway a few years earlier had been met with great interest from the Swedish left, and it was a feature which, as in Värmland, received renewed interest in the press in the aftermath of the 1887 elections.[18]

The only problem was that the introduction of parliamentarism depended not only on the secession of monarchical power in relation to the executive, but also on the formation of durable factions and transparent, political agendas. At that stage the focus of opinion-making had shifted in the direction of political reform, but the controversy over tariffs was still alive. The rhetoric of 'the people' as well as a more collectivistic perspective on democratization clearly moved up to the front stage of political debate. Rhetoric drawing on the notion of 'the people' was frequently used by radical liberals and social democrats alike when they organized the franchise movement in 1890 and cooperated in mobilizing the two so-called 'Folkriks-dagarna' in Stockholm, in 1893 and 1896 (the word 'Folkriksdag' translates literally as 'people's parliament', although 'people's assem-blies' is probably more accurate). These assemblies preceded the general elections held in the same years (for an extensive analysis of the Swedish franchise movement, see Lundberg 2007).

Mass-mobilization by means of proxy

When organized labour emerged in the 1890s, this confirmed that political cleavages in society had become more sharply drawn. Liberals and conservatives alike formed new support organizations, and compared to the 1880s there were also more tangible signs of mobilization at the rural grass-roots level. Particularly among the liberals, the possibility of an urban–rural alignment became of critical importance. On the one hand, opinion in the rural constituencies, among the landed peasantry, drifted towards a more conservative position on the matter of suffrage, since greater inclusion would threaten the delicate balance of power achieved through the 1865–66 reform of parliament. Universal suffrage, on the other hand, was, needless to say, demanded by the disenfranchised, and by urban radicals, progressive liberals, and socialists alike. At the core of this radicalization of liberalism were the formation of the franchise movement and the organization of people's assemblies.

Although it is, of course, impossible to 'measure' precisely the impact of these factors in terms of 'organizational efficacy', it should be stressed that the franchise movement – which was not formally affiliated with the liberal faction in the Second Chamber – did serve as its campaigning platform in the 1893 as well as the 1896 general elections. Local liberal electoral assemblies ('valmansföreningar'; similar to the German 'Wählervereine') had started to form in the major cities (in Stockholm, 1883, and in Gothenburg, 1892), whereas campaigning in the provinces was contingent on the efforts of the franchise movement and its organizational framework. Perhaps precisely because of the lack of formal ties to party, the franchise movement and the idea of summoning a 'people's assembly' met with substantial interest. The issue was, after all, of general interest and, so it could be argued, transcended the traditional factionalism of politics.

Discursively transformed by references to 'the people' and the 'rights of the people', the franchise could be launched as a universal interest. This universal interest bridged egoistic class interests and, therefore, made possible an appealing form of cross-class, non-partisan politics (cf. Lundberg 2007: 401–405; Lundberg does, however, also stress that the franchise movement gradually lost its grass roots attachment and became more elitist). That the franchise at the same time *was* a political issue was, however, beyond doubt. To a considerable extent it was class-related, and with differences in opinion corresponding to left/right ideological conviction. This situation added further to the increasing public interest in politics that had begun to accumulate in the previous decade, during the debates on protective duties.[19]

Certainly the idea of widening the movement by including more issues than just that of suffrage found support. Still other voices, such as *Karlstads-tidningen*, warned against what it saw as a perilous move, viz. creating a broadly based, left-wing organization on unnatural foundations.[20] The idea of a grand left-wing coalition was in part inspired by the Norwegian pattern, but a generally held suspicion among the Swedish liberals towards too close an alignment with the social democrats was a main reason why the proposal fell through (Rönblom 1929: 62–71). A coalition, therefore, was considered too risky by many liberals because of the ideological diversity and the internal divisions typical of the Swedish left. The franchise movement appeared largely as a liberal proxy, and it involved the popular movements as key actors, but still on the basis of only one single issue. In effect, if not by design, the result was a two-tiered structure. Värmland represented a prominent example of this pattern, and developments in the region illustrated both the advantages of the approach as well as its drawbacks.

To begin with, the formation of a national franchise movement in 1890 drew on the efforts previously made by a large and diverse number of local associations, united by the aim of promoting extended rights to vote. This process had been initiated by the formation of 'Allmänna rösträttsföreningen' (1886) in Stockholm, and 'Östergötlands rösträttsförening' (1887) (Lundberg 2007: 36–37). In Värmland, too, the formation of a regional franchise organization preceded organization at the national level: the former had, in fact, come into effect as early as March 1889, and by the end of the year no less than 32 local branches had appeared throughout the province.[21] The annual report of the branches for 1892, i.e. as preparations for the first of the two people's assemblies in Stockholm were in progress, proudly stated that the people of Värmland had earned themselves 'a seat of honour among their comrades from other parts of the country'. According to the report no less than 17,000 people had petitioned in favour of the upcoming assembly. In no other region, the board noted, did such a large proportion of the population display open support for the movement. In addition no fewer than 18 new local branches had also formed during the previous year.[22]

It is important to note that the franchise movement often grew strong organizations precisely in those areas where nonconformism and teetotalism had first struck root and, before these movements, where early nineteenth-century forms of association had made inroads. This was the case in, among other areas, southeastern Värmland, in the previously mentioned districts of Visnum, Väse, and Ölme (chapter 2). Considering nonconformism and teetotalism, the former of these popular movements traced its roots in the area back to at least the late 1850s, when a chapel, which later became part of the Mission Covenant Church, started in Väse, in 1859 ('Väse Missionsförsamling'; this particular expression of nonconformism started out as low Church, but seceded in 1878). In Visnum a chapel had been opened in January 1871 ('Visnums Missionsförsamling'). From the 1880s onwards the nonconformists were followed, first, by the Good Templars and, then, in a second wave, by the Blue Ribbon. In 1889–90 alone, five lodges of the IOGT were established. As for the Blue Ribbon, one of the very first local branches, the one in Ölme, was supposedly formed in 1892.[23]

The franchise movement followed suit. While the Karlstad branch of the organization – the largest one – had 289 members by the end of 1889, the one in Visnum mustered a substantial number as well, viz. 121 members. During the following year, local branches were also established in Ölme and Väse.[24] These areas were by and large agricultural, although Visnum, south-east of Ölme and Väse, was also part of the Bergslagen mining region (Kåpe 2005: 73–76; Carlsson 1953: 410 classified the district as dominated by small-scale family farming); in fact the 'Björneborg' IOGT lodge in Visnum seems to have related to a village with the same name, and where an iron works had been established as early as the 1660s (Kåpe 2005: 26; Furuskog 1924: 417). The deputies elected to parliament from these parts, such as Lars Anderson in Ölme and, between 1887 and 1908, Olof Andersson from Hasselbol, were farmers. The same was the case, for instance, with Olof Olson, who represented the neighbouring Mellansysslet judicial circuit in the period 1887–93. This reflected the requirements for owning property built into the electoral system. But at least Andersson and Olson were also closely connected to the franchise and popular movements. For instance, Olson was elected to the regional board of the former organization in 1889, and, later on, was a ranking member of the Blue Ribbon. Both he and Anderson were also active in the Mission Covenant Church.[25]

Be that as it may, the interests of the well-to-do farmers and other, less fortunate groups among the rural population were diverse, not least on the issue of the franchise: examples such as these could certainly be taken as evidence of political modernization rooted in horizontal power relations and consensual bargaining. However, 'Swedish model' cross-class alliances of this kind were as much possible simply because a multitude of organizational arenas just happened to synchronize with one another at a particular point in time, i.e. the 1890s. Possible explanations for the subsequent successes of liberalism in areas such as the above may have included anything from peasant individualism and economic self-interest to radicalized grass roots demands for justice and equality. What temporarily brought them all together were, as Lundkvist (1977) has pointed out, the challenges brought on by modernization; a matter indeed open to many interpretations. An example of this was apparent at a Blue Ribbon meeting at Ransäter, Mellansysslet, in February 1900.There it was said that the immense societal changes that had taken place in the last twenty-five years had not only been beneficial. In the wake of progress had followed 'arrogance, sloth, extravagance, banking credits [sic], infighting between individuals and entire peoples, drunkenness, counterfeiting and, consequently, suicidal tendencies'.[26]

Needless to say, this scenario did not necessarily imply deep and heartfelt solidarity among the majority of the heterogeneous rural population itself. Neither did it imply a need for the creation of proper institutional mechanisms for securing organizational commitment and trust, let alone the formulation of uniform doctrines. Rather, the profound societal changes typical of the late nineteenth century, and with them an increasing polarization in the countryside, were in the long run detrimental to the kind of ad hoc organization depicted here.

With regard to the urban–rural dimension, the above problems were not least echoed in the different meanings read into modern individualism and citizenship by countryside grass-roots and city advocates of liberalism. In this case, too, the first signs of controversy appeared in connection with the 1890s elections. By the time of the formation of the franchise movement, the editorship of the *Karlstads-tidningen* had passed from Anders Jeurling to Mauritz Hellberg. Beginning in 1890, Hellberg gradually became the main contender of radical liberalism in Värmland and formally remained editor of the newspaper until 1939. Born in the province in 1859, the son of a land surveyor, Hellberg had studied at Uppsala. There he joined 'Verdandi', a radical organization of students formed in 1882 by Karl Staaff. Its aim had been to build a bridge between intellectual liberals and the emerging labour movement. For instance, Hjalmar Branting, leader and subsequent chairman of the Swedish social democrats, was one of its members. After his return to Värmland, Hellberg became editor of the *Karlstads-tidningen*; since his time at school he was also a close friend of Gustaf Fröding, who, from 1887 to 1894, periodically worked for the newspaper. Hellberg's ideas and values had been firmly established during his years in Uppsala. Above all the idea of individuality appealed to him. To Hellberg individuality possessed a value in its own right, regardless of the ambition or achievements resulting from that individuality (Örnklint 1993: 12).

Unlike farmer deputies such as Olof Olson and Olof Andersson, and unlike other leaders of liberalism in the region, such as Anders Henrik Göthberg, or Carl Björling and August Lindh, who both emerged as leading functionaries around the turn of the century, Hellberg's ideas on individuality caused problems. Although in principle in accordance with both nonconformism and teetotalism, in reality they brought him in conflict with precisely these increasingly influential groups. He was not an abstainer, nor was he, because of his view on matters of religion, credible among nonconformists (Kvick 1977: 216–20, in particular 220; Örnklint 1993: 23 characterizes Hellberg as an agnostic). Throughout his career he proved himself a formidable adversary when defending his ideas. With an instinct which in hindsight seems almost telepathic, Hellberg always displayed a capacity for choosing the approach best suited to the occasion, and the argument best suited to puncture his opponent and exploit the weakness of his arguments. Qualities such as these invariably created animosity, not only within the liberal camp. For instance, in 1911 the Church pessimistically noted that 'political liberalism', skilfully promoted in the radical spirit of the 'Verdandi' tradition, was probably stronger in Värmland than anywhere else in the country.[27]

The first people's assembly was held in March 1893, with Hellberg acting as one of the two vice-chairmen. The main line of action decided was, as previously indicated, against the formation of a more broadly based left-wing political organization, and a continued focus on the single issue of suffrage (although this strategy would, in effect, prove impossible to sustain once the election campaign had started). A manifesto on the results of the assembly was issued to the Swedish people, and a strategy was set for the general elections to parliament.[28] The campaign was to be boosted by press coverage, and involved test elections as well as petitioning in order to provoke reform of the election laws. Certain novelties, compared to previous elections, were also included in the preparations, such as canvassing and the use of professional, out-of-town speakers ('resetalare'). The 1890s were therefore characterized by a new intensity in terms of campaigning, which meant jettisoning the deeply rooted suspicion of organizational involvement in the elections (Esaiasson 1990: 86–91). This change was all the more important since it indicated new, external conditions for political organization and mobilization.

Yet within the franchise movement opinion was also divided on crucial issues, such as the notion of 'citizenship' and the inclusion of women in the assembly – an issue with important implications from the point of view of suffrage. According to the chairman of the 1893 assembly, Dr David Bergström, citizenship included both men and women, whereas others wanted women to be excluded from the proceedings. One female representative, however, was present. This was Emelie Rathou, subsequent founder of the Swedish branch of the Women's Christian Temperance Union (WCTU), i.e. the White Ribbon ('Vita bandet'). Using the Good Templars, among whom she was at the time active, as an example, Rathou pointed to the fact that it was precisely the cooperation between men and women that accounted for the success of that movement. By way of clarification, the assembly finally voted in favour of using the terms 'men' and 'women' so as to avoid any confusion on the issue.[29] Hence, despite the ambitions expressed at the March assembly, variation in opinion, as well as heterogeneity in terms of grass-roots level involvement, became characteristic of the election campaign.

As the general elections approached, the movement sprang into action. Local committees were formed across the country to orchestrate the campaign along the lines decided by the national assembly. From this point onwards, though, different sources give somewhat different pictures of the outcome in Värmland. The regional board of the franchise movement recorded noticeable effects of the campaigning only in certain parts of the province, more specifically Mellansysslet, Södersysslet, Nyed-Älvdalen, Visnum, Väse, and Ölme. Furthermore, according to the board, only in regard to the election of Olof Andersson in the last three districts was the turnout successful.[30] In Mellansysslet, for instance, two moderate liberal candidates, both belonging to same nonconformist chapel of the Mission Covenant Church, competed with each other. The above-mentioned, pro-suffrage candidate Olof Olson finally suffered defeat against Anders Henrik Göthberg, who held a less radical position on the issue. Because of this, Göthberg in effect became a substitute candidate for the conservatives in the constituency, at the same time as he had widespread support among the many iron workers in the area.[31]

Regarding Mauritz Hellberg, finally, he as well had been personally involved in the campaign and initiated the organization of three new local branches of the franchise movement. The board did, however, conclude that, with respect to the actual elections, they had expected failure from the very outset and were thus not surprised by the meagre outcome. Probably the board had taken into account the specific social and organizational conditions in the region. For instance, financial problems – a recurrent feature of liberal political organization – had hampered work.[32] By contrast, *Karlstads-tidningen* made a much less pessimistic assessment of the results, and warmly greeted the election of pro-free trade candidate Olof Andersson as the best outcome one could possibly have hoped for. Still, even this victory was marred by infighting, since

Map 4. The Väse, Ölme and Visnum judicial circuits.

the opponents had been able to recruit a nonconformist teetotaller to run against Andersson.[33]

The available sources, then, give a mixed picture of the political climate during the elections. As with the report in *Karlstads-tidningen*, they also shed some light on the ideological heterogeneity of the franchise movement and its complicated extensions into the various popular movements. What the comments reflect, more or less directly, were the difficulties involved in creating coherent standards not only for nomination procedures and issue structuring, but also that the franchise movement faced problems of societal integration and social representation (cf. Gunther & Diamond 2001). But regardless of the pessimistic opinions in the aftermath of the elections, the actual turnout did, however modestly, swing the composition of the

Second Chamber somewhat to the left. Firstly, according to Carlsson (1953: 148), the number of left wing deputies increased from 73 to 76 of a total of 228. Secondly, on the regional level, interesting patterns come to the fore if we consider the various constituencies in a somewhat different light compared to the above. In agricultural constituencies such as Visnum, Väse, and Ölme, but also Fryksdal, there was a clear majority of left-wing votes; and so was, according to Carlsson's estimates, the case also in regard to more industrialized rural areas, such as Mellansysslet and Älvdal-Nyed (Carlsson 1953: 410, 413). These included areas where the franchise movement, on the one hand, noted the effects of its campaigning but, on the other hand, detected only sparse tangible results in terms of turnout, such in the case of Mellansysslet and Göthberg's subsequent victory there. Despite the fact that a moderate such as Göthberg succeeded in upsetting political opinion in Karlstad, this does not negate the overall impression that the 1893 elections, meant that an important step had been taken towards a more radicalized political climate in the region, albeit on the foundations of an occasionally extremely diverse social basis.

In fact, one of the most important outcomes triggered by the 'external challenges' (Panebianco 1988) of the 1893 elections was the formation in parliament of the People's Party (1895–99). As a progressive faction it was a direct predecessor to 'Liberala samlingspartiet' (1900), which two years later was supplemented by 'Frisinnade landsföreningen' as its nationwide extension. This development was a befitting illustration of the extra-parliamentarian but at the same time intra-parliamentarian roots of Swedish liberalism, following Duverger's description (1967 [1954]) of two, basically juxtaposed paths towards modern party systems.

As it happened, the new faction in parliament appeared just in time for the next, 1896, campaign. At that stage, though, it was also a disheartened franchise movement that went into action. Plans and strategies were roughly the same as in 1893 and the actual results similar to those of the previous election. The general level of turnout, however, dropped, and the press was less actively involved this time. Yet, in July 1896, *Karlstads-tidningen* remarked, in a fit of optimism, that the upcoming elections, after all, marked a turning point in Swedish politics. Among other things the increased polarization between left and right was viewed in positive terms, since this made it easier for the voters to distinguish more clearly between the various candidates. Consequently, among the results which the newspaper was looking forward to was the demise of 'amalgamated' factions, based on conflicting interests in parliament, and the establishing of an 'influential and truly liberal party' on the political stage.[34] Although considered too radical, and too left wing by some influential candidates – for instance, A. H. Göthberg this time also remained on the moderate side[35] – the election and the formation of the People's Party still became incremental to liberal organization.

With respect to the contributions made to party campaigning by the franchise movement, they did play an important part, but political development had also made clear, firstly, that liberalism and socialism did not, as some had hoped, share an organizational future together. Secondly, it was clear that liberalism had somehow to develop and consolidate its own grass-roots framework. In this process, the rank and file of the popular movements would, as within the franchise movement, become crucial. However, as the formation of the franchise movement and, not least, the 1893 campaign illustrate, in this they also became a topic of conflict between liberals and socialists and, particularly so in Värmland, a battleground for infighting among the liberals themselves. Nonconformism, to be sure, was for the time being a steadfast ally of the liberal movement. Organized teetotalism and, above all, the trade unions were another matter. That the trade unions opted for the social democrats was, perhaps, not surprising. However, in political terms organized teetotalism wavered between left-wing options, and in particular the Good Templars, if not the Blue Ribbon, became increasingly inclined towards the socialist camp (Edqvist 2001). Hence the lessons learned from political organization in the 1890s gave cause for alarm, as they demonstrated not only the merits but also the perils of organization by means of proxy. What, then, were the consequences of this strategy in the next stage, as ideologies and programmes started to make a more profound impression on the electorate?

The 1911 elections

With regard to nonconformism and teetotalism I have previously suggested the emergence of a new kind of modern and radical individualism, which, although in principle compatible with liberalism, was still more clearly orientated towards the collective compared to the traditional liberal mindset. Such an argument is compatible with the classic interpretation of the Swedish popular movements and their organizations. According to this line of argument they became important tools in the formation of new group identities and social integration in a rapidly changing society (Lundkvist 1977); viz. they performed functions which up to a certain point made them similar to political parties. Yet further similarities may be noted. Importantly, Lundkvist also stresses that the popular movements served as 'training grounds' for democracy, and for collective bargaining along democratic lines. This was because their formation required adaptation to more or less strict organizational standards, such as respect for majority rule. This pattern differed from early middle-class and liberal voluntary associations, where organizational standards were poorly developed. Another similarity to political parties proper should also be noted, especially considering their impact on the socio-economic composition of the Second Chamber in parliament: for example, by 1890 almost 15 per cent of the deputies were organized nonconformists (Lundkvist 1977: 175). In fact, compared to other regions, Värmland was quite unusual. Following the 1893 elections, no less than six of this province's ten deputies belonged either to the Mission Covenant Church or 'Evangeliska Fosterlands-Stiftelsen' (EFS, a low-church, non-secessionist forerunner of the former movement).[36]

Together with teetotalism, nonconformism rapidly became a critical factor in the formation of liberalism, not least by shaping public opinion out in the consituencies. For instance, in Värmland the *Ansgarii-Posten* newspaper (1887–1920) became important as a voice of nonconformist, regional radicalism. However, as previously pointed out, in many respects there were at the same time substantial differences in outlook between liberals such as Mauritz Hellberg and the representatives of the popular movements. Somewhat paradoxically, Hellberg's concern for the grass roots of society went hand in hand with a fundamental lack of understanding of the very same groups, reflecting, among other things, his underestimation of nonconformism and teeototalism and their impact on local society.

Whereas Hellberg and his fellow urbanites would on occasion give historical lectures, such as on the topic of 'Witches and witch-craft', but also talks on subjects of more immediate interest, such as unemployment – in the Lecturing Society of Karlstad ('Karlstads föreläsningsanstalt') – it remains doubtful whether such efforts really engendered a genuine and permanent interest among the groups concerned.[37] Rather, for instance among members of the Good Templars, it had been noted, with some curiosity, that the movement failed to attract any serious attention from the middle classes and the intellectuals – as in a discussion held at an lodge meeting in the town of Arvika, western Värmland, in March 1893. There the participants observed that in the US or UK the educated classes, and not least women, were much more active in supporting the fight against liquor and drinking than their counterparts in Sweden. The discussants, however, also expressed the hope that teetotalism would attract a corps of doctors, clergy, and schoolteachers who could participate in its efforts more decid-edly in the future.[38]

Note that the discussants did not take into consideration the pre-1850 attempts made, most notably by the Swedish Temperance Society, to stem drinking, and which had originated in efforts by precisely the same professions as those mentioned in the above, and in particular the clergy. More than implying an outright negative attitude, the statement simply suggests that the rank and file of the popular movements were often quite unaware of their predecessors. In this particular aspect history did, indeed, not matter. Rather, if we look for traces of any contemporary, sequentialist interpretation of Swedish political modernization, such a reading can be found in the Temperance Society itself (chapter 2), or the Liberal Debating Society in Karlstad (see the introduction to this chapter). Ultimately it symbolized an attempt to redefine and adjust middle-class con-ceptions of individualism to the new demands brought about by rapid social and economic change. Many nonconformists, Good

Templar activists, and Blue and White Ribbon members, though, did remain wary towards and uncertain of the ambitions of the liberals; something which, of course, only proves that the latter had considerable ground to cover before they could lay a firm foundation for party affiliation. That temporary alliances were possible had been shown in connection to the 1890s elections, but as the new century approached, not only did new such possibilities appear. Difficulties, too, mounted, as an effect of the marriage between two basically different organizational strategies – organization by means of proxy and mass-based organization – and the increasing political radicalism, not least of the IOGT.

When the Liberal Party finally appeared in 1900 and, two years later, its national organization ('Frisinnade landsföreningen'), the latter set out on an ambitious attempt to organize liberals, or 'frisinnade', all around the country. These were ideas that, among others, Mauritz Hellberg had approved of since the heyday of the franchise movement and the 1893 and 1896 elections (see above). Above all, though, 'Frisinnade landsföreningen' was the creation of Karl Staaff, who was inspired by the British liberals. At the constituent meeting of the latter, held in Birmingham in 1877, the ambitions had been to create not only a basis for the national elections but, importantly, also a 'liberal parliament' outside parliament (Staaff 1917: 144–60; Kihlberg 1962: 259–63). This was certainly echoed in the emphasis Staaff repeatedly put on the importance of the 'will of the people' in relation to parliamentarism, such as in a speech in Dalarna during the 1911 campaign (Staaff 1918: 174–75). However, while this strategy meant recognition of the autonomy and activities of the individual citizens, it also ran the risk of creating tensions between the party convention, and the parliamentarian group of the party.

Therefore, among the many tasks left for the executive committee of 'Frisinnade landsföreningen' to grapple with, was coordinating itself with the Liberal Party; indeed, as late as 1904 some 80 out of a total of approximately 1,000 members of 'landsföreningen' (a number which, importantly, did not include the members of the various local branches around the country) had still refrained from joining the party.[39] Furthermore, it also had to encourage the many local level associations to integrate with the national organization, and stimulate liberal opinion-making in the regions,[40] or, in other words, instigate rules of social cooperation and organizational mechanisms securing commitment, monitoring, and accountability along the lines suggested by Ostrom (1990).

Considering organization by means of proxy, all this represented a break with tradition. Yet progress was slow. Regional differentiation in itself posed one hurdle, something the executive committee in Stockholm was also quite well aware of: from the outset of its formation, 'Frisinnade landsföreningen' had distributed a series of pamphlets entitled *Political characters* ('*Politiska fysionomier*'). Navigating a delicate course between satire and parochialism, these pamphlets can be regarded as a plea to what the executive committee viewed as the regional political cultures and colourful activists typical of different parts of the country; admittedly, though, Värmland was not included among the regions approached.[41] Also, as will become clear, liberal organization and electoral mobilization to a great extent remained contingent on the organizational networks of nonconformism and teetotalism. Although the immediate effects of this, such as in connection to the 1911 general elections, were far from clear, in hindsight it is, again, obvious that the drawbacks of such an approach outweighed the advantages. The kind of organization needed to balance grass roots and leadership was never fully implemented. The grass roots were very much left to their own devices.

In fact, the subtle differences signalled by the labels 'liberal' and 'frisinnad' capture something of the essence of what would rapidly become the most important dividing line within early twentieth-century liberalism. 'Frisinnad' literally means 'broad-minded', although any precise translation from Swedish to English is difficult. The expression had a corresponding notion in German, i.e. 'freisinnig', but in this case the context differed from what had become typical of Swedish 'frisinnade'. Originally, liberals of all persuasions laid claim to being 'broad-minded'; this had, indeed, been considered more radical compared to 'liberal' and was therefore, at the recommendation of Staaff, included in the name of the national organization of the party (Kihlberg 1962: 261). As time passed, though, 'frisinnad' increasingly came to designate a more or less distinct variety of liberalism, characterized by connections to rural society, and to nonconformism and teetotalism. Hence yet another feature was added to the conventional urban–rural division of Swedish liberalism (a feature which, importantly, was if not synonymous so in any event closely related to the intra-parliamentarian/extra-parliamentarian cleavage depicted by Duverger, 1967 [1954]; also cf. Vallinder 1984). The quality of emerging as a 'soft party' in Panebianco's terminology (1988) thus spelled the roots of a conflict – over prohibition – that would eventually be the undoing of the party in 1922–23 (see below).

A similar development was typical of party formation in the provinces. In Värmland a regional office of 'Frisinnade landsföreningen' opened in June 1907 ('Värmlands frisinnade länskommitté), although a permanent secretary, or 'ombudsman', was not appointed until 1916. Although local liberal assemblies had, in some instances, formed in advance, these remained more or less autonomous bodies until the formation of 'Frisinnade landsföreningen' and its regional network. Contrary to the situation in Schleswig-Holstein, therefore, liberal party organizations did not develop in parallel on the regional *and* national level at one and the same time; a circumstance which underlines both the difference in institutional settings between Sweden and Germany as well as the specificity of Schleswig-Holstein as a region.

In Värmland the regional office was supplemented by an executive committee and three subordinate organizations for the northern, western, and eastern constituencies of the province, as well as a number of local branches (the number of constituencies had been reduced from ten to three since the 1890s). This organization remained more or less intact until 1922, when 'Värmlands frisinnade valkretsförbund' was created. Whether this change resulted in any real centralization of the party organization is difficult to judge. The context does not, however, suggest this. Rather, the main impression of liberal organization remains that of improvisation and haphazard management; for instance, the executive committee itself had to be reinstituted as late as in 1918, as it had somehow fallen out of service.

Step by step, liberal organization nevertheless expanded during the first two decades of the twentieth century. Although not necessarily executed in any coordinated manner, this development reflected ambitions to cover all those aspects which were considered crucial to the life and activities of a political party. Quite naturally, an initial concern was to manage the campaigns, viz. the tasks of nomination and mobilization, mainly by rallying supporters to the cause.[42] While interest aggregation and issue structuring became a concern at the central level, once a national organization had formed it still remained an important task of the regional and local assemblies to filter back the decisions made, and to communicate the party programme to the grass-roots level. But, as indicated, at the same time the executive committee in Stockholm recognized the difficulties involved with imposing centrally formulated directives. For practical purposes, the committee noted, it was possible only to make requests, more or less urgent, occasionally by telephone when possible.[43] Indirectly, therefore, functions of social representation and social integration, to follow Gunther and Diamond (2001), posed important and, most likely, unresolved issues from a national perspective. Despite its intentions, the allegedly universalistic liberal outlook was really a regionally entrenched outlook.

Precisely in regard to local and regional self-government, however, coordination of policies took place, though only gradually, and this left organizational imprints, at least on the regional party structures. For instance, in Värmland a specific branch of the organization was created for coordinating liberal policy-making in the Provincial Council. Furthermore, women were gradually included. Their inclusion began in 1909, with the formation of an autonomous organization for the promotion of women's suffrage. Although formally non-partisan, this body was closely tied to the liberals, and the first elected chairperson of its executive committee was Gerda Hellberg, the wife of Mauritz Hellberg.[44] Eventually it evolved into a regional women's branch of the party in 1919,[45] and in the new, 1922, organization several women were also elected to the board of the various local branches of 'Frisinnade landsföreningen'.[46]

When all was said and done, though, the core of the party was still its local branches. The national board had difficulties controlling these, not least when factionalizing on the local level continued to pose a problem. In Värmland, most notably the Mellansysslet area and the supporters of Anders Henrik Göthberg remained a regular source of irritation, at least from the point of view of *Karlstads-tidningen*. Göthberg's position on the 1893 and 1896 elections are two examples; his manoeuvres in connection to the 1908 elections yet another. According to the newspaper, Göthberg had demanded that a conservative candidate should, against the rules of the party, be allowed to run in the test election organized by the Liberal Party, since prospective voters included people inclined to the right as well as the left.[47] Underpinning the conflict were, again, the tensions between radical and more moderate factions within the party, and between urban 'liberals' and rural 'frisinnade'. However, not only the countryside but also the cities, such as Hellberg's own Karlstad, were a matter of concern: as the 1906 elections to the provincial councils approached, Karlstad was, on the one hand, considered an easy win by the executive committee of 'landsföreningen'. On the other hand, the victory was conditional since the committee felt uncomfortable with the candidate – Gullbrand Elowson – who, though part of the local establishment, would have 'to be discarded' and replaced.[48]

Difficulties implementing discipline along the lines laid down by the party also originated in the reluctance of some prospective parliamentary deputies to embrace the very idea of centralized organi-zation throughout the 1910s and the First World War. When Emil Rylander accepted his nomination as one of the liberal candidates in the northern constituency of Värmland in the 1917 elections, he did so reluctantly. He explained his doubts in terms of the need to choose between personal conviction and practical necessity (chapter 1). At a meeting held in Torsby, Rylander declared, firstly, that he had never fully accepted the programme of the Liberal Party since it was, in his opinion, much too imprecise. Secondly, however, there were also the effects of the new, proportional electoral system to consider, and with it the 'inevitability' of modern political parties. This was Rylander's main thrust. Since the current situation forced candidates to join formally with parties, it also put ever-increasing pressure on them to declare their position on the political issues addressed to them. It was the decided opinion of Rylander that the latter was to the good of the legislative work in parliament, i.e. it provided an antidote to political renegades. However, the downside was, according to him, also obvious. The ideological compromises necessitated by formal affiliation to a party posed a new kind of moral dilemma for the individual deputies – in Rylander's case more specifically in regard to prohibition, something which he personally advocated.[49]

In light of the pressure brought to bear on the local liberal assemblies by formal organization or, perhaps, the institutionalized tension between local tradition and party, it is worthwhile to dwell at some length on the issue of what the average partisan in Värmland was like in the early twentieth century. The membership lists which were annually submitted by the local branches provide interesting information on this matter. Unfortunately the material is incomplete and, as far as the northern constituency is concerned, lacking entirely. In the two other constituencies, far from all branches bothered to file the requested information, and the main bulk of it pertains to the late 1910s and early 1920s. Though marred by inconsistencies, what remains still provides us with a skeleton key to the make-up of liberal partisanship shortly before the split of the party. Although the questionnaires differ somewhat in design between years, returned data includes not only the total number of members, but also the proportion of women as well as nonconformists and teetotallers among them. Usually the regional branch also asked for a breakdown with respect to occupation. (Particularly the latter data is sketchy, though, but in cases where it does exist it indicates that a majority of the members were, in fact, farmers.)[50]

In 1920 the western districts reported a total of 865 members spread among 26 local organizations.[51] In the east, though, a mere ten branches reported a total of 373 members by 1922.[52] This certainly does not correspond to the image of these areas, such as the Visnum, Väse, and Ölme districts, as traditionally simmering with civic and political association of all kinds. However, the data was compiled only a year before the conflict on prohibition in the Liberal Party culminated, and therefore in all likelihood reflects what had at this stage become a general problem to the party – an increasing number of members were defecting because of the conflict (Johansson 1980: 60). And in which direction the secessionists chose to direct their faltering loyalties we can only guess. As for those remaining we should, however, note that evidence, although circumstantial, does indicate affiliations and networks similar to those of parliamentary deputies such as Anders Henrik Göthberg, Olof Olson, and Olof Anderson thirty years previously.

Firstly, the overwhelming majority of members belonged to organizations based in the countryside. Despite the fact that the local branch in Karlstad (included among the eastern districts) had the largest number of members – 151 (1922 figures) – the majority of members were still organized in rural areas: 76.4 per cent in western Värmland (1920 figures), and 59.5 per cent in eastern Värmland (1922 figures).[53] Secondly, women were in the minority, but in eastern Värmland 12.3 per cent of all party members in these areas were women, mainly because of the relatively speaking large number of females in the Karlstad branch.[54] Thirdly, in western Värmland 7.1 per cent of the party members were nonconformists whereas 13.2 per cent were teetotallers; in the eastern districts the proportion was 7.8 per cent and 29.0 per cent respectively (as previously indicated, the former were usually affiliated with the Mission Covenant Church).[55]

Table 3. Membership of 'Frisinnade landsföreningen', c. 1920. Proportion of members in urban and rural districts (per cent).

District	Urban districts	Rural districts
Western Värmland	23.6	76.4
Eastern Värmland	40.5	59.5

Sources: Föreningsrapporter till valkretsförbundet 1920. Vol. 7, Inkomna handlingar från lokalavdelningar 1918–21. Västra Värmlands frisinnade valkretsförbund; Föreningsrapporter till valkretsförbundet 1922. Vol. 8, Inkomna handlingar från lokalavdelningar 1919–26. Östra Värmlands frisinnade valkretsförbund. Folkrörelsernas arkiv för Värmland, Arkivcentrum Karlstad.

The figures still require some further comment. To begin with, we should particularly note that only a minority of all liberal voters were actual party members. In the country as a whole the ratio was approximately 17.5 per cent at the time of the 1911 general elections.[56] Figures for the local branches are, as I have pointed out, impossible to calculate; although outside Stockholm, Värmland had the highest number of members directly joined to the national level organization by 1910: 155 out of a total of 2,127 members.[57] In any event, the Swedish pattern almost certainly indicates a more successful case of grass-roots organization compared to Schleswig-Holstein. In *this* region the liberals managed to organize only 5.0–10.0 per cent of their supporters (left-liberals and national liberals respectively, Schultz Hansen 2003: 473). At the same time party organization on the grass-roots level still lagged behind compared to the social democrats, who organized roughly one-third (32.0 per cent) of their voters in the 1911 elections.[58]

Finally, we do not know the precise extent of overlapping membership in the case of nonconformist and teetotalist liberals, although more generally this combination of affiliations was far from uncommon, and in particular with regard to the Mission Covenant Church, and the Blue Ribbon. But, as a reflection of the omnipresent and unresolved tension between different strands of political individualism, the conflict within the party in some cases seems to have spread to these organizations as well. For instance, among the former, Göthberg's own congregation at Munkfors (Ransäter) simply split in the autumn of 1923,[59] only a few months after the division of the party into two factions. In even other respects some of the alignments between civic and political associations had most probably started to dissolve long before the concluding battle on prohibition. Anders Henrik Göthberg, one of those who had originally answered the call to gather in Stockholm for the constituent meeting of the Liberal Party in 1900,[60] had left the IOGT as early as 1892 (*Svenska folkrörelser*, I, 1936: 450): as opposed to the Blue Ribbon, the IOGT had become both more radicalized in political terms and more secularized by the end of the nineteenth century. Among some of the former, though, affiliation with the Liberal Party and, at the same time, teetotalism and nonconformism remained, as for ombudsman Carl Björling, a viable option at least up to the 1923 split (*Svenska folkrörelser*, I, 1936: 278).

As the September 1911 elections moved closer, the new regional organization of the party was put to a critical test. An important innovation was also that the electoral system had now been reformed from a majoritarian to a proportional system. Portending Emil

Rylander's shrewd observation some years later, this meant that party organizations, however weakly developed, henceforth became more important to campaigning activities. Indeed, immediately following the reform of the electoral system, the efforts on the part of 'Frisinnade landsföreningen' to strengthen their grass-roots organization had surged, and included renewed activism and the formation of new, local branches.[61] Among other things, this also meant that the 1911 campaign was initiated earlier – in June – compared to previous elections. Preparations for the campaign on the regional level started as early as January, though. For example, the liberals in eastern Värmland then stressed the necessity of making the new citizens 'aware' of the liberal credo. Since the conservatives had 'unlimited' financial resources at their disposal, and since the social democrats could rely on their organizational skill and equally substantial funds, it was necessary for the liberals to make a vigorous effort not to fall behind. Regardless of how realistic the latter's analysis of the competing parties was, the executive committee pleaded with its voters to raise money to be used for the election campaign.[62]

Although, technically speaking, it was still possible to run in the election without a party label, candidates seldom seem to have used this opportunity (Esaiasson 1990: 110–13, including n. 17, 134–35). Rather, with the 1911 elections, campaigning entered a more 'modern' phase and in terms of issues focused on military expenditure, constitutional reform, socio-economic reform (including the agricultural sector), and the alcohol issue. The extent to which the different parties were successful in adapting to the new conditions did, however, vary. For instance, the social democrats started using motor cars to transport speakers between rallies; a move that was replicated by the conservatives. In particular the latter, though, still suffered from the lack of a centralized coordination of the campaign. The same was the case with the liberals, despite the efforts previously made by the executive committee in Stockholm (Esaiasson 1990). Particularly in the countryside, the absence of efficient communications also remained an impediment to campaigning. As late as the mid-1930s, the executive committee in Stockholm proposed, among other things, using motorboats for campaigning; predominantly in the coastal regions, one assumes, but probably in the extensive inland lake districts as well.[63] Some confusion, finally, occurred because liberals and social democrats entered the election in the form of cartels in fifteen constituencies, including four parishes in the western constituency of Värmland (Trankil, Silbodal, Skillingmark, and Järnskog),[64] thus provoking conservatives such as Albert Petersson to complain about 'improper forms of campaigning' (see introduction).

It appears, however, that the liberals devoted some time and energy to 'improper campaigning' among themselves, too. The tensions between, on the one hand, the Liberal Party and the urban liberals, and on the other hand 'Frisinnade landsföreningen' and its supporters, surfaced at an early stage of the preparations. They included the role of the nonconformist faction in the party. In March the executive committee in Stockholm pondered an official letter – one couched in very careful words, however – from the local branch in Kristine-hamn. Unfortunately, the original document has not survived, but it is clear that in this town on the eastern border of Värmland some dispute had arisen regarding 'the attitude among some of the liberal newspapers towards the nonconformists'. The executive committee probably decided that the matter was too sensitive, since it simply filed the complaint.[65] One important reason for this might have been that, considering the upcoming elections, it felt impelled to be guided by organizational necessity rather than ideology – this because, as Esiasson (1990: 111) points out, the popular movements still had well-developed organizational networks for campaigning and, in that capacity, continued to exercise considerable influence on the behaviour of the political parties.

Among the liberals the lion's share of campaigning did, in a strictly formal sense, fall on the local branches. Tasks included the recruitment of campaign workers and preparation for the nomina-tion of candidates (Ransäter). Meetings were held at which, as in the town of Filipstad, the issue of women's suffrage was discussed.[66] At Munkfors attempts were made to invite Karl Staaff himself to hold a rally, since it seemed likely that he would anyway visit Karlstad during the campaign. That the branch experienced some difficul-ties in attracting speakers, though, is clear from the proceedings.[67] In effect, however, the outcome of the campaign depended heavily on the activities of both the nonconformists and the teetotallers. Similarly to earlier campaigns, the venues of these movements were used to hold liberal campaign meetings.[68] One important distinction compared to earlier elections, though, was that the difference between civic and political association had become more blurred.

Not only the IOGT but also the Blue Ribbon had thus become more overtly politicized. The IOGT had already undergone a radicalization, and its loyalties were not unanimously orientated towards the liberals (Edquist 2001). And they coordinated the election preparations behind locked doors, as in Arvika where the Good Templars decided to organize a closed, member-only deliberation on the elections.[69] In the Blue Ribbon similar opinions were voiced. Carl Björling, who would become a regional ombudsman for 'Frisinnade landsföreningen' in 1919 (*Svenska folkrörelser*, I, 1936: 278), was chairman of the Högerud section of the Blue Ribbon when some among his sixty-odd members suggested nothing less than an entirely new 'Christian and political temperance party' in order to advance their cause. The keeper of the minutes concluded, somewhat wearily, that the issue was best resolved by latching onto the established political parties.[70] It was as if the pattern typical of the 1890s elections had been replayed, only in reverse, with the popular movements permeating the Liberal Party, and pressing for commitment, rather than the other way around.

When election day in September was approaching, *Karlstadstidningen* nevertheless conveyed optimism, considering the intense campaign.[71] And the actual results did, indeed, once more confirm the dominant position of liberalism in the province. Although the elections were an all-out success for the social democrats on the national level, the liberals in Värmland received a 46.1 per cent result compared to the national average of 40.2 per cent (Table 1, chapter 1). By comparison the social democrats won 29.5 per cent of the votes in Värmland, which, although a very substantial increase, was not above the national average for the party – unlike the case of the liberals.[72] *Karlstads-tidningen* commented on the results under the headline 'The People's Verdict' ('Folkets dom').[73] However, in light of the noticeable advances made by the social democrats, this very verdict could also be read as a warning to the liberals of what might be in store for them in future elections should they fail to ride the rising tide of popular radicalism.

Difficult as it is to explain electoral behaviour, it probably had less to do with organizational factors at this stage. It is possible that voting liberal had in fact become something of a political–cultural tradition, despite the difficulties and factionalism within the party. This might not have been the case among the workers, who, rather, tended to move towards the social democrats. However, it almost certainly applied to the farmers, a crucial group in the rural districts. On the one hand, the problem – that of preserving agriculture and, not least, small-scale family farming in a rapidly industrializing society – reflected the traditional urban–rural split among the Swedish liberals. On the other hand, this was an issue which, from the point of view of the individual voter, was not necessarily enmeshed with the never-ending controversy on prohibition and, hence, the tangled web of alignments between various forms of civic and political forms of association. As much as these two strands of organization had mutually reinforced each other since the late nineteenth century, analogous to what Tocqueville had suggested (2003 [1840]), the result was at the same time a stark illustration of the perils of political self-interest.

Therefore, an important factor on the regional level was presumably the, relatively speaking, greater homogeneity among the peasantry in Värmland compared, for instance, to the eastern and southern parts of the country, or Schleswig-Holstein, where manorial economies were still prominent at the turn of the century (chapter 4). This is not to say that the rural population had not differentiated along the lines suggested in the above (see also Olausson 2004), but only that this feature was probably less extreme compared to many other regions. Indeed, Carlsson (1953: 407–15), who studied national voting patterns in the general elections up to 1902, including the socio-economic composition of the electorate, identified no constituencies in the region which were dominated by large-scale farming. Rönblom (1929: 174) might well have exaggerated when he claimed that rural workers to a great extent opted for liberalism by the turn of the century. What remains a fact, though, is that from 1900 onwards the established political parties, the liberals included, increasingly tried to attract these workers as well as the farmers, not least the small-scale family farmers. Focusing on the liberals, the interest taken in agriculture and its modernization became part of their new progressivism – for example, when the executive committee of 'Frisinnade landsföreningen' started its preparations for the 1911 elections, it also discussed the matter of creating a 'non-biased organization for the rural workers'.[74] Although the incorporation of agrarianism with 'non-biased', viz. cross-class progressivism, might in the long run have failed to attract the workers and, rather, driven them towards the social democrats, it is nonetheless likely to have appealed to the practical, or 'utilitarian' needs of the farmers.

Certainly, the sharpened focus on agriculture had already stimulated the landed interests and peasantry alike to create their own interest organizations. This movement had begun with the formation of 'Svenska agrarföreningen' (1895), which was fiercely protectionist in outlook, and directly inspired by the German 'Bund der Landwirte' (Carlsson 1953: 162–63). Later on the farmers also created their own political parties: 'Bondeförbundet' (1914) and 'Jordbrukarnas riksförbund' (1915; the two parties amalgamated in 1921 under the former name). In general terms, therefore, the liberals again seemed trapped in their traditional, uneasy position in-between political chairs. However, if we extend the perspective somewhat, beyond the 1911 elections, it does at the same time become clear that 'Bondeförbundet', which was more clearly orientated towards the smaller farmers – a crucial category in Värmland – had great difficulties establishing itself in the province. In the 1917 elections the party received virtually no votes at all in Värmland (it formed too late to participate in the 1914 elections). In the 1921 elections the result was only half the national average, and only in the 1924 elections did 'Bondeförbundet' reach 10.8 per cent of the votes in the province.[75] Recently split in two factions, the 'frisinnade' still fared much better compared to the country as a whole and, after the social democrats, became the second largest party in the region.[76]

In general terms the 1911 elections were instrumental to the formation of the modern, Swedish party system. From a liberal point of view, though, the elections had also highlighted the complicated relationship between the national leadership of the Liberal

Party/'Frisinnade landsföreningen' and its grass roots; a problem to a considerable extent related to its organization by means of proxy. Part of this problem, too, was the differentiation between urban liberalism and rural 'frisinne'. But as much as this differentiation signalled different outlooks, and different approaches to citizenship and the challenge of modernity, it also reflected a generational shift within the liberal movement (insofar as this description is valid at all after 1911). In brief, around 1910, old-style liberal candidates of the nineteenth century mould, moderates and radicals alike, had become a dying breed, something which went hand in hand with the increasingly important role of ideology, of programmes, and of mass-based organization in Swedish political life.

In Karlstad, Gullbrand Elowson, who had joined the liberal camp during the 1880s, had departed in 1908. By the end of his carreer considered expendable by the executive committee in Stockholm (see above), he had been succeeded in 1906 by Axel Schotte, a high-ranking official in the provincial administration, and a more up-to-date liberal by the standards of the executive committee. Mauritz Hellberg, of course, had involved himself in the 1911 campaign, and he did so in part on the strength of his own seat in the prestigious First Chamber, which he had finally been able to secure the previous year. More stalwart than Elowson, Hellberg was nevertheless also at odds with social and political developments. On the threshold of a new era, his intellectualism and particular views on individuality had made him increasingly detached from the grass roots of the party. Originally considered too radical to fit in with mainstream liberalism, it was significant that he became a deputy only at a late stage in life. In a 1917 letter from his old friend, professor Johan Bergman, the latter was regretful about Hellberg's late entry into parliament, but at the same time tried to strike a jesting tone: Sweden had, according to him, indeed become a 'country for old men'.[77] Instead, liberal leadership on the regional level had gradually moved into the hands of younger people, such as Carl Björling and August Lindh, who had both been brought up in environments ideologically close to the popular movements and a more collectivistic conception of political individualism. These were among the men who were destined to play prominent roles in the 'frisinnade' faction when the Liberal Party finally split.[78]

The winding road to destruction

During the First World War and the outbreak of the revolution in Russia, food rationing and shortages led to social unrest and political crisis in Sweden. In March 1917, at the same time as the first phase of the revolution culminated and the Tsar abdicated, one conservative cabinet replaced another after fierce opposition from socialists and liberals. On the domestic scene the social democrats had gathered strength during the war, but nonetheless split in May 1917; one faction remained reformist whereas the other, the left-wing faction of the old party, included the core of what later on (1921) became the Swedish Communist Party. As the 1917 general elections approached, demands for the introduction of universal suffrage increased. The elections resulted in victory for the social democrats, but also in a recovery for the liberals, who had declined in the previous, 1914, elections. Consequently, the social democrats and the liberals joined forces and formed a coalition government.

The latter were in for some nasty surprises, though. As the 1920 elections had turned out to be a political parenthesis, the 1921 elections, viz. the first in which universal suffrage for men and women was applied, became the more important. To the liberals – although the *Karlstads-tidningen* among other newspapers tried to refute this – the immediate threat was that of being cut to pieces in the struggle between the social democrats and the conservatives; thus, the 'brute clash of interests between class-based parties [simply] was a reflection of the [recent] war between nations'.[79] In reality, the onslaught came from within the ranks of their own party.

The main competition for voters came from the social democrats. But the tool with which to match this challenge – the party organization – was slowly crumbling. For one thing, the matter of prohibition continued to put a strain on the efforts to coordinate policies. Teetotalism had culminated in terms of organized members around 1910 (Lundkvist 1977), but within 'Frisinnade landsföreningen' itself, teetotallers together with nonconformists continued as a formidable and, as it would prove, subversive lobby. Furthermore, the liberals had suffered from yet other internal conflicts since 1914, one of which was on defence issues and military expenditure. In connection to the elections that year, a right-wing faction actually left and eventually joined the Conservative Party. Finally, Karl Staaff had died in October 1915. With his replacement by Nils Edén, a professor from Uppsala and leader of the liberal deputies in parliament, the party entered a severe leadership crisis. Staaff had guided the party wisely and paid more than lip service to its grass roots in an attempt to maintain a balance (Johansson 1980: 22–25). Although skilful, Edén lacked these qualities. He failed to keep together a movement and an organization which, to follow Rönblom (1929: 96–97), more than anything else was a cross-class coalition of ideas.

Compared to Staaff, Edén was more elitist, in the sense that he was much less prone to let the party conventions and, thus, the grass roots, decide on matters pertaining to the orientation of the party; importantly, following such a line also meant tying the deputies in parliament to the decisions made by the conventions. The latter, Edén had argued in the spring of 1916, simply lacked the necessary insight and knowledge to decide on complicated political matters (in this case specifically on military expenditure) (Johansson 1980: 24–25). When put to it, Edéns perspective in effect implied a centralization of 'Frisinnade landsföreningen', which, whether by necessity, considering its organizational pedigree, or by creed, had been open to diversity in local and regional opinion. Edén's strategy could – perhaps – have posed a harsh but nevertheless useful remedy for the tensions between 'liberals' and 'frisinnade'. Under current conditions, however, it created an organizational crisis which brought out this conflict in full. His resistance towards accepting the leading role of the party conventions thus seemed to confirm the problem of party alignment touched upon by Emil Rylander during the 1917 elections.

By the time of the 1921 general elections, these competing ideas of party came out into the open. The hardliners among the 'frisinnade', led by editor Carl G. Ekman, mobilized their teetotalist supporters and demanded prohibition. In this they also found support among the social democrats, who by this time had become well entrenched in the organizational network of the teetotallers, and in particular the Good Templars. The moderate minority led by Edén favoured restrictions and control, but only based on existing legislation. Their approach was therefore not entirely dissimilar to the strategies used by the 'Deutscher Verein' (see chapter 2) in Germany. Prohibitionists and moderates were, however, unanimous on the need for a referendum to decide the extent of public support for prohibition. The conflict culminated at the party convention in June 1920, although a compromise was eventually negotiated. It was, as Johansson (1980: 51) has stressed, to great extent a conflict over the right of the majority to set the party programme. Since the moderates insisted on the right of the minority to veto any too far-reaching proposals on prohibition – a position that was reflected in the final compromise – in effect the majority rule of the convention was overruled.

The bitterest struggles took place among the Stockholm liberals, but the conflict inflicted damage on the organization across the country. In Karlstad the local branch of 'Frisinnade landsföreningen' was divided, but at a meeting held in August several moderates claimed that the prohibitionists tried to impose a 'much too narrow-minded view' on the matter. Even though the prohibitionists were in the majority, they did not have the right to suppress the party minority's views.[80] Opinion in the countryside was likewise divided, but more generally tended towards the protectionists, i.e. the 'frisinnade'. This reflected the close connections that still existed between the party and organized teetotalism and nonconformism.

Old organizational networks were once again activated in the 1921 elections. For example, as early as March the nonconformists of the Mission Covenant Church closed ranks on the matter. Formally nonpartisan in political matters, all congregations in Värmland decided, firstly, that any member who for any reason possessed ration coupons for alcohol (alcohol rationing had been introduced nationwide in the previous year) should immediately return them to the proper authorities. Moreover, the members in Väse decided to sign a mass petition in favour of temporary and all-out prohibition.[81] Secondly, it seems that in some parts of Värmland the teetotalist organizations of the

Good Templars and the Blue Ribbon had by this time tried to join forces by forming joint committees, such as in the Ölme district.[82] As the elections approached, campaigning in favour of prohibition was extended. On 13 August, the IOGT lodge Heijkensköld in Älvsbacka, west of Filipstad, decided to hold an open session on the issue, prompted by the upcoming elections. The meeting was to be organized in cooperation with other lodges in the area.[83] And at an extraordinary meeting three weeks later, in September, the lodge 'Björneborg' of the IOGT in Visnum pondered the position on prohibition among the candidates from the various parties. The keynote speaker was Gustaf Svensson, a prominent Good Templar member and social democrat from Stockholm.[84] The double-edged political role of the popular movements had become fully apparent.

On the one hand, all of these organizations had an intensely mobilizing effect on the electorate. On the other hand, their party affiliations were more than ever before uncertain. For every successful move that could be noted by, for instance, the teetotallers, there was a corresponding defeat of the idea of a synchronized election campaign among the liberals. These difficulties had long been reflected in the brief reports – and briefer they became as the elections approached – from the local branches. As early as the previous year, Adolf Carlsson, head of 'Frisinnade landsföreningen' at Värmskog, western Värmland, succinctly pointed out to the regional office that it was 'not easy to keep a local branch here'.[85] We can note two things in relation to this. To begin with, social cooperation is never easily achieved. Even in small-scale associations of the kind typical to the early nineteenth century or, as here, small, local-level party branches, successful cooperation requires repeated and continuous experience within the framework of the organization and its ideological values and beliefs. It remains a statistical fact that this pertains particularly to the formation of mutual or horizontal trust between citizens (Åberg & Sandberg 2003: 116–117).[86] Such conditions were no longer in place as the activities of the local branches of 'Frisinnade landsföreningen' dwindled to a minimum, or simply ceased.

Furthermore, the tensions among the liberals on the issue of prohibition suggest more deeply running ideological controversies, which ultimately pertained to competing conceptions of political individualism. Urban liberals had, indeed, moved closer to the popular movements in their views on citizenship as an effect of the turn towards progressivism, but obviously not close enough. These were differences that dated back to at least the 1890s and the endeavours of the suffrage movement, and later contributed to the increasing divide between liberals and social democrats. To some extent the same kind of differentiation also characterized the struggle between the liberal party conventions and the parliamentarian group around Edén. In a sense, therefore, the upheaval most notable among the teetotallers was in actual fact an expression of a more deeply rooted disagreement on fundamental matters of civic and political association and political modernization. Hence, when viewed from the perspectives of 'Frisinnade landsföreningen', the situation looked ominous when the 1921 elections began.

In several respects these elections were unique. They had been triggered by the 1918–21 constitutional reforms which, to follow Kahan (2003), marked the passing from a politics of 'limited suffrage' to that of democracy. For one thing, this meant an enormous increase in eligible voters, mainly by the inclusion of women in the political system. Also, although social and economic issues played an important role as an effect of the post-war crisis, no single issue dominated the campaign if we consider the emerging party system as a whole (Esiasson 1990: 127). This feature confirmed that doctrines and programmes had become more important at the expense of single issues. Still, precisely the single issue of prohibition was rapidly tearing up the liberal front, this at a time when competing parties devoted their efforts elsewhere. If not sooner, so in any event when the nomination procedure was completed in early August, it was clear that factionalism would obstruct the elections: the liberals in Värmland entered the elections with no less than three, separate lists: one rural list, one for the towns, and one for anti-prohibition candidates, with A. Zachrisson from Karlstad as primary candidate.[87]

Not surprisingly, the most distinguishing feature of the elections on the national level was the victory of the Social Democratic Party, which attained a national average of 36.2 per cent. Another prominent feature was the overwhelming defeat of the Liberal Party, with a result of 18.7 per cent. As in previous elections the liberals, however, still fared much better in Värmland with a 29.5 per cent result *but*, importantly, simply because of the overwhelming support from the rural and, in effect, prohibition list.[88] Clearly, this showed how political events had overtaken the position held by 'classic' liberals, now among the moderate camp, such as most notably Mauritz Hellberg. Indeed, the rhetoric of *Karlstads-tidningen* as the first election results were made public serves as an pertinent illustration both of this and the fact that the ideological leadership of the party and its members now stood very far from one another. Rather than dwelling on the issue of prohibition and intra-party factionalism – obviously too embarrassing a topic to be discussed – the newspaper identified the lack of 'class-related prejudice' as a main source of defeat. It stressed that, contrary to the socialists and the agrarians ('Bondeförbundet'), the Liberal Party fomented no such ideas to profit politically from.[89] This line of argument, viz. rooted in a late nineteenth-century middle-class morality of cross-class cooperation, became a smokescreen intended to conceal the bitter factionalism within the party.

If anything, the prohibitionists now gathered strength from the results in the belief that the demands for a ban on liquor would prevail, not least since a date for a referendum on the issue was set in the aftermath of the elections: August 1922. Any hopes the prohibitionists had for a ban on alcohol, though, proved to be wishful thinking considering the outcome. Värmland was among those regions where the majority voted in favour of prohibition, but in the country as a whole a narrow majority of 50.7 per cent voted against the idea (Johansson 1980: 74–77). It is certainly true, as Johansson (1980) argued, that internal divisions had hampered the Liberal Party from the outset, and that these were at the core of the conflict. However, drinking as a social issue had been part of liberalism and its predecessors since the very beginning – including among the intra-parliamentarian factions in the second half of the nineteenth century, but also, even more importantly, among the non-political, civic associations outside parliament which had once provided the base for the extra-parliamentary branch of the movement.

Both phalanxes now recovered and redeployed for the final show-down. It unfolded in conjunction with the May 1923 party convention in Stockholm. The proceedings have been dealt with in detail by previous research (see Johansson 1980: 193–253), but to outline them briefly, opinions were divided on how the results of the referendum should be interpreted in relation to the party programme and, consequently, how strongly the demands for prohibition should be formulated. More important from our point of view were the consequences, in particular on the regional level. As an effect of the conflict, the moderates left the party, although many delegates warned against the consequences, among them Mauritz Hellberg. Would not the effect of a split marginalize the liberals similarly to what, according to him, had proved to be the case with the agrarians? Hellberg instead favoured the idea of a united party and, in this respect, also quoted the women's and youth organizations of the party as examples to be followed.[90]

Alas, a split was virtually impossible to avoid at this stage. Following the negotiations on 27 May, some 70 delegates immediately gathered – at 10 p.m. – to elect a working committee that would prepare the formation of a new Liberal Party. From now on, then, the Swedish liberals would be divided between, on one side, 'Frisinnade folkpartiet', containing the majority of the old 'Liberala partiet/Frisinnade landsföreningen', and, on the other side, 'Sveriges liberala parti'; the latter was formally established on 7 October, although the process was not fully completed until the following year. The split also meant that Nils Edén in effect retired from political life, although he retained his seat as deputy to parliament until 1924. While Carl G. Ekman took the chair of 'Frisinnade folkpartiet', a lawyer from Stockholm, Eliel Löfgren, became the chairman of 'Sveriges liberala parti'. Mauritz Hellberg sided with the latter faction.

If anything, the 1923–24 events gave final proof of the deficiencies of weakly developed party organizations *cum* organization by means of proxy. Not surprisingly, professor Nils Alexandersson, who had joined in the efforts to organize the new 'Sveriges liberala parti', emphasized the need for a coherent programme. In his view it was 'unsound' for political association to be based on privately negotiated opinions alone. Rather, the 'spine and backbone of a party must consist of a mutual and carefully considered doctrine'.[91] Though the former option had been feasible, to some extent, in the nineteenth century, it was an untenable position in the era of democratic mass politics and modern party systems. However, when considered in hindsight, ideology as such was only one of two problems faced by the new party. An equally pressing concern was that of the organization. As secessionists, the liberals had been forced to leave the 'frisinnade' in possession of the established organization of the old 'Frisinnade landsföreningen'. Of course the new party rallied to put together a roster of reliable people who could mobilize prospective members, but as the central registers for 1923–24 suggest, it met with considerable difficulties in doing so. Värmland was no exception.[92] On the regional level, no actual material has been recovered for 'Sveriges liberala parti'.

By contrast, the 'frisinnade', which continued to operate through the organizational framework of the old party, suffered from the split to a much lesser extent. This was amply demonstrated by the first post-split election results of 1924. Between them, 'Frisinnade folkpartiet' and 'Sveriges liberala parti' yielded a better result in Värmland compared to the national average (21.3 per cent as compared to 16.9 per cent). However, the absolute majority of votes were in favour of the 'frisinnade' and only a small minority of voters aligned themselves with the new Liberal Party. Out of a total of 1,578 votes cast for 'Sveriges liberala parti' (2.8 per cent of the overall results in the elections), 531 of these were from cities and towns, whereas 12,116 of 14,176 'frisinnade' votes were cast in the countryside.[93] From the late 1920s things went from bad to worse. For instance, in the 1932 elections the liberals received a result of 1.9 per cent (1.8 per cent in Värmland), and the 'frisinnade' 9.8 per cent (13.0 per cent in Värmland). Simultaneously the social democrats consolidated as the largest party in parliament.[94]

Something had to be done, and it came in the shape of a reunion between the two factions in 1934. The liberals still considered themselves a left wing option;[95] and to 'strengthen and stabilize' the organization quite naturally became the main task of the new party – 'Folkpartiet' (the People's Party; distinct from the 1895 intra-parliamentary faction bearing the same name).[96] About this time, however, liberalism as an ideology had lost political momentum; something that would trouble it for some considerable time.

Rather, in parliament the liberals would now increasingly become reduced to what Lindström and Wörlund (1988: 273) have called 'the politics of unholy alliances', i.e. politics more concerned with how to squeeze the most from its parliamentary position than politics guided by ideological conviction.

A transitory phenomenon

Ironically, the formation of a modern party system, and the increased role of political organization, programmes, and doctrines, spelled the demise of liberalism as an ideological movement. The principle of organizations by means of proxy had clearly proven to be a transitory phenomenon at the same time as it tended to shape indeterminately many a liberal's view on how to mobilize grass-roots support. This is all the more ironical since liberalism and its ideals of civic and political association had been *the* major radical alternative in nineteenth-century society. In the main, liberalism certainly moved further to the left during the crucial years around the turn of the century, the only problem being that many of its supporters moved on once the party decided to stop. By the 1930s liberalism had been surpassed by the social democrats and lost its prerogative to identify, aggregate, and structure the major political issues in society. Yet this development was at the same time part of a more profound modernization of politics. Once universal suffrage was introduced everybody, except the most truculent of conservatives and communists, subscribed to those basic civic values which had originally nurtured liberalism. These no longer provided enough of a platform from which to form and sustain a government, to follow Gunther and Diamond (2001).

There is one final point to made with respect to this, viz. the development of liberalism in relation to the idea of a specifically 'Swedish model' for political modernization and democratization. While it is beyond doubt that the organizational weaknesses of liberalism and, looked at from the other end of the spectrum, the organizational skills of the Social Democratic Party, played important roles in the changes of political culture, other aspects of the problem make less sense, at least judging by the case of Värmland. To begin with, the 'organizational skills' of social democracy, however formidable, had yet to be cemented in a more long-term strategy. As most notably Schüllerqvist (1992) points out, the 1920s remained a period of probing different options in this respect. From that point of view it would not, perhaps, have been entirely impossible for the liberals to regain political momentum. Had it not been for their internal weakness, there was nothing inevitable about their defeat. Related to this, too, is the matter of the composition of the liberal electorate.

Since the assumption of a 'Swedish model' rests heavily on the relative independence of the peasantry as well as the political feebleness of the middle classes and, therefore, implicitly that of liberalism (Therborn 1989), it is worth stressing that the self-reliant peasantry were, indeed, the body and soul of the Liberal Party: As late as the early 1920s, nearly eight out of ten liberal voters in the country were rural dwellers, and close to nine out of ten in Värmland (chapter 1). Even though far from all of them were farmers, of course, the latter still had a strong voice in the party organization, both as passive members and as activists. There was certainly nothing feeble about the farmers as such. What one finds lacking in the 1850–1920 period were coherent organizational and ideological mechanisms that could bridge the urban-rural divide and, later on, the related separation of 'liberals' and 'frisinnade'. Where such cross-cultural alignments were possible, such as in Denmark (see Thomas 1988), liberalism continued as a vital political force. Where they proved unfeasible, as in Sweden, liberalism failed.

Adding to this were the increasing doubts among many farmers about the true value of liberalism from the point of view of what they came to consider as agricultural necessities, such as state support and protection. It is this perspective that adherents of the 'Swedish model' have made into one of their most important points: the fact that the peasantry finally discarded what had become a much weakened middle-class liberalism and, instead, opted for alliance with the social democrats, in 1933, in exchange for protectionist legislation, has very often been interpreted as a victory for consensual bargaining. Yet, while the 'Swedish model' adherents have a point, not only the weaknesses of the middle classes should be considered an important factor, but also the *inability* of the farmers to extend their perspective and look beyond their 'class interests', rather than their *contribution* to consensual bargaining as the linchpin of parliamentary politics. If anything, it was the class interests of the farmers that provided the rationale for their alliance with the social democrats, not political universalism. At the same time as their position may be described as being closer to the economic individualism of early liberalism, their apparent reluctance, at least in Värmland, to immediately shift their support to agrarian organizations and parties also suggests that liberal, cross-class politics were, after all, possible up to a point. Whether by force of culture, tradition, or the socio-economic composition of the peasantry, events in Värmland were not an historical inevitability. They suggest the possibility of alternative paths in the development of grass-roots democratization.

CHAPTER 4

Schleswig-Holstein

'Linksliberalismus' one step to the right

Reich on the rise

Compared to Sweden, the institutional and organizational framework of the first all-German elections was different in several ways. First of all, the two-tiered structure of provincial diets and a national assembly made political life more diverse. Furthermore, all elections from 1871 onwards were held against a background in which party organizations, however flimsy, were a political reality, not something which had yet to be created. Indeed, the two most important parties, the Progressives (1861), and the National Liberals (1867), had already formed on the basis of the dominating factions in the Prussian 'Landtag'. Similarly, the Schleswig-Holstein liberals had, as previously pointed out, organized independently, in 1863, in the 'Schleswig-Holsteinische Landespartei' under Wilhelm Beseler; a faction which eventually turned into the left-liberal LPSH/F of Albert Hänel.

As far as left-liberalism in Schleswig-Holstein is concerned, a regular party thus appeared earlier compared to Värmland. Neither was this the result of initiatives at central level. The organization of the left-liberals in Schleswig-Holstein developed parallel to that of the Prussian Progressives, and the LPSH/F remained more loosely integrated with the national organization of the former for most of the period considered. This structure was an effect of the federalistic make-up of the empire with its many, competing regional identities. In fact, the Schleswig-Holstein left-liberals had originally refrained from joining the Prussian party organization simply because the latter had been in favour of annexing the region in 1866 (Schultz Hansen

2003: 465–66). Therefore Lipset & Rokkan's (1967) observation that modern European party systems were formed on the basis of a merger of competing, regional elites is very applicable to the German pattern. One difference between Germany and countries such as Sweden or the Netherlands was that these rifts in the political fabric of the emerging nation-states were never properly mended. Rather, to many Schleswig-Holsteiners incorporation with Prussia simply meant the introduction of higher taxes and a new, military element hitherto unknown to local society.

Integration of the new Germany into a consolidated political community in the decades to follow, for instance by means of notions such as 'Heimat', was achieved only to a certain extent with respect to the establishing of party systems. While keeping some distance to more radical, autonomist factions, such as the Particularists, the Schleswig-Holstein liberals in LPSH/F had close links to the Progressives from 1870, and even managed the inclusion of the 'Liberale Vereinigung' (national liberal secessionists) in an alliance in 1884. Despite this coalition, which eventually broke up in 1893, the two party organizations of LPSH/F and the Progressives still remained formally independent of each other up to 1910 (Thompson 2000: 296). Instead of an integrated left-liberal organization, alliances of this kind became a second best option to manage electoral mass-mobilization, and the strategies of obstruction aimed at them by the conservatives and Bismarck in particular.

Originally, new elections to parliament were scheduled for every third year and, after 1888, every fifth year. Among these I have targeted the 1871, 1884, 1898, 1907, and 1912 campaigns as being of particular interest. They bring out another important feature of German liberal parties – but also an important similarity with Sweden – i.e. the circumstance that the parties to a great extent continued to operate by means of proxy. In 1871, liberal opinion in Schleswig-Holstein was put to a first, crucial test during the nationalist fervour that surrounded the ending of the war with France, and the proclamation of a unified Germany. Indeed, even in Schleswig-Holstein, traditionally in favour of autonomy, the Franco-Prussian war had, as we remember, provoked patriotic outbursts, as illustrated by the adolescent Ferdinand Tönnies (chapter 2). Importantly, his case reflected more than just youthful excitement. It also captured the tensions typical of German liberalism, vacillating between different strands of individualism and various old and new modes of collective identification, in the latter case nationalism. Although the nation-state undoubtedly was the result of socio-economic modernization, this was not necessarily the case with the 'nation' itself, according to what Tönnies later wrote in his famous treatise on 'Gemeinschaft' and 'Gesellschaft'.

Similarly to the notion of 'Heimat', the 'nation' was ultimately an expression of 'natural will' rather than the product of a modern, 'rational will'. It drew on ideas of archaic, more genuine and, perhaps, even arcane bonds between people. We need only consider Tönnies' opinion of the 'common people', viz. those among whom the fulfilment of life depended on life among family, friends, and neighbours 'in home, village and town' (Tönnies 2001 [1887]: 173):

> if the common people and their labour become subject to trade or capitalism, beyond a certain point they cease to be a people or nation. They adapt themselves to alien influences and conditions and become "civilized". Science, which is really the province of the educated, is continually fed into them in various forms and combinations as a medicine to cure their boorishness (Tönnies 2001 [1887]: 174).

In regions such as Schleswig-Holstein, always a major source of inspiration for Tönnies' sociological thought, and a region in which, congruous to Värmland, local culture revealed both parochial as well as modernizing traits, these tensions became particularly obvious during the last decades of the nineteenth century.

The complex ethnic and linguistic make-up of Schleswig-Holstein also added to emerging modes of political behaviour and nation-building. On the one hand, insufficient organization and emigration had, by the time of the First World War, pushed the demographic boundary between Danes and Germans further north into Schleswig. On the other hand, ethnic tensions increased with the attempts of forced assimilation and the countermeasures adopted by the Danes (Schultz Hansen 2003: 476–83). Among other things this presented the established parties with an important electoral group which could not be absorbed along conventional lines of issue aggregation and societal representation, to follow Gunther and Diamond (2001). The very same ethnic tensions simultaneously provided sustenance to the Danish lists in the general elections. All the way up to the last pre-war elections in 1912, the first constituency of Hadersleben-Sonderburg continued to send Danish deputies to Berlin (Schultz Hansen 2003: 464).

Economically, as well, Germany was a land of striking contrasts between industrial districts and rural areas. In addition, the agricultural sector as such was quite diverse, a feature which came to colour the debates on tariffs from the late 1870s onwards. Whereas grain-producing areas were more inclined (although not always) to accept tariffs, farmers who were heavily involved in the production of livestock turned more easily towards the free trade camp, since their domestic markets were less vulnerable to foreign competition, and since tariffs meant an increase in prices of fodder. The latter became typical of Schleswig-Holstein, although the issue was not in itself decisive for the political orientation of the farmers. In fact, Thompson suggests that any stress put on the free trade argument would be 'simplistic' and 'at odds with the political situation in the province' (Thompson 2000: 293–94, quote at 293).[1] More specifically, taking stock of this 'political situation' implies assessing the autonomist and regionalist traditions prevalent in Schleswig-Holstein throughout the period in question (see below). Moreover, once tariffs had been implemented, it became politically impossible to argue in favour of a complete turnaround on the matter. Thus the extent of the system rather than the principle of tariffs came under debate.

More importantly, however, the 'Second Reichsgründung' spelled more than just controversies over protective duties. Tariffs were a symptom rather than a cause of Bismarck's ambitions finally to crush the opposition in parliament, and in particular the liberals; to stem the rising tide of social democracy and to consolidate the new state by means of a series of administrative, fiscal, and commercial reforms. The most important consequence as we approach the 1880s, therefore, was the end of a liberal era and the emergence of a more authoritarian phase in German domestic political life

(Sheehan 1978). Effectively, the liberals were shattered as a result of Bismarck's policies and the 1884 elections were one pertinent illustration of this – but not in Schleswig-Holstein, where not least the left-liberals fared much better compared to the national average. National liberals and left-wing liberals together received a total of 62.1 per cent of the votes in the region compared to a 36.9 per cent national average (Table 2, chapter 1).

However, the pressure exerted from the right only represented one out of two extremes in the liberal dilemma. The following period, mirrored by the 1898, 1907, and 1912 elections, was when the social democrats gradually came forward as the largest faction in parliament. It was also a period during which Schleswig-Holstein to an increasing extent became industrialized. Whereas Schleswig-Holstein at the time of its incorporation with Prussia was overwhelmingly rural and agrarian, by the end of the First World War one-third of the population lived in industrial cities and towns such as Kiel, Altona, Flensburg, Neumünster, and Wandsbek (Ibs 2006: 129). For instance in Flensburg, in 1895, the Socialist Workers' Association there had numbered only 222 members, but by 1912 the number had swollen to 1,788, including 263 women (Pust 1975: 144). Not only the urban environments were transformed by this development. It was also reflected in an increased political awareness among the rural workers. Class-based political cleavages came to the fore.

As Schleswig-Holstein simultaneously retained much of its rural character, the dual challenge of national unification and socio-economic modernization provided fertile ground not only for the rise of 'Heimatkunst' but also for the emergence of new political divisions. In a sense these were more complex in their make-up compared to those involved with the emerging party system in Sweden. In brief, not only were the liberals more severely faction-alised compared to Sweden; they also faced organized socialism at a much earlier stage in the election campaigns. Finally, throughout the period the conservative, Prussian royal administration in itself posed a major obstacle. Yet, both the 1907 and, in particular, the 1912 elections signalled a left-liberal comeback, judging from the turnout. The left-liberals somehow managed to defend and reinforce their traditional position as a main political force in the region, despite hapless organization. One key to understanding their dominance was the deeply rooted fear of socialism and revolutionary upheaval; another was the design of the electoral system; a third explanation was, however, the left-liberal influence among the peasantry, fragile as it nevertheless proved to be on many occasions.

To begin with, this 'peasantry' was much more diverse in its composition than in Värmland, where small-scale family farmers formed a dominant group. The western districts, by the North Sea, were traditionally home to groups of independent farmers (such as Tönnies' family), which, historically speaking, had been able to maintain their freeholding liberties and features of self-government all the way up to the Prussian annexation. It was a bucolic yet dynamic environment which produced not only the father of modern German sociology, but also the famous historian Theodor Mommsen, who was born in Garding, Eiderstedt. These areas specialized in rearing beef cattle on large farms with the help of hired labour. Politically speaking, farmers and labourers were divided between, on the one hand, national liberals and conservatives and, on the other hand, left-liberals. The mid-section of Schleswig-Holstein was characterized by backward, small and middle-sized farming, where the so-called 'Geestbuer' ('Geestbauer') tilled the sandy soil and were involved in a mix of grain and cattle production; political opinion was inclined to the left. The east, finally, was generally speaking dominated by large manors but also well-to-do tenant farmers, diversified in terms of production, and dependent on the labour of cottagers and day-labourers. As in the west, political opinion reflected the socio-economic cleavages in the area: estate owners followed conservative tradition, whereas labourers, tenants and small farmers had liberal and, increasingly, socialist convictions (Tilton 1975: 20–29).

Since liberal leadership in the region at the same time was overtly urban and academic in composition, the urban–rural division was a defining characteristic of the movement (Beyer 1968; Thompson 2000) in much the same manner as in Värmland. Important differences, though, were that the economically dominant groups of farmers were much more volatile, politically speaking, and, eventually, also much more prone to support right-wing parties. Precisely in this dimension, the liberal flaw of weak formal organization proved fatal in the long run. This became obvious not least once universal suffrage was introduced in 1918. As Tilton points out (1975: 10–11), one should therefore also consider that, despite the more generous electoral laws compared to Sweden, these still excluded a majority of the adult population before the First World War. Neither women nor men under the age of 25 had the right to vote; thus, at the time of the 1874 general elections still only a fifth of the population (21.2 per cent) were eligible to vote.[2]

The 1871 elections

The likely results of the first all-German elections, scheduled for March 1871, were not entirely promising from a liberal point of view. One week before the proclamation of the German Empire, in the Hall of Mirrors at Versailles on 18 January, *Keiler Zeitung* commented at some length on the issue. Citing an article in the Trier-based *Volksfreund*, a newspaper with close ties to the newly established 'Zentrum' party, the time chosen for the elections seemed not only unfavourable but virtually impossible to the liberals. Indeed, many among the electorate stood fully armed in France while the election campaign back home was about to take off. Of these, the best and brightest among the younger generation, a majority were potential liberal voters. Looked at the other way around, the *Kieler Zeitung* questioned whether political conservatism really was the certain outcome among voters as they grew older. But although there was reason for concern, considering the gravity of the situation, the election also represented an opportunity to steer the new nation down the right tracks of constitutionalism. According to the newspaper, the context of the election if anything highlighted the need to de-militarize German society, including, if possible, a shortening of the three-year conscription.[3]

The assumptions made as to the connection between age, voting, and military service, however, must be understood in light of the following: conscription applied to all men of military age, i.e. from the age of 20, but given the restrictions built into the electoral system the issue of voting still remained a purely theoretical matter to these groups of young men. What the *Kieler Zeitung* obviously referred to, then, were the large cadres of reserves which also made up the army. Furthermore, to a left-liberal ear the risks of 'militarization' of society could be read not only in terms of a devaluation of civic values through the extended military service of its citizens; in any event this feature became more prominent only after 1871, when it reflected, among other things, in a rapid growth of veterans' associations and various military clubs. 'Militarization' could also be defined in budgetary terms, as 'high taxes and potentially unchecked state expenditure' (Clark 2006: 599). All in all the newspaper conceded that the task lying ahead was a formidable one, since the election was hampered not only by the war, but also by the restrictions imposed on the press and on civil liberties, such as the freedom of assembly.[4] These were features which quite naturally complicated campaigning.

The newspaper captured several of the main points of the LPSH/F programme which had been launched in May 1870, viz. the peaceful uniting of north and south Germany, cuts in military expenditure, a halt to tax rises, extended civil rights, and self-government. On the issue of northern Schleswig, with its Danish population, the position was also clear: it must at all costs remain an integral part of the region and should not be ceded (Kiehl 1966: 28–31). Apart from the paragraph on northern Schleswig, this programme was roughly in line with the demands previously adopted by the Progressives in other regions, such as Württemberg (the latter related in Eisfeld 1969: 203–204). Differences between parties and factions, though often blurred and confusing, were thus more contingent on a combination of doctrine and party programmes rather than opinions on singular issues, the latter being the case in Sweden during this period. Ideology had made its way into politics, albeit it would often be harnessed by pragmatic considerations in the years to follow. Electoral competition on the basis of party programmes and, simultaneously, restriction of the press and lack of civil liberties was, however, only one feature which made campaigning different compared to Sweden. A third difference still was the very design of the electoral system (see Diederich 1969).

Apart from what has already been said about the restrictions surrounding the right to vote, neither did the electoral system favour the formation of centralized parties. Rather, historically speaking, electoral systems based on single-member constituencies and majoritarian elections usually favoured local or regional elite factions (chapter 2), the latter a prominent feature of political culture in Schleswig-Holstein. At the same time, however, the German system also had positive features. Most notably Suval (1985) has argued that the electoral system was, indeed, inclusive enough to facilitate at least a certain amount of group-specific identification among the voters, based on party affiliation and voting practice. The German social democrats are a strong case in point. Among the positive features, later noticed by among others the Swedish liberals, were also direct elections and the principle of absolute majority (chapter 5).

Whether Suval's reasoning applies to the much more heterogeneous groups of voters that made up the liberal parties is questionable, though. Confirmation of the rules of the political game by means of the electoral system and, at the same time, affirmation of one's own interests does seem a process based on principles similar to those suggested by Ostrom (1990). However, the electoral system was only one, if crucial, component of this structure. Compared to the social democrats the liberals lacked important features, and more specifically organizational arrangements and party institutions, on the foundations of which ideological identity and issues could be properly negotiated. Quite naturally this left less room for the liberal parties to perform functions of societal representation and social integration (cf. Gunther & Diamond 2001). We need only in this context consider the organization created by LPSH/F in 1867, which included a general assembly and an executive committee of seven persons, assisted by local representatives, but sparsely so in the countryside (Kiehl 1966: 23–25; Thompson 2000).

Local 'Wählervereine' (electoral assemblies) added to this structure, as in Sweden, but these were nevertheless separate entities in relation to the party organization. Any bodies corresponding to the network of local party branches in Sweden were virtually non-existent. Therefore the Schleswig-Holstein liberals were almost certainly less successful in organizing their voters compared to what was the case in Värmland: as late as 1911, the left-liberals had succeeded in enrolling only 5.0 per cent of their supporters (Schultz Hansen 2003: 473). Indeed, they were worse off in this respect compared, most notably, to the

left-liberals in Baden, who organized about one-third of their supporters at the same time. Yet, more than Baden, Schleswig-Holstein
was typical of the average German organizational pattern amongst
the liberals (Thompson 2000: 281–82). Also, the system of second
ballots made what were already fragile party alignments even more
volatile among the liberal factions. In addition, candidates in the
elections were not required to reside in their respective constituencies.
This may certainly have provided an antidote to parochial elitism,
but at the same time it also widened the gap between voters and
their parties in cases – such as with the liberals – where there was
no organizational or ideological cement with which to bond grass
roots and leadership together.

Against the left-liberals stood the national liberals and, increasingly so, the socialists. When the 1871 elections were announced,
the latter had begun to pose a real threat to the established political factions. Contrary to what became the case among some of the
Swedish liberals when the franchise movement formed in the early
1890s, the German liberals never seriously contemplated any form
of cooperation with the socialists; that they did try to sway the
workers by addressing the social issues of emerging industrialism,
such as at a national liberal meeting in February 1871, is another
matter.[5] Neither did any of the centre-left parties have any illusions
about a grand left-wing coalition.

Campaigning in strategically targeted areas, such as the western
parts of the province, and organizational resolve was part of the
socialist strategy (Regling 1965). This was an endeavour that was
only fuelled by the introduction of Bismarck's Anti-Socialist Laws
a few years later. By the time of the First World War, the remarkable effort made by the German socialists had, in the words of
Watt (1968: 114), resulted in a strong, working-class sub-culture
of its own: 'The Social Democrats had given to him [the worker]
his own fraternal and sports organization, his own singing groups,
and clubs for his wife and his children. He could read any of more
than ninety Social Democratic newspapers, led by the vigorous
Berlin daily *Vorwärts*.' In contrast to the liberals, therefore, they had
successfully managed to become a mass party, including efficacious
institutional arrangements for interest aggregation, issue structuring,

and mobilization. By that time the social democrats had organized from 12.8 to 52.6 per cent of their voters in Schleswig-Holstein, depending on constituency (Thompson 2000: 282).

By the 1870s the socialists were quite well aware of their potential. For example, they did not hesitate to strike a messianic chord when appealing to the voters; and, in fact, such allusions were all the more important to campaigners operating in strongly religious environments. It was, as Regling (1965: 159) points out, not unusual to compare Ferdinand Lassalle, the late founder of the 'Allgemeine Deutsche Arbeiter-Verein' (ADAV, 1863), to Christ, in order to justify the gospel of socialism and, slowly, make it a replacement for religion. In connection to the 1871 elections, therefore, the socialists introduced themselves to the voters in the eight Altona-Stormarn constituencies (Holstein) with help of a motto coined by Lassalle, i.e. that 'the worker is the rock, upon which the Church of our time will be built'.[6] Such confidence was, at this stage, direly needed since the strength of socialism, however threatening from the point of view of the establishment, still left a lot to be desired. Hence the fears of the Prussian government, too, concerning the socialist 'menace' in the province, were rather exaggerated. In Rendsburg, northern Holstein, for instance, ADAV had, indeed, a local assembly, but in the early 1870s it still included only a limited number of active members, and they led a rather quiet life as far as politicking was concerned (Regling 1965: 122–23, 172–73). Among their activities were commemorative celebrations of Ferdinand Lassalle's birthday.[7]

During the 1865–70 period ADAV managed to extend its activities across the whole of Holstein, and for the voters, the Altona-Stormarn appeal claimed, a great moment had now arrived. The workers were now about to elect their very own representatives to parliament. In contrast to Bismarck's contempt of parliamentary procedure and protocol, the appeal stressed that the deputies represented and exercised the ultimate legislative power of the Reich (reflecting the more positive appreciation among the Lassallean socialists of the state and its institutions, compared to more orthodox Marxists). And not only that: parliament was, indeed, also ultimately responsible for the implementation of this legislation.[8] In matters constitutional the message was therefore in a sense comparable to that of Albert

Hänel and, thus, the left-liberal position. Political power was to be wielded by the people through their elected parliamentary institutions. At the same time a major difference compared to the liberals was, of course, the attacks made on capitalism and the explicit ambition to unlock the doors of parliament to deputies recruited from the working classes, not only their alleged representatives from the established political elite. Socialist policy posed a threat not only to the creed of the 'invisible hand', typical to economic individualism, but also to the liberal ambition to be the vanguard of the working classes by means of example and cross-class alliances. Indeed, one could therefore say that the 1871 socialist programme in a sense spelled the demise of a liberal era in German politics a few years later, during the 'Second Reichsgründung', although this was an end that, somewhat paradoxically, was to come about not because of socialist campaigning, but rather as a result of Bismarck's determination to rout the liberals.

The Danish issue, viz. Northern Schleswig, as well as lingering separatism among the German population, also complicated the election campaign. Difficulties faced by the parties pertained above all to the dual differentiation of the voters by socio-economic *and* ethnic identification. For instance, since the Danes entered the elections on the basis of their own candidates, campaigning among them was considered a lost cause from the outset by the liberal and right-wing parties. Eventually the Danes also won the Hadersleben-Sonderburg constituency in the northernmost part of the province (Schultz Hansen 2003: 464), and although the national liberals secured the second, Flensburg-Apenrade, constituency they met significant resistance from the Danish candidate, farmer H. A. Krüger from Bestoft. Krüger, in turn, had been nominated by among others Gustav Johannsen, a bookshop owner in Flensburg, who would himself become a popular name among the Danes but also many German voters in the following elections.[9]

As for the particularists, they, too, blurred the political front lines among the liberals. One case in point is the non-socialist workers' association in Schleswig, which decided to nominate a secessionist (particularist) candidate, Count Eduard von Baudissin, whereas the local 'Bürgerverein' favoured the national liberal candidate Theodor

Reinke.[10] Certainly, *Schleswiger Nachrichten*, which supported Reinke's candidacy, was blunt as to the prospects of Baudissin: these were 'now, as before, completely lost'.[11] This statement, however, underestimated the strength of particularism in the constituency, since Baudissin carried the day by 3,776 votes to 2,282 for Reinke.[12]

The press, therefore, however crucial to campaigning, was on occasion well off-target when assessing the public climate. As for the organizational proxies of the parties, these usually continued to be modelled on the 'classic' pre-1848 patterns of middle-class association. They included most notably the 'Bürgervereine' and different kinds of cultural societies including, particularly in northern Schleswig, nationally orientated ones such as the 'Harmonie' society in Flensburg. In this case the association simply shifted from a pro-Danish to a pro-German position after 1867 (Kretzschmer 1955: 282). In yet other cities, such as Hamburg, some of these citizens' associations were eventually attached to party organizations (Thompson 2000: 283), but this was far from always the case. Equally often their efforts resulted in some confusion on matters political, which only goes to show the malleability of ideological affiliation and the narrow distinction between 'civic' and 'political' association.

As a case in point, Reinke's and, in particular, Baudissin's candidacies in the 1871 elections pose two examples of the ambiguous role played by civic association in relation to political association: a formally non-political assembly, a workers' association, chose to take a clearly political position with respect to the legal and administrative status of Schleswig-Holstein in relation to Prussia. The case of J. Pauls in Bredstedt, in the fourth constituency of Tondern-Husum-Eiderstedt, who eventually declined nomination, is another example. In his case the platform was an anonymous 'Delegiertenversammlung', and not one of the regular liberal electoral assemblies.[13] Yet a third example was the society of the 'Schleswig-Holsteinischen Kampfgenossen', which convened in Itzehoe.[14] Associations such as these did, however, not only intervene in the nomination procedure, by screening and putting forward possible candidates. Whether successful or not, they also helped disseminate ideas and created opinion on current issues, such as on the matter of the infallibility of the Pope,[15] declared by the Vatican in the previous

year – a matter of no small importance in the subsequent unleash-
ing of Bismarck's 'Kulturkampf'. Although Catholicism was of no
particular relevance to political conditions in Schleswig-Holstein per
se, generally speaking anti-Catholic sentiments, often deeply rooted
(Gross 2004), were still emblematic to post-1870 German liberalism.

In regard to the role played by the newspapers, and in particular
the *Kieler Zeitung* under the aegis of Hänel's close ally Wilhelm
Ahlmann, as well as considering the use of proxies, the 1871 campaign reveals certain similarities to the pattern typical in Värmland
and Sweden. Other similarities included appearances by individual
speakers, seen as crucial to electoral mobilization. In fact, the paramount importance of this feature was almost certainly due to the
poor organization among the liberals; left-liberals and national
liberals alike. Canvassing, though, does not seem to have been a
regular part of campaigning; something which, again, was hardly
surprising considering the limited financial resources of the parties.
Finally, as in Sweden, the campaign was also of relatively speaking
short duration. It took place in the last couple of weeks, or even
days, before the actual elections. One exception was the nomination of Albert Hänel, in early February, first by the local electoral
assembly of LPSH/F in Kiel, later by the electoral assembly in the
seventh constituency of Kiel-Rendsburg. In the opinion of the *Kieler
Zeitung*, Hänel, who since 1867 was a deputy to the parliament of
the North German Confederation, was the man best suited to avert
any tendencies towards factionalizing within the party.[16] One such
source of factionalism, indeed, was represented by the particularists,
including names such as Baudissin, who had left the main party
only recently and, at about the same time as Hänel received his
nomination, convened at a rally in Rendsburg,[17] precisely where
the provisional government of Schleswig-Holstein had once been
formed in 1848.

As stands clear from evidence, factionalism was very much part
of the elections. Also, there was the competition not only from
the socialists but also the national liberals and the conservatives to
consider. In the long run, and in part as a result of the system of
second ballots, the left-liberals and the particularists were forced to
join forces in some constituencies, since neither of the candidates

of these parties was able to collect enough votes in the first round of the election. All in all this reflected what gradually, in the years to follow, became the hallmark of Hänel's policies, viz. an ambition to always manoeuvre between the Scylla of liberal factionalism and the Charybdis of socialism.

Albeit at the expense of ideological clarity, this strategy proved successful in yet other respects. Joining together particularist candidates and the LPSH/F secured mandates in seven out of nine constituencies, i.e. all except Flensburg-Apenrade and Hadersleben-Sonderburg (Schultz Hansen 2003: 464). Lauenburg, where the national liberals also won, was not administratively joined with the region until 1876 and then formed a tenth constituency. The outcome stood in stark contrast to most other regions. There the national liberals generally achieved a better turnout compared to the progressives (Sheehan 1978: 125, Table 9.1). Indeed, the left-liberals received a national average of only 16.0 per cent, compared to 30.1 per cent for the national liberals,[18] the single biggest faction in parliament. Also, the threat posed by the socialists was contained, although tobacco worker Carl August Bräuer, the social democratic candidate in the eighth constituency, made it as far as the second ballot.[19] This circumstance nevertheless spelled important changes which were to occur in connection to the next, 1874, elections, when not only the national liberals advanced their positions at the expense of the left-liberals, but also the social democrats secured two deputy posts, one for Altona-Stormarn outside Hamburg, and, following massive campaigns, one for the ninth constituency. This area included the Segeberg district, which was traditionally dominated by the liberals (Schmidt 1985; Schultz Hansen 2003: 464).

Which features did, after all, make the liberal mode of mobilization by means of weak organization and proxies work? Liberal doctrine, as reflected in the party programme, was certainly important, although it included pragmatic concessions which were not necessarily intrinsic to liberalism as an ideology. This is illustrated by the stress put on the integrity of Schleswig-Holstein as region in the 1870 programme. On the one hand, this item could certainly be read as an appeal to the idea of the right of self-determination. On the other hand it could, however, also be understood in terms of unchecked parochialism, and simply as a conservative reaction to modernization, its foundations being not entirely unlike the kind of belief system Tönnies (2001 [1887]) found typical of pre-industrial communities. What still made this paragraph appealing to left-liberalism was the federalistic framework of the German nation-state which, in turn, could be used to link the idea of liberty with regionally embedded notions of 'Heimat'.

Regardless of its status as a 'Honoratiorenpartei' or 'Professorial party', the LPSH/F therefore made a serious attempt to channel public opinion on the matter of regional identity. Not least Albert Hänel was repeatedly accused of intellectual aloofness (see below), but regional pride and independence still became regularly exploited by the party in the following election campaigns. But nevertheless the role of the party elite, as opposed to the structures typical of 'Frisinnade landsföreningen' in Sweden, must be stressed. For all its shortcomings the latter left ample room for grass-roots opinion to be funnelled directly into parliament. In addition, the fact that the proxies used by the left-liberals in Schleswig-Holstein, unlike the Swedish popular movements, lacked the properties of mass organizations further helped to narrow the organizational basis of the LPSH/F. Consequently, Duverger's notion (1967 [1954]) of parties with intra-parliamentarian roots fits better, if not entirely, as a description of left-liberalism in Schleswig-Holstein than of conditions in Värmland.

As in Sweden, albeit for partly different reasons, the left-liberals in Schleswig-Holstein failed to institute organizational mechanisms securing commitment, transparency, and accountability in a manner that facilitated trust in the party among its heterogeneous groups of followers (cf. Ostrom 1990). Similarly, too, doctrine never seems to have been substituted for formal organization as the cement of social cooperation. Despite rhetoric, political pragmatism and alliances between the elites of the competing factions remained more important factors to the structuring of left-liberalism. When we add to this the particularistic, ethnic, and socio-economic realities of Schleswig-Holstein, the success of liberalism appears all the more enigmatic. Which factor could span the classic urban–rural divide within the Schleswig-Holstein liberal movement; a divide further increased by the design of the electoral system and, in our particular case, more sharply drawn because of the divergent positions taken with respect to relations with Prussia?

Again, individualism, although drawn from different sources, provides an important part of the explanation. From that perspective, too, there were both differences as well as interesting similarities compared to Sweden and Värmland. Beginning with the differences, German liberalism after 1848 never seriously attempted the transformation to mass politics in the same manner as the Swedish liberals did; but neither were they forced to do so by mounting pressure from within a framework of regular mass-movements such as in the Swedish case. To begin with, nonconformism failed to spread extensively, let alone make an impact on political life in the same manner as in Sweden: for example, roughly 6 per cent of the population in Värmland was organized in different nonconformist churches by 1905, but around 1910 only 0.3 per cent of the population in Schleswig-Holstein (chapter 2). Neither did mass-based teetotalism, such as the Blue Ribbon or the Good Templars, play any significant social, let alone political, role in German society, although they did eventually spread, primarily in the northern parts of the country from the 1880s onwards. In fact, Schleswig-Holstein and Hamburg became strongholds of the German Good Templars, but even so the movement was numerically weak compared to Värmland, and most likely it became more typical of Danish than German civic associations in the region.

The very first lodge appeared in the Danish-speaking district of Hadersleben, in 1883, whereas the first German lodge followed in Flensburg, in 1887. Ten years later the *Nordslesvigs Good Templar* reported a total of 48 lodges, which comprised 1,232 members.[20] All of the localities mentioned in the material pertained to northern Schleswig, but at the same time the statistics ranged up to lodge no. 64 (the higher the number, the more recent its date of formation).[21] This might imply that a further 15 lodges – perhaps German ones – were excluded from the report, closed down, or in any event had failed to submit data. Assessing the level of membership relative to the population as a whole is difficult, but we may remember that in Värmland there were a total of 18,451 organized teetotallers by

1905, 10,520 of whom were Good Templars.[22] Also, judging from the issues addressed by the *Nordslesvigs Good Templar*, the organization was largely non-political, at least up to the turn of the century, contrary to what was the case in Sweden.[23]

As I have previously stressed, German public life therefore lacked important, mass-based proxies that – and this was the essence of the Swedish popular movements – could function as inroads to political influence *and* simultaneously help formulate a more widely defined conception of modern citizenship, despite the limitations of the electoral system. Most notably in the case of organized temperance, the brunt of anti-alcohol campaigning continued to fall on the efforts of the state-aligned DV, which, in Schleswig-Holstein around 1900, also included many prominent liberals as members, such as Albert Hänel and Wilhelm Ahlmann.[24] Although the DV expressed itself benignly when taking stock of the Good Templars,[25] any actual, let alone extensive, cooperation, does not seem to have evolved before well into the twentieth century.[26] In addition, whereas for instance the baptists and methodists made some inroads in local society, they do not seem to have been able to penetrate to any significant extent a confessional environment which was dominated by the Lutheran Church and the 'Innere Mission'. As Hahn-Bruckart notes, they were not particularly successful in transmitting what he depicts as a specifically American nucleus of civil association to German soil (Hahn-Bruckart 2006: 246–49). (Interestingly, the same juxtaposition between 'American' and 'German' civil society had been made eighty years previously, in an essay by Dr Hans Fraenkel, 1922, when taking stock of the new Weimar Republic in a *Festschrift* dedicated to the famous liberal historian Friedrich Meinecke; see later in this chapter.)

Instead, religious life was shaped by other influences, and with far deeper historical roots. Unlike Denmark, Germany lacked a Grundtvig, viz. the Danish nineteenth-century theologian Frederik Grundtvig, who successfully reformed the Church along modern lines (see, for instance, Claesson 2003). And unlike Sweden, low church and nonconformist movements were weakly developed. Yet, the same pietistic awakening, originating in Saxony and Prussia, which had swept north, including to parts of Sweden, in the seventeenth and eighteenth centuries, had left an imprint on the social environment of Schleswig-Holstein as well. As in Sweden, where nineteenth-century nonconformist movements represented an alternative path towards the individualization of society, so did pietism in Schleswig-Holstein, historically speaking, exercise the same pressure and, furthermore, on the foundation of non-Enlightenment and non-secular ideas (Hejselbjerg Paulsen 1955; Jakubowski-Tiessen & Lehmann 1984; Weitling 1992). As we have seen in chapter 2, it was the German Enlightenment that took colour from pietism, and not the other way around. Also, similarly to Tocqueville's observation of the relation between civic association and Protestant dissent in America (1981 [1835–40]; Eckstein 1994), pietism at the same time represented a counterweight to excessive self-interest: it taught that individual experience was crucial both to religious awakening and personal responsibility. In the long run pietism therefore promoted the individualization of society, but individualism informed by a sense of responsibility which, contrasted in particular to the atomized economic individualism of emerging liberalism, put more stress on the role of the individual as part of a community.

The kind of morality that religious awakening aimed at was not alien, for instance, to the ideas underpinning Kant's notion of categorical imperatives, considering morally just acts among modern citizens, or C. F. Gellert's conception of individual responsibility. And since pietism had challenged established Lutheran orthodoxy, in the long run it also eroded trust in the official authorities. Paradoxically, it facilitated what eventually became modern and secularized rationalism. By doing so pietism did, in a sense, become a forerunner of Enlightenment ideas and also liberalism. As society assimilated these generally different yet in crucial respects similar strands of thought, they gradually crystallized into various types of civic associations in the cities and towns of Schleswig-Holstein, all according to the middle-class conception of social cooperation founded on individual effort *but*, simultaneously, closely-knit circles of peers. Not surprisingly, we can note a basic similarity between this way of thinking and acting and Tönnies' reasoning about the importance of local context to the fulfilment of the 'common people' (see above).

Two of the organizational expressions of this aspect of local culture were the 'Bürgervereine' and – as in Sweden – the emergence of small savings banks (on savings banks in Schleswig-Holstein, see Kopitzsch 2003: 318–21). Certainly, geographical data should always be interpreted with care, but under any circumstance it remains an interesting coincidence that at least some of the first 'Bürgervereine' in Schleswig-Holstein appeared precisely in localities (Flensburg and Husum) where pietism had made strong inroads as far back as the 1670s (Jakubowski-Tiessen & Lehmann 1984: 321–22). Also, pietist centres such as the above-mentioned were among the places where early savings banks appeared; at the same time, though, the very first ones were actually run by reform-minded estateowners in Dobersdorf and Knoop, in the Kiel area (Kopitzsch 2003: 321).

Whether the local peasantry had much to say on the subject of Kantian philosophy, and of categorical imperatives, may remain a matter of dispute; that some of them, indeed, were familiar, for instance, with Gellert and his writings is clear (chapter 2). But the main point is: when traditions such as this merged with a social and cultural environment in which attachment to the land and a deeply-rooted sense of independence, symbolized by the unique position that the province had for centuries upheld against the Danish crown, this could easily result in the peculiar blend of utilitarian individualism, political radicalism, but also conservatism that has been noted by Tilton (1975), Thompson (2000), and others before them. But at the same time, all this also represented a different culture compared to that of Albert Hänel and his colleagues. With or without the help of organizational proxies, electoral mobilization of the rural electorate was not easily coordinated by the parties. In fact, individualism itself among the more well-to-do farmers often hindered organization on an extensive level when it came to interests that extended beyond farm, family, and village community. In the same way as among the Swedish liberals, individualism both stimulated partisanship and became an obstacle to cooperation and collective agency. Also, similar to the situation in Värmland, it was not unusual that the left-liberals had to accept the nomination and election of deputies who were more right-wing than their liking, following the inclinations of the voters. This was a move made to avoid the election of outright conservative candidates or, in more industrialized constituencies, social democrats.

The efforts made by Hänel to secure the re-election of national liberal Georg Beseler, the brother of Wilhelm Beseler (see above), in the sixth constituency of Pinneberg in the 1877 and 1878 elections is a case in point (Beyer 1968: 158–59). This was, as Beyer (1968) noted, a tactic facilitated by the system of second ballots, this system continued to be favourable to the liberal parties during the whole period up to 1914. If liberalism, therefore, turned into a makeshift belief in values and outlooks not easily translated into modern political language and a modern left-right comprehension of society, at the same time it had the ability to appeal to people, since its basic tenets of freedom, self-determination, and individualism were attractive to everyone but, alas, trusted by no one. The clearest example of the latter was the farmers.

As much as the liberal creed of self-determination could easily be appreciated by the farmers, their economic interests were guided by a different rational, which found other outlets than those represented by the liberal parties. The clearest expression of this came in the shape of the 'Bund der Landwirte', which was established in 1893. This was an agrarian interest organization sponsored by the conservatives, and with its main basis of operations in central and northern Germany. Among the well-to-do farmers in Schleswig-Holstein, many a voter would still opt for the left-liberals or the national liberals in the parliamentary elections,[27] but in matters economic their sympathies often lay elsewhere. Features such as these also explain why the liberals in the region were less successful, compared to Sweden, in integrating the peasantry within the organizational framework of the modern political party. Rather, the fact that the left-liberals remained a force to be reckoned with during the 1880s was in part a result of deliberate organizational changes in the LPSH/F, in part a reflection of the personal leadership skills of Albert Hänel.

Split, merger, and success

A main objective and long-desired goal of Bismarck was to undermine the liberals in parliament (this and the following paragraph, Sheehan 1978: 181–88, 199). Controversies concerning the accountability of the imperial administration to parliament, as well as Bismarck's proposal for fiscal reform and protective duties, provoked the desired split. The left-liberals became more and more isolated at the same time as the moderate and right-wing elements of the liberal factions were pushed closer to the conservatives. In the spring of 1878, tensions had escalated. The crisis culminated following two attempts to assassinate the emperor, William I. The blame was put on the socialists, since 1875 united in the 'Sozialistischen Arbeiter-Partei', when ADAV had merged with a competing faction at the Gotha conference (only with the reorganization of the party in 1890 did the official name of the party become 'Sozialdemokratische Partei Deutschlands'). In this situation parliament was dissolved and new elections declared. The outcome was a defeat for the liberals – national liberals and progressives alike – and the introduction of the Anti-Socialist Laws. By the end of the year the protectionist programme of the government was consolidated and it was accepted by parliament in the following year, although, in fact, agricultural interests continued to remain uncertain about the usefulness of tariffs.

Principles of free trade were defended by radicals on the left wing with the help of the argument that economic and political freedom, the classic item on any liberal agenda, were too closely connected to be separated in the manner implied by the shift towards protective customs: the right of political representation went hand-in-hand with freedom from economic regulations. The alignment of political individualism and economic individualism was, however, always uneasy and could be criticized for being far too doctrinaire. In effect the 1878–79 events shattered the German left and the liberals in particular. One important result was a general turn towards the right in domestic political life. Another outcome was increased factionalizing among the liberals themselves. As in 1867, when the liberals had split in progressives and national liberals, in turn the national liberals now split on the issue of tariffs. The left-wing faction seceded and formed the 'Liberale Vereinigung'. As a whole the liberals moved from defeat to defeat in the following 1881 and 1884 general elections, and with national liberalism at the core of the changes. Under the leadership of Johannes Miquel a clear-cut protectionist agenda was finally adopted by the latter in March 1884. In what became known as the 'Heidelberg Declaration', the paramount importance of agriculture to the German national economy was stressed.

This was a move which would seem to have made voters in Schleswig-Holstein more susceptible to the National Liberal Party, and less inclined towards the left-liberals under Albert Hänel. This, however, would prove not to be the case. During what was as usual a short campaign – effectively it began in September, and the nomination procedure was completed by early October,[28] whereas the date for the elections was set for 28 October – the problem of tariffs, and constitutional as well as social reforms, formed the agenda. Indeed, the last item could not escape political attention,[29] since not only did Bismarck try to fight off political radicalism with the help of the Anti-Socialist Laws and a confrontational policy towards the liberals: his move to sway the working classes by proposing state-managed social insurance must also be considered as part of the attempts to wrestle the political initiative from the hands of the opposition. Approval of the package, though, was not unanimous. The initial proposal of 1881, which covered work injuries, had been contingent on centralized control by the imperial administration as well as subsidies by the federal states. It was eventually accepted in 1884, but only on the basis of a less centralized, corporatist structure. In turn the proposal for health insurance for the workers had a less controversial design, whereas that of pensions raised the issue of taxation and, indirectly, state control over society (Edebalk 2003).

Precisely because of factors such as these, the 1884 election campaign to great extent focused on taxation and tariffs. These were considered emblematic of Berlin's attempts to strengthen its administrative grip on society. On the matter of protective duties, the exchange between left-liberals and national liberals had actually begun the previous year; something which only goes to show how flammable this issue still was, five years after the 1878–79 stand-off between Bismarck and the opposition. Yet for the farmers in Schleswig-Holstein the choice to opt for tariffs was, as I have previously pointed out, far from obvious. Rather, this issue must be understood in light of the ideological and organizational development among the liberals in 1883–84.

In a speech which Hänel addressed to the voters in the seventh constituency (Kiel-Rendsburg) in 1883, he had emphasized the liberal demands for increased civil liberties but also his reluctance about tariffs. These, he claimed, would only benefit big business. He therefore appealed to the common sense of 'the people' – including the farmers – on this matter, similarly to what would become the case among free traders and protectionists in Sweden only a few years later. In addition, Hänel made clear that he was firmly opposed to any form of 'factional politics' (Kiehl 1966: 46–47, quote at 47). Probably this argument was not primarily rooted in anti-party sentiments of the traditional kind, but was a tactic and, in this respect, a reflection of the fear of further faction in connection with the impending elections. Rather, Hänel prepared the ground for the great left-liberal coalition of 1884, i.e. the merger of the progressives and the 'Liberale Vereinigung' into the 'Deutschfreisinnige Partei'. By this configuration the left-liberals tried to ward off the 'external challenge' (Panebianco 1988) posed by Bismarck and to unite what remained of the liberal opposition in parliament.

Unlike Eugen Richter, the leader of the progressives, Hänel was therefore not alien to the idea of cooperating with national liberal dissenters. Only in 1884, however, did this become an acceptable solution to Richter. It then emerged as an opportunity to reverse the electoral defeats of 1878 and 1881 by amalgamating the left-liberals with the national liberal dissenters. Based on the alliance between the progressives/LPSH/F and the new 'Liberale Vereinigung', Hänel continued to defend his view on tariffs during the campaign. Although sympathetic towards social reforms – but, importantly, based on the self-determination of the workers – he spared no effort in vehemently criticizing the protectionist agenda of the national liberals.

Hänel's criticism of protective duties was not to remain unchallenged as the general elections approached. The opposition, though, was of a kind which, perhaps, had not been expected. Shortly before the elections, the *Schleswiger Nachrichten* not only rebuked Hänel's entire mode of liberalism as being too theoretical and, ultimately, disloyal from the perspective of the Reich's interests. Indeed, the newspaper also raised the question whether an issue such as that of tariffs should be politicized at all.[30] Two points can be made here. Firstly, viewed from a certain perspective the coalition of interests that made up the 'Deutschfreisinnige Partei' could certainly be interpreted as nothing more than just a shrewd attempt at politicking by Hänel and the progressives. In other words, the left-liberals were simply unreliable opportunists. Secondly, however, there was also a more profound meaning to the criticism voiced by the newspaper. Although campaigning had developed in the direction of competition between regular party programmes earlier compared to the situation in Sweden, viz. spelled the 'politicization' of politics at an earlier stage, obviously some issues could, given the circumstances, still be considered as being above factional strife.

To begin with, the ideological position of the newspaper itself should be considered. Søllinge and Thomsen (1989: 656–57) describe the *Schleswiger Nachrichten* as 'apolitical', but at least as far as the 1870s and 1880s are concerned this label should more correctly be read as a euphemism for a national liberal bias. Importantly, this also meant signalling a greater degree of allegiance to the new German state and its leadership. Tariffs, having been defined by Bismarck as a reason of state, were by definition above electoral strife. With the help of a slightly Hegelian reading of the kind of relationship between the state and the citizens that this implied, the position of the newspaper could therefore be understood as radical and at the same time informed by the highest of reason – that of national interest. Consequently, the *Schleswiger Nachrichten* discarded Hänel's views as being much too aloof to German political logic. More precisely, it suggested that his position was untenable since the left-liberals grounded their reasoning in an economic theory which was basically 'unsound', and on the basis of this rejected 'all *practically* minded men' as 'illiberal' and 'reactionaries'.[31] In fact, on the contrary, the national liberals and their supporters comprised precisely the kind of 'practically minded men' who correctly understood the needs of the country. Hence Hänel's opponents also tried, more or less directly, to whet the interest of the farmers, practical men as they no doubt were. As Germany rapidly industrialized, so did the market for produce expand, and tariffs, so it would seem, provided the farmers in Schleswig-Holstein, as elsewhere, with valuable protection from outside competition. So the national liberal and conservative arguments read.

This was a position that was anew criticized by Hänel. A week after the remarks made in the *Schleswiger Nachrichten*, Hänel spoke polemically against government policy and, above all, the national liberal programme. Sceptic towards the German 'ecstasy' for colonies, resentful at military expenditure and the monopoly on tobacco, he questioned whether the Reichstag should really continue to approve one new tariff after the other. Particularly on this point, national liberal policies and the 'Heidelberg Declaration' were questionable. Many national liberals in Schleswig-Holstein, he pointed out, were actually free traders by conviction, but in practice had their hands tied by the Declaration. What, then, was really the position of the national liberals?[32] They had, Hänel stated emphatically, only two options. They could continue to side with the government and the conservatives in an ambition to 'pile one tariff upon the other', as well as continue to thwart governmental accountability on budget matters, and corrupt the electoral laws. This would indeed be in all 'consequence with the Conservatives and their enmity with Liberalism'. Or they could, like the left-liberals, turn in opposition against these foul policies.[33] Rather than appealing to 'reasons of state', Hänel struck a different chord: the bureaucratized, top-heavy Prussian conception of state was, after all, something completely different than the more loosely integrated, federalistic idea of Germany hailed by Hänel. In essence Hänel's rejection of the national liberals and the pro-tariff camp played on the deeply rooted suspicion in Schleswig-Holstein of anything that smacked of centralized government from Berlin. The matter at hand was as much about preserving independence from Prussia as it was, such as in the case of social insurance, about the classic credo of 'liberating the individual from the chains of restrictions in the name of civilization'.[34] By conflating these two positions, Hänel made a case which probably was more appealing to the Schleswig-Holstein mindset.

In an open letter to the voters in the seventh constituency, the liberal voting committee had drawn a clear line between, on the one hand, conservatives and national liberals and, on the other, left-liberalism. The difference, the *Kieler Zeitung* pointed out, was that the former put state and government before the people, whereas the latter put the people, the grass roots, before the government.[35] This perspective was, as had also been the case during the 1871 elections, easy enough to amalgamate with the age-old autonomist sentiments in the region. When linked to the issue of tariffs it could also appeal to voters in an area which, particularly around Rendsburg, was predominantly agricultural.[36] Furthermore, at an early stage in the campaign the *Kieler Zeitung* had also been careful to point out that, in its opinion, support of the national liberals would in the long run only profit the social democrats.[37] It was, all in all, a clever case of structuring critical issues and strategic deliberations in such a manner that the integration of disparate groups of voters into the party ideology was promoted (cf. Gunther & Diamond 2001). The cross-class approach in combination with the appeals made to self-determination obviously worked. Hänel secured his victory in the constituency with an overwhelming majority of 10,747 votes.[38]

However, striking a balance between the national liberals and the social democrats only represented one facet of left-liberal campaigning. Certain events during the campaign in the third constituency of Schleswig-Eckernförde provide an illustration of the delicacy required of the left-liberals. In the town of Schleswig, a new association had formed in the Friederichsberg district the previous year. It was the 'Friedrichsberger Bürgerverein'. Immediately, it had involved itself in the preparations for the local, 1883 elections[39] and, if less obvious, it seems to have played a part in building opinion in conjunction with the 1884 general elections as well. On 25 October, three days before election day, the members convened to enjoy a lecture given by a photographer, Schnittger, on 'the life of the German *bürger* one century ago'.[40] The lecture was also announced in the local *Schleswiger Nachrichten* the same day.[41] Mundane as the event was, the proceedings did however also include the planning of an Augustenburger seminar, discussions of which involved the participation of Schnittger.[42] And this part of the agenda had not been publicly advertised. Which meaning can be read into this event?

As we have seen previously, appeals to self-determination remained a powerful tool in regional political life; and as for particularism, although much less flammable at this stage, it was still a topic of some controversy, not least among the liberals. Traditionally the Augustenburger cause held some appeal in the Schleswig area. A door-to-door poll conducted almost twenty years earlier, in March 1865, had shown that a majority of the townspeople were sympathetic to the idea (Petersen 2000: 119), and as we also remember, Count Baudissin, a particularist candidate, had more recently won the elections in this constituency in 1871. In light of this, the arrangement of an Augustenburger seminar could well have been an attempt to stir up old sentiments on the matter in connection to the elections.

At the time of the 1884 elections the liberal candidate was Asmus Lorenzen, a farmer of free trade persuasion from the village of Büdelsdorf,[43] whereas Christian Wallichs of the free conservatives ran as his main opponent (the free conservatives were a faction rooted in the royal bureaucracy and, thus, signified loyalty to Berlin first and, only secondly, to Schleswig-Holstein). While losing the city districts of Schleswig to Wallichs, Lorenzen did however win the constituency as a whole.[44] The choice of a left-liberal candidate from among the ranks of the farmers may well have reflected grass-roots sympathies not only for the party's position on current issues, such as tariffs. Possibly, the outcome also reflected some of the traditional autonomist sentiments *cum* agrarian outlook on life that continued to exercise an influence on political life in the region.

However, the case of Lorenzen is also interesting from a different point of view. Albert Hänel himself appeared at the nomination meeting. There he assisted in the introduction of Lorenzen to the audience. The latter, he said, was a man who would not blindly follow the party line, although he had accepted all aspects of its programme. According to Hänel, Lorenzen, to be sure, was 'no puppet, but a *Landmann* and also a man',[45] and therefore worthy of trust, one may assume. Personal appearance was, of course, important to prospective deputies. However, as in Sweden, personal appearance also seems to have gone hand-in-hand with a certain hesitation about associating oneself too closely with a formal party and fixed programmes: individual citizenry and its virtues were more important to a deputy than his loyalty to the party. What remains particularly striking, though, is that this tension between personal conviction and affiliation to party was brought up by none other than the party chairman himself.

Reminiscent of Eduard Lasker's 1876 description of his national liberal faction as a 'great political community', characterized by unity but at the same time also diversity of opinion (chapter 1), Hänel's statement captured the ever-present dilemma among German liberals: should they remain a loosely integrated 'Bewegung', a 'movement', or turn themselves into a coherent organization? Last but not least, Hänel's introduction of Lorenzen was not only an admission of this problem and an acknowledgement of the personal qualities of the latter. It was also a symbolic act of reassurance in the sense that the allusions made to Lorenzen's earthbound qualities obviously aimed at satisfying the utilitarian approach to politics among the farmers. In Lorenzen, therefore, the left-liberals had found precisely the kind of practically-minded candidate who could rebuke the criticism of their programme as being too theoretical and detached from everyday life and practice.

The campaigning in Schleswig does not only indicate the intricacies of regional political culture and the ambiguous nature of party affiliations, but also the importance of civic associations formally independent from party structures. Various 'Bürgervereine', liberal workers' associations, and other civic arenas played a role both in building opinion and by breeding the kind of enlightened citizens that the liberal creed hailed, as well as filtering these citizens out as suitable candidates for the elections. This pattern was not unique to the Schleswig-Eckernförde constituency. For instance, in the sixth constituency of Pinneberg the liberals nominated the teacher Johannes Halben, born in Lübeck in 1829. Among his greatest assets was that he had not only founded the 'Klub Fortschritt' (the Club of Progressives), in 1863, but had also profited from 30 years' experience of the Workers' Educational Society in Hamburg.[46] Admittedly, his was a background quite different from that of Lorenzen, but nevertheless one more in line with the socio-economic and cultural conditions in a district which for all practical purposes was evolving into an industrialized suburb. In addition to examples such as these, there also emerged other associations and spheres, positioned somewhere between being regular proxies and outright secondary organizations to the party, such as the liberal 'Kirchenverein' in Schleswig-Holstein (Kiehl 1966: 457).

In all these respects the liberals were better prepared compared to the conservatives, who became the last political faction to form a regional umbrella organization, as late as 1882 (Kiehl 1966: 459). Yet left-liberal organization, although encompassing the entire region, was still thin on the ground by modern standards. In addition, economic problems continued to haunt the LPSH/F throughout the campaigns of the late nineteenth and early twentieth century. Small cash amounts could be collected through the local committees of the party, but most of the funding was provided by the members of the executive committee in Kiel, including Wilhelm Ahlmann, who, apart from owning the *Kieler Zeitung*, was also a banker (Kiehl 1966; Thompson 2000). Newspaper coverage was also of great importance, much in the same manner as the Swedish liberals made systematic use of their connections with the press. In particular the *Kieler Zeitung* – a newspaper which (at the price of 4 Marks 50 Pfennig per quarter) 'remained true to the ancient, Schleswig-Holstein ideals of freedom, the rights of the nation, and prosperity of the people'[47] – was important. It was used not only to market the party programme but also advertised for campaign contributions during the elections.[48]

Lack of formal organization and lack of financial resources put great stress on the individual performance of the party leadership. Above all Hänel, one among a small group of natural candidates, was kept busy touring the region during the 1884 campaign. On 1–2 October he was scheduled to speak not only in Husum and Bredstedt, but also Tondern, in western Schleswig.[49] This was only three days before he was expected to deliver a keynote speech at the party convention of the LPSH/F at Neumünster.[50] The venues of such events as well as for the regular nomination meetings of the party, though, were not, as often was the case in Sweden, those of the supporting civic associations themselves. Rather, political meetings among left and right alike usually convened at hotels, inns, and restaurants.[51] Political culture in Schleswig-Holstein was one of local village taverns *but* at the same time universal doctrines, whereas political culture in Värmland to a greater extent revolved around mass organization *but* at the same time singular issues.

At the Neumünster convention the party consequently gathered at the local railway hotel. [52] Beginning by outlining the history of the old 'Landespartei' and the path towards the 1884 coalition with the 'Liberale Vereinigung', Hänel summarized the main points of the left-liberal programme. What risked being a bland, scholarly digression turned out, in fact, to be a cleverly designed thrust into the traditions and culture of the region. It was important, Hänel noted, to understand the historical specificity of Schleswig-Holstein in order to properly appreciate the party's position in relation to the conservatives. For one thing, the latter had no real grasp of concepts such as 'duty' and 'honour' (harsh words, indeed, to a conservative ear). Rather, they continued to consider the freedom fighters of 1848 simply as 'rebels' and 'traitors', and, furthermore, only held the Augustenburg particularists in contempt. Similar volleys were fired at the national liberals, ending with the declaration that the party programme of LPSH/F, indeed, had nothing to do with 'capitalism and factional strife at all costs, nor with abstract Manchester doctrine, nor with the implementation of a fully-fledged free trade system.' No, the keystone of liberalism, as Hänel saw it, was the well-being of the nation on the basis of rule by a free people.[53] The message paid off.

Firstly, the alignment of the progressives with 'Liberale Vereinigung' was, as such, an organizational feat which strengthened Hänel's position in the party. Secondly, there was the virtue of self-determination to be considered. In Schleswig-Holstein this line of argument was compatible with the historical and socio-economic identity of the region. It could certainly strike home among the urban middle classes but could, at the same time, appeal to the proud and self-reliant farmers. One important flaw, though, in this individualistic and anti-etatist agenda was that it made the left-liberals less ready to embrace a more progressive perspective on social reform, unlike Swedish liberals around the turn of the century; to an increasing extent they accepted the idea of state-managed social reforms, but then again, the nature of the state apparatus differed between Sweden and Germany. Put simply, while the left-liberals in Schleswig-Holstein, for obvious reasons, were convinced that the state was really nothing more than a disguise for Bismarckian authoritarianism, any equivalent to this was absent among the Swedish, including the Värmland, liberals.

As the election results began to be reported back, it was clear that the liberal coalition had held the ground more successfully compared to other Prussian provinces – but so had the national liberals, too (chapter 1, Table 2). More specifically, the coalition received 34.2 per cent of the votes in the region, and the national liberals 27.9 per cent (Ibs 2006: 152). Out of ten constituencies, the left-liberals held sway in four and the national liberals in two. In the remaining four, the vote fell in favour of the conservatives/free conservatives (two), the social democrats (one), and – as usual – the Danish list, in the first, northern constituency of Hadersleben-Sonderburg (Schultz Hansen 2003: 464).

Proxies had played a part in the mobilization of liberalism. Yet their role was not unequivocally positive, albeit for slightly different reasons than in Sweden. Compared to Värmland, they could not equal the kind of public involvement in political life that was made possible by the popular movements in the 1887 elections or, most notably, those in 1893 and 1896. Certainly the German proxies were, as in Sweden, collective expressions of an individualized society, and of different strands of political individualism. However, political individualism as such was also, in principle, quite feasible without the underpinnings of civic association. This was not least the case as long as citizenship remained restricted because of the design of the election laws. As I have previously stressed, the main problem was that liberal proxies were not mass-based and, hence, left the electorate in Schleswig-Holstein even more volatile than what became the case in Värmland. This observation in turn begs the question of why the German liberals did not seriously pursue mass-organization by means of party instead. Paradoxically, political individualism provides the answer in this context, too. The very stress put on individual freedom, effort, and performance, whether interpreted from an urban, middle-class perspective or a rural perspective more or less automatically steered campaigning along old, established, and well-trodden paths.

Interestingly, these old and well-trodden paths had a specific feature which made liberal rhetoric sound quite different compared to the that of, most notably, Mauritz Hellberg in Värmland. His was a radicalism which, not least by the force of his anti-clerical views, tried to execute a break with history and tradition. (Then again, sequentialist interpretations of political modernization could be voiced in this context as well, such as in the liberal debating society in Karlstad, of which Hellberg was a member; see chapter 3.) Yet by comparison, Albert Hänel, possibly in part because of his professional background, made much more frequent use of the past as a value in itself, and as means of legitimizing liberalism to the voters in Schleswig-Holstein. It was, as with the 1884 elections, a regionally specific expression of 'Historismus'. Liberalism was the defender of regional identity and tradition rather than the liberator from outdated traditions.

Momentum lost

The 1898 elections reflect two processes of equal importance to national and regional political culture: firstly, the step-by-step growth of the Social Democratic Party into the largest faction in the German parliament; and, secondly, the increased importance of ethnic orientations to nationalism and national identity. In the first case the lifting of the Anti-Socialist Laws in 1890 also led to a reorganization of the party; it thereby became a platform for a distinct working-class sub-culture, but also a political machine which soon enough was criticized because of its monolithic structure and oligarchic tendencies (Michels 1983 [1911]). Largely at the expense of the liberals, the social democrats went from 27.2 per cent of the vote and 56 mandates in 1898 to 34.8 per cent and 101 out of 397 mandates following the 1912 elections.[54] In the second case the emergence of 'Völkisch nationalism' combined the elements of 'Heimat' ideology with Prussian militarism and the increasingly imperialistic ambitions of Wilhelmine Germany. Although this process was not completed by the turn of the century, it nevertheless provoked fundamental changes in political life during the 1890s, most notably expressed in the appearance of new right-wing parties. Finally, internal fragmentation gained impetus among the liberals during the 1890s. One reason was the return of the old, pre-1884 divisions, while another factor was the growing discontent with Eugen Richter, the party chairman of the German Progressive Party. At heart of the problem was Richter's leadershipstyle in parliament, which many considered too oppositional. Tensions culminated with disputes over military expenditure and a split of the 'Deutschfreisinnige Partei' in 1893. While one faction remained under the leadership of Richter, now under the name of the 'Freisinnige Volkspartei', the other faction, 'Freisinnige Vereinigung', included the Schleswig-Holstein liberals (Sheehan 1978: 265; Ibs 2006: 153).

If we begin by scrutinizing more closely the advances made by the Social Democratic Party it is, of course, clear that this reflected the socio-economic changes sweeping through Schleswig-Holstein. Still, industrialization did not engender the same dramatic changes as in many other parts of the country. Although the population employed in agriculture and forestry fell from 41.0 per cent in 1882 to 34.0 per cent in 1907, employees in industry only increased from 27.0 per cent to 31.0 per cent during the same period; the figures for commerce, transportation and services reveal a similar pattern of gradual rather than abrupt change.[55] Throughout the pre-war period and the Weimar Republic era the region retained its agrarian character. Importantly, therefore, a substantial proportion of the new, social democratic electorate comprised the rural working-class, including employees of the large farms and manors in the region. Although liberalism had traditionally succeeded in attracting parts of these groups, they increasingly shifted their allegiance in favour of the social democrats. With this also followed the kind of tightly-knit, working-class sub-culture that has been described above. The SPD and its secondary organizations came to permeate not only the politics of the working-class, but all aspects of their everyday life. Local branches of the party formed in all the cities and towns of Schleswig-Holstein, accompanied by women's associations, cooperatives, bakeries, building societies and a range of cultural and sports societies (Schultz Hansen 2003: 469–70). This development became the ultimate confirmation that the middle classes had failed to improve the workers by setting a good example by their allegedly moral and intellectual superiority (cf. Hurd 2000). This failure to create an inclusive cross-class civic sphere, hierarchical and elitist as it may have been, was an ill omen for the future, considering the sharp social conflicts that were emerging in German society.

It is emblematic that in the long run not even Albert Hänel could mobilize sufficient electoral support to secure his traditional seat in the Kiel-Rendsburg constituency. With the exception of the 1898 elections, the constituency voted social democratic from the 1893 elections onwards. In fact, in 1898 it was only by a narrow margin of 99 votes that the social democrat candidate, Carl Legien from Hamburg, failed to win the first round of the elections. In the second ballot, the tables turned in favour of Hänel.[56] Judging by the situation this was not because of any overwhelming support for the left-liberal party, but simply because national liberal and right-wing voters preferred the election of Hänel to that of a social democrat. It was an ominous sign of the times that these right-wing voters were organized by the 'Deutsch-sozialen Reformpartei', which had formed in 1894 and included a motley collection of disgruntled middle-class voters and 'Kaisertreue' under the umbrella of an anti-Semitic, anti-capitalist, and anti-socialist agenda.

At the same time Carl Legien, the vanquished candidate, was, for all the dread of socialism expressed by liberals and conservatives alike, by any standard a moderate. For instance he was, like many German social democrats at this time, critical of the dogmas of Marxist ideology and opposed to the idea of using mass strikes as a political tool. The key to reforms and self-determination of the workers was 'organization' rather than 'insurrection' (Schultz Hansen 2003: 469–70). Despite this, though, the socialists continued to be anathema in political terms, including among the liberals. While the Swedish liberals and social democrats on occasion joined in cartels in the general elections (chapter 3), no such cooperation evolved in Schleswig-Holstein, although there were differences between the national liberals and the left-liberals: While the election meetings of the former were closed sessions, those of the latter were open to the public, including social democrats and right-wing followers (Thompson 2000: 292). Yet German liberals never considered themselves as radicals in the same manner as the Swedish liberals.

Instead, fear of socialism provided fertile soil for unholy alliances among the centre and right-wing parties – at the same time as these right-wing parties were also the sworn enemies of liberalism. Compared to the 'Deutsch-sozialen Reformpartei', however, 'der Bund der Landwirte' (1893) became a more serious competitor, in particular to the left-liberals. This was because of their dependence on the support of the farmers. Adding to the increasingly confusing political map was the lingering uncertainty about the actual party affiliations of many candidates even as late as in the 1890s. This was not least the case among new right-wing factions precisely such as the 'Bund' and the 'Reformpartei', which, in effect, joined in close cooperation. All of this was reflected in the 1898 campaign. Count Reventlow, one of the main candidates in the Kiel-Rendsburg constituency, is a case in point. He was simply put down as an 'anti-Semite' in the official records, i.e. as a candidate of the 'Reformpartei'. By the *Kieler Zeitung*, however, Reventlow was first announced as running for the 'Bund' in early June, but a week later as a candidate of the 'Reformpartei'.[57]

In the opinion of this newspaper, though, Reventlow's candidacy was at the same time met with suspicion even among the major landowners in the area. Primarily, as the *Kieler Zeitung* saw it, this was not because of his anti-Semitic agenda, but rather doubts as to whether the economic interests of agriculture really would profit from the programme of the 'Bund'.[58] However, on other occasions the newspaper also clearly stated that 'parochial anti-Semitism' and the liberal creed were by no means compatible with each other.[59] In addition, the newspaper assured its readers that conditions in agriculture were by no means as desperate as the 'Bund' claimed. As for the problems that undoubtedly did exist, it should prove no difficulty to manage them under present conditions with the help of 'diligence' and 'intelligence',[60] i.e. the standard, liberal antidote to social, economic and any other among a plethora of possible problems. Contributing to what proved to be a rather confusing campaign was the competition among the left-liberals, between the 'Freisinnige Volkspartei' and the 'Freisinnige Vereinigung' (Hänel's faction), although the latter in effect also tried to support the candidates of the former, such as Dr Duus in the second constituency of Flensburg-Apenrade: it was, the *Keiler Zeitung* hoped, perhaps possible to bring Duus as far as to the second ballot, if only every 'freisinnige' voter in the district did his duty in the elections.[61]

Judging by the election results it is nevertheless clear that the left-liberal bloc in Schleswig-Holstein had been shattered. Compared to the national average the two left-liberal parties fared reasonably well with 18.2 per cent of the votes (11.1 per cent in the country as a whole),[62] but mandates were secured only in the third and seventh constituencies, in Schleswig-Eckernförde and in the above-mentioned Kiel-Rendsburg districts. It did not, for instance, prove possible to carry Duus to victory in Flensburg-Apenrade. Rather, in this part of the region, where the voters were traditionally divided between, on the one hand, national liberal and conservative opinions and, on the other hand, pro-Danish sympathies, the 'Deutsch-sozialen Reformpartei' managed to win with the support of the 'Bund'. As for the national liberals themselves, they also won two constituencies, whereas, as usual, the Danish list prevailed in the north. The remaining four seats were divided between social democratic and conservative deputies (Schultz Hansen 2003: 464, 467). Although it was possible for the left-liberals to reinforce their positions in the following decade, the turn of the century spelled a definite turn in domestic political life.

The 'Deutsch-sozialen Reformpartei' lost its seat as early as in the following, 1903, elections, but its appearance on the political stage clearly demonstrated that an anti-Semitic profile was, indeed, not beyond the political imagination of the Schleswig-Holsteiners. Among the demands of the party was a ban on Jewish immigration. In essence, if not to the letter, a similar message was repeated by the 'Bund der Landwirte'. For instance, during the 1912 elections, in the ninth Oldenburg-Segeberg-Plön constituency the 'Bund' pleaded to the farmers, the German people and the German Fatherland for resistance not only to the 'Red International' but also to the 'International of Gold'; these being, it thought, the main enemies of the people.[63]

The preoccupation with ethnicity and the idea of ethnic purity would increasingly come to pattern German political thinking. Anti-Semitism had to greater or lesser extent always been part of public life, although historically speaking this was nothing unique to Central Europe. A similar development occurred in the case of anti-Polish sentiment particularly so in the mixed borderland regions of Prussia, in areas such as West Prussia and Poznania, which had been acquired after the first partition of the Polish Commonwealth in 1772 (Tighe 1990). Certainly a wish for assimilation had become typical of most Prussian Jews in the nineteenth century, and many Poles, too, had originally been prepared to consider themselves at least as Prussian subjects. One important reason for that was that Prussia, for all her vices, never really posed as a 'nation' by modern standards (Clark 2006). The important shift was when Prussia increasingly acquired the leading role in German unification and a nation, yes even an empire, of Germans was, to follow Anderson (1991 [1983]), 'imagined up' from Prussians, Baviarians, Schleswig-Holsteiners, Jews, Poles, Danes and other groups (Mommsen 1995). Therefore, by 1900 ethnicity had become an important key to the understanding of German political modernization, regardless of where the threat to political and cultural unity was seen as coming from. This was reason behind the emergence of extreme right-wing parties within the framework of the established party system. The 'Reformpartei' as well as the 'Bund' reflected the increasing xenophobia in social and political life, and the established parties in part chose, in part were driven, to take positions on the issue.

What made the ethnic issue in Schleswig-Holstein specific, though, was not so much anti-Semitism as the age-old question of Danish–German relations. Similarly to what became the case among the Prussian Poles in the East (see, for instance, Kulczycki 1981; Suval 1985; Tighe 1990), stricter government policies to assimilate the Danes proved counterproductive. They reinforced Danish nationalism, something which among other things had been reflected in the formation of the 'Sprogforeningen' in 1880, an association aimed at the preservation and promotion of the Danish language in northern Schleswig. In addition, a Danish electoral assembly had been formed in 1888 on the initiative of the journalist Hans Peter Hanssen. This meant that Danish political opinion in the region became organized along stricter lines by the end of the nineteenth century compared to what had previously been the case. Although German–Danish tensions did not peak until shortly before the First World War, in a manner similar to anti-Semitism the increasingly ethno-nationalistic colouring of the Danish–German issue divided political parties and blurred left–right oriented and class-based divisions. Perhaps the most obvious illustration of this was the workers' movement.

With respect to the social democrats specifically, the SPD declared in 1902 that they supported Danish demands for a referendum and agreed to protect the Danes from forced assimilation. The split of the workers' movement along national lines could still not be avoided, however. A separate Danish workers' association formed (1911) and, as yet another reflection of this process, the 'Indre Mission'/'Innere Mission' in northern Schleswig also split into two branches: one nationalist, and one pietist and non-nationalist (Schultz Hansen 2003: 479, 481–83). But ethno-nationalism also brought confusion to the established liberal and right-wing parties. Among the liberals in particular it contributed to the further fragmentation of what was traditionally the core of their electorate, the urban middle classes and the farmers.

The 1898 elections and their outcome in Flensburg-Apenrad illustrate the situation. For example, when the *Kieler Zeitung* commented on the campaign in this constituency, it did so by pointing to the importance of the historical division of the area between the northern part (Apenrade), which included a Danish majority among the population, and the southern (Flensburg) area:

> Between the northern and southern parts of the second constituency there are well-established differences in the sense that, among the German electorate in the north, party-based cleavages play a negligible role, whereas in the south, such party-related issues divide the electorate, in like manner as the rest of the Reich. This is explained by the circumstance that above all the nationalities problem captures the attention and interest of the voters in the north, whereas in the south issues of nationality are not immediate but, on the contrary, are pushed into the background in favour of differences on economic matters.[64]

Map 5. The Flensburg-Apenrade constituency.

These circumstances all played into the hands of the 'Deutsch-sozialen Reformpartei', if only temporarily. It is also interesting to note how the newspaper did not seem to consider the 'nationalities question' a political issue proper. Somehow removed from the realm of politics, it had at the same time become the defining characteristic of partisanship in parts of the region. At the same time, though, the matter of national identity was closely related to the classic issue of citizenship and, therefore, also ultimately contingent on the conception of the German state, its application, and institutional underpinnings. The ethno-nationalist interpretation, with its stress on unity and homogeneity, was clear enough in this perspective. Some left-liberals, though, including Albert Hänel, continued to emphasize the federalistic underpinnings of post-1871 Germany. Herein lay the true importance of the thousand-year legacies of the empire, in Hänel's opinion. Indeed, this trait was typical of his outlook on Germany throughout the 1890s.

184

For instance, Hänel had stressed the federalistic conception of Germany in his 1892 inaugural speech as rector of the Christian-Albrechts-Universität (see chapter 2), and he followed the same line of thought a few years later, in 1896, in another speech to commemorate the twenty-fifth anniversary of the new nation. To him the matter of ethnicity seems to have been less important. In fact he did not bring the matter up at all. Reiterating his 1892 ideas, he said that the new Germany should rightfully be considered a federation rather than a unitary state ('Einheitsstaat'). As I have previously pointed out, in principle this interpretation fitted just as well with the idea of 'Heimat' and differentiation as with 'Heimat' and the notion of a homogeneous people. Importantly, though, while stressing the institutional make-up of the state, institutions as such were, according to Hänel, still no more than mere human constructs. They were ultimately contingent on the responsibility of individual citizens in relation to one another, and to God. This applied to rulers and statesmen as well as to the common citizens, regardless of their political orientation (Hänel 1896: 13).

The reference made to the relationship between man and God is an interesting coincidence, considering the socio-cultural context of Schleswig-Holstein and its pietistic heritage. It is, for instance, difficult to imagine Mauritz Hellberg in Karlstad conceptualizing the idea of individuality and citizenship in the same manner as Hänel did. The stress put on such links arguably brought Hänel closer to a civic-minded, republican rather than ethno-nationalist perspective, regardless of any pragmatic concessions the left-liberals may otherwise have been prepared to make in parliament or in the election campaigns. However, except for the religious dimension, Hänel's perception of citizenship and the state still remained that of an intellectual and educated middle-class individual.

By contrast, most accounts of the political development at the turn of the century tend to emphasize the turn towards ethno-nationalism among the liberals, rather than alternative features such as the above. With some exceptions, such as Alsace, where republican perspectives prevailed, much because of the ties and proximity to France, most notably Kurlander argues that this became typical of regions such as Schleswig-Holstein, and Silesia (Kurlander 2002a, 2002b,

2006a, 2006b). But although this certainly holds true on a general level, the case of Albert Hänel indicates that there were noticeable exceptions to this pattern.

In addition, ethno-nationalism as such was, albeit a necessary factor, probably not sufficient to swing liberal voters in favour of right-wing parties. Most notably among the peasantry, pragmatic considerations rather than lofty appeals to 'diligence and intelligence' helped to drain support for the left-liberals in times of economic hardship. Analogous to Moore's analysis (1967; see also Tilton 1975) of the flawed modernization of agrarian societies, such as Germany, Japan, and Russia, economic and political individualism along the lines suggested by Hänel and others was not enough to secure the support of the farmers. In the long run the farmers obviously rejected these ideas and with them civic, democratic values. Lack of proper organization by which rural opinion could otherwise have been integrated, modified, and represented in a democratic manner (cf. Gunther & Diamond 2001), as well as – increasingly – accusations of complacency and autocratic tendencies within the left-liberal party, added to the difficulties (see below).

Despite these contingencies the main threat among, in particular, the left-liberals was perceived as coming from the socialists rather than from the right-wing, or from internal strife, or due to increasing ideological confusion. To the political establishment, to the 'Mittelstände', and to the press, the social democrats were, as the *Flensburger Nachrichten* put it, a threat to all that was dear in terms of religion and morality, culture and economy.[65] Now, middle-class anxiety and insecurity about their role and position in a rapidly changing society – equally as much as, on occasion, childish optimism about the future that lay ahead – was pretty much typical of these groups in all modernizing countries in Europe. Characteristic of German society was that these fears resulted in reaction steeped in 'Historismus' and idealized stereotypes about 'Heimat', rather than reform and a proactive perspective on change. This, too, shaped the development of liberalism and explains its increasingly conservative outlook. An important consequence of these inconsistencies, therefore, was a series of electoral defeats on the regional level both in the 1893 and 1898 elections as well as those in 1903.

Liberalism rejuvenated?

Considering the turn of events in the 1890s, it seems paradoxical that left-liberalism made a remarkable recovery in Schleswig-Holstein in the last two elections before the First World War, in 1907 and 1912 respectively. In 1907 the LPSH/F secured five mandates, and seven in the 1912 elections, largely at the expense of the social democrats and the national liberals (Schultz Hansen 2003: 464). These results marked a brief return to the situation in the 1870s and early 1880s when left-liberalism had been *the* political movement of the region. Whether this comeback also implied the rejuvenation of liberalism as an ideology and political party is quite another matter.

Viewed from one perspective, the electoral successes in 1907 and 1912 are difficult to understand. The formal organization of the liberal parties still retained traits of improvisation. Among left-liberals and national liberals alike, local branches and a nucleus of full-time appointed officials developed, but only slowly, particularly so in the countryside, and largely by emulation of the Social Democratic Party. Although, for instance, the left-liberals in Hamburg developed a much denser organizational framework, including city, local, and suburban levels as well as youth and women's associations, the administrative staff of the party as a whole was kept to a minimum. Only by the beginning of the twentieth century did the left-liberals and the national liberals appoint regular party secretaries. Each party stationed one secretary in Hamburg and one in Schleswig-Holstein (Thompson 2000: 283–84).

As a consequence, mobilization by means of proxy remained a characteristic feature of campaigning strategies, at least so in connection with the 1907 elections. For instance, in Bordesholm it was the 'Verein für nationale Bestrebungen und Wahlen' (which convened at the 'Alten Haidkrug' inn) that decided to support the left-liberal candidates. This was not a local party branch, strictly speaking.[66] Similarly in Itzehoe, traditionally a left-liberal stronghold (Nicolai-Kolb 1991: 171), local branches of the 'Alldeutscher Verband', the 'Reichsverband gegen die Sozialdemokratie' and the 'Evangelischer Bund' all served as electoral platforms. However, they performed this function in a coalition for *all* centre-right parties, rather than for the liberals specifically.[67] The latter, therefore, might have been a sign of what had, at this stage, become a state of increasing fragmentation and disruption among the left-liberals in Itzehoe (Nicolai-Kolb, 1991: 171). Once innovative, when applied to conditions within a political culture of limited suffrage (cf. Kahan 2003), organizational strategies based on informal networks between independent bodies and proxies now belonged to the past.

Indeed, the attempts to topple the liberals, in particular by the right-wing, also became more aggressive in the early twentieth century. In an advertisement for the new year and the upcoming elections, the *Itzehoer Nachrichten* – traditionally a promoter of regional interests – invited subscribers by presenting itself as 'German in every sense of the word', but at the same time as 'Schleswig-Holsteinian to the core', pro-agriculture, and anti-Catholic. At the same time, it resented 'autocratic liberalism', viz. the kind of liberalism which 'by deliberate efforts tries to infuse our culture with new meaning and, rather, reaps its best fruits from obstruction.'[68] Contrary to what had been the case, for instance, in the successful 1884 campaign, left-liberalism obviously no longer had a monopoly on interpreting the true identity and political orientations of the Schleswig-Holsteiners. Not least the farmers were a crucial group in this context.

Lamenting the fact that many a 'Landmann' in the second, Flensburg-Apenrade constituency had preferred 'to stay at home rather than to vote liberal' during the 1912 campaign, a letter to the editor of the *Kieler Zeitung* tried to get to the bottom of the problem of why it would really be such a disaster to elect a 'Freisinnig'.[69] Certainly, the constituency eventually fell to the left-liberals (Schultz Hansen 2003: 464), but only after the second ballot; and although betraying the left-liberals was tantamount to betraying one's duty to the Fatherland, according to the letter,[70] it is at the same time obvious that liberal inertia with regard to the requirements of agriculture had opened the way for candidates such as Count Reventlow, this time running for the 'Bund der Landwirte'.[71] Yet, compared to the social democrats the liberals were still considered the 'lesser of two evils' by conservative opinion (Schultz Hansen 2003: 473). The recovery of the liberals in the last pre-war elections was therefore probably not so much a case of the rejuvenation of liberalism, but rather a confirmation of the inbuilt limitations of what had increasingly become an anti-democratic political system.

If any one factor should be considered decisive in the 1907 and 1912 victories of the left-liberals, it was the design of the electoral system and the system of second ballots. In fact, the conservatives and the extreme right had counted on the second ballot, rather than the first rounds of the election, when they assessed Reventlows prospects; at least this was the case according to the district commissioner in Flensburg.[72] While this kind of strategy reflected the fact that the gap between liberals and right-wing candidates in terms of electoral support was gradually closing during the pre-war period, in contrast the social democrats steadily increased their turnout. Presumably much due to the efficacy of their party organization, they received 40.4 per cent of the votes in Schleswig-Holstein in the 1912 elections. However, because of the absolute majority requirement they secured only two mandates, in Kiel-Rendsburg and Altona-Stormarn respectively (Schultz Hansen 2003: 464). We need only consider the case of the sixth constituency of Pinneberg, in which the social democratic candidate, von Elm, received a plurality of votes – 47.6 per cent – compared to 28.9 per cent for his main opponent, Dr Braband of the left-liberals. In the second ballot, however, Braband won a narrow victory with 51.7 per cent of the votes against 48.3 per cent for von Elm (Table 4). Considering the results in the respective rounds, the outcome did not necessarily reflect deeply-rooted support for the left-liberal programme in itself.

Table 4. The 1912 elections, Pinneberg constituency. Votes by candidate in the first and second ballots (per cent).

Ballot	Social Democratic	Left-liberal	National Liberal	Conservatives/ Bund der Landwirte
First	47.6	28.9	17.9	9.5
Second	48.3	51.7	–	–

Sources: Summary of the election results in the sixth constituency of Pinneberg. 6759. Reichstagswahl 1912. Oberpräsidium und Provinzialrat der Provinz Schleswig-Holstein. LAS. Note: the Conservatives and the Bund der Landwirte both promoted the same candidate, Count Baudissin-Borstel.

Compared to Sweden, where liberals themselves were divided on the issue of the design of electoral systems, the battle lines in Germany were, in a sense, more clearly drawn. Lacking the kind of radicalism and grass-roots extensions that had become typical of Swedish liberalism by the turn of the twentieth century, German liberals more systematically exploited the majoritarian *cum* second ballot system precisely to avoid the radicalization and democratization of the elections. Like the hesitance displayed in relation to progressivism in matters social and economic, the usage of the electoral system, too, was an illustration of the increasing conservatism of liberalism in Schleswig-Holstein. Certainly, this stood in stark contrast to liberal rhetoric, as expressed by Albert Hänel; once again, the reluctance to opt between left and right among the 'left'-liberals left their movement more and more uneasily positioned in the political landscape, despite the electoral successes of the early twentieth century.

Setbacks of the kind experienced in Pinneberg or, for that matter, Flensburg-Apenrade, quite naturally had a knock-on effect among the working population across Schleswig-Holstein. Six months after the 1912 elections, in June, the district commissioner in Rendsburg reported that he had denied the Social Democratic Bicycle Club in Büdelsdorf permission to arrange an excursion. Not only did the date of the excursion coincide with the festivities of the local 'Kriegerverein'. Referring to a meticulously drawn map of the planned routes of the respective parties, it was clear that they would eventually converge upon each other. This was because the destination of the social democrats – the 'Schmoock' inn – was adjacent to the 'Spitzkrug', where the 'Kreigerverein' planned to gather after their procession. After much ado the district commissioner concluded in his report – map attached – that the whole affair must certainly have been planned as a deliberate provocation by the socialists. He therefore dispatched the Gendarmerie to Büdelsdorf to secure public order. The situation was, he thought, even more serious since not only were the majority of the population in Büdelsdorf industrial workers, the town had also experienced the outbreak of a 'particularly severe strike' the year before.[73] By 1914 left-liberalism was therefore tainted because of its lack of credibility among the working-class, but also hampered by the traditional suspicions expressed by conservatives, nationalists, and the farmers.

Europe was engulfed by war. As Germany effectively was left without civil government during the last months of the war, political developments meant a chaotic passing of power from the duo of Hindenburg and Ludendorff to Ebert and Noske. However, not to simplify matters entirely, it should also be noted that Schleswig-Holstein or, more precisely, Kiel was also where the attempted German revolution first ignited, with the mutiny of the sailors in the High Seas Fleet on the night of 28–29 October 1918 the seminal event. Although it proved possible for Gustav Noske, who had arrived in the city by train on 4 November with an imperial commission to investigate the situation, to calm things down, the mutiny signalled the outbreak of military and civil unrest across the country. It eventually fell to two social democrats – Noske, minister of defence in-the-making, and Friedrich Ebert, from 9 November the new chancellor – to take command of the state as the emperor abdicated; to make the necessary compromises with the military establishment; and to erect the foundations of what would soon become the Weimar Republic. As chaos ensued, events in Berlin, where the Spartacist rising erupted in January, were clouded by confusion. 'What is happening in Berlin?', *Kieler Zeitung* asked in its evening edition of 6 January.[74]

What happened – in Berlin and elsewhere in the country – had far-reaching implications for political culture in Schleswig-Holstein. As late as the 1919 elections to the new national assembly the liberals held sway. Together with the social democrats and the Catholic centre, it was these liberals, now under the label 'Deutsche Demokratische Partei', that were among the guardians of the new republic. It was an uneasy alliance, though, considering the relationship between these factions before the war. Soon enough it also became apparent precisely how fragile the new liberal democracy and its constitution were. Democracy after all was, as one of Friedrich Meinecke's pupils, Hans Fraenkel, noted in 1922, something that had been handed to the Germans by their conquerors (1922: 294). From the 1921 general elections onwards, electoral sympathies began to polarize between, on the one hand, the socialist camp, now including the social democrats and German Communist Party, and, on the other hand, the extreme right. The latter was, among other factions, represented by the right-wing conservative and anti-Semitic 'Deutschnationale Volkspartei' (DNVP), which peaked in the two 1924 elections with above 30 per cent of the votes. To echo Weitz (2009: 10), it was groups of this kind, rather than the liberals, that represented the true challenge to the republic and, as sworn enemies, finally toppled it. From the 1928 and, particularly, the 1930 elections onwards, the Nazi Party, by extensive campaigning, established itself as the dominant party in the region.[75] By the time of the 1932 elections in July, when its results were a massive 52.7 per cent (chapter 1), townspeople and countryside dwellers had been taken in by the Swastika.

How was it that a development which, in many respects, had started in a manner so promising in the nineteenth century ended so badly in the following century? The weak organization of the liberal parties is certainly part of the explanation. The liberals could not, in the long run, handle the onslaught of the more well-organized extreme left and right options. In the same way as the left, the German right realized that the key to power was mass-mobilization (Weitz 2009: 116). Also, changes in party leadership among the liberals played a role (cf. Panebianco 1988). If not for any other reason than the mere passing of time, critical changes occurred in the early twentieth century. Wilhelm Ahlmann, all-round supporter and financier of the left-liberals had died in 1910. As for Albert Hänel, who died in May 1918, he had long since (1903) completed his last term as deputy to the parliament for his old constituency, Kiel-Rendsburg.[76] In brief, the last generation of politicians that had been directly involved in the fateful events in 1866–67 was long gone by the time the Weimar Republic was instituted. With them an elitist but at the same time genuinely reform-minded liberalism evaporated. Details such as these at the same time illustrate how individual actors and local context reflect more fundamental shifts and changes in society and culture; a feature which directs attention to explanations provided as to the German path towards political modernization.

To some contemporaries the answer became obvious as soon as the Weimar Republic was launched. Although displaying some bitterness over the 'betrayal' by Woodrow Wilson and his Fourteen

Articles, Hans Fraenkel saw it as a duty to reconcile the people and the state with each other within the framework now provided by the new republic. In this his opinion was no different from that of many other defenders of the new order. Yet, in what was basically a reverse expression of 'Historismus', he also identified some of the difficulties. For example, although it was true that Prussia had bred an 'absolutist–bureaucrat lifestyle', it had also been the origin of democratic ideas on local self-government. Alas, unlike the Americans, Germans were by and large less prone to political individualism, and whereas American democracy as well as capitalism were ultimately a Calvinist product, filtered through English culture, this was not the case in Germany (Fraenkel 1922: 296–97, 304).

Steeped in traditionalism

Later, after the Second World War, assessments such as this provided some of the fabric of the 'Sonderweg hypothesis'. In some respects it coloured the seminal work of Sheehan (1978) on German liberalism. Pertaining to Schleswig-Holstein, this kind of 'inverted' sequentialism, if one may say so, also informs explanations such as those of Tilton (1975). Apart from stressing obvious features such as economic crisis and deficient government policies in fighting this, Tilton also emphasized ideological factors, i.e. the ability of the Nazis to exploit 'nationalist and reactionary currents in the rural people's traditional view of the political world' (1975: 136). Likewise, Thompson has more recently underlined the inherent traditionalism and conservatism of the rural voters (2000: 303). In both cases they follow a strand of argument that, indeed, was not unfamiliar to contemporary analysts who, like Hugo Preuss (1916, see chapter 1), or Fraenkel (1922), had spoken of the 'political innocence' of the Germans, and of their 'lack of individuality'. This also brings to mind Moore's observations (1967) about the defunct modernization of the peasantry in countries such as Germany and Russia.

However, at least in respect to Thompson's assessment (2000: 303), rural conservatism was at the same time of a kind that did not necessarily, or by definition exclude the possibility of modern, political individualism, if only because it was ultimately rooted in 'rural pride and independence'. Of course many among the Schleswig-Holstein farmers were of conservative stock but – as indicated in this chapter – it was a kind of conservatism which, given the right conditions, could just as easily be turned in the direction of more democratic options. One important factor which thwarted these ambitions was, as Kurlander has stressed, the rise of ethnic nationalism in the 1890s, which, as far as liberalism is concerned, drove them closer to an outright reactionary position (Kurlander 2002a, 2006a). In part restoring some of the credibility of the 'Sonderweg hypothesis', Kurlander raises a crucial issue:

> If the German bourgeoisie were just as dynamic as the French and as modern as the British – and there is plenty of evidence to support both assertions – then why did the vast majority of progressive, middle-class Germans defect to Adolf Hitler's NSDAP, a party which not only rejected the liberal tenets of free trade, individual rights, and parliamentary democracy, but likewise endorsed a *völkisch* utopia that excluded hundreds of thousands of German citizens on decidedly racist grounds? (Kurlander 2006a: 85)

His answer is simple. '[T]he vast majority [of liberals] were ethnic (*völkisch*) nationalists', and had been so long before the First World War (ibid.). This is an important argument. Yet there were also important exceptions, at least during the crucial pre-war period; exceptions such as Albert Hänel. In fact, this circumstance underlines the importance to regional liberalism of the generational shift among the liberal leadership around the turn of the century. Among those who more clearly belonged to the 'post-1867' generation, the shift towards ethno-nationalism was all the more dramatic. For instance, even left-liberals such as the theologian Johannes Tiedje, who, before the war, criticized the German assimilation policies vis-à-vis the Danes, turned and embraced an ethno-nationalist perspective (Kurlander 2006a: 88). In fact, even Kurlander's own and most important illustration of a more universalist and republican strand of liberalism – Hans Peter Hanssen (Kurlander 2006a: 87–88) – actually seems to have fitted into this pattern. Although pleading for the coexistence of Danes and Germans, he did so on the basis of a movement which at the same time evolved into a particularistic political one. In what was, of course, an extremely turbulent situation, and informed by the reluctance to let any part of northern Schleswig slip away to Denmark – the classic left-liberal position – in 1919 the *Kieler Zeitung* identified Hanssen as the foremost propagator of secession.[77]

To recognize the undisputable fact that German society and liberalism turned out 'illiberal', or in any event displayed 'illiberal' traits, is not the same as to say that it lacked liberal features entirely; nor that society, as in the case of Schleswig-Holstein, had an original and fatal deficit in terms of modern individualism, and therefore wholly lacked beliefs in modern, civic values. For instance, in a more recent analysis of the 1924 elections, Omland (2007: 170–71), stresses that the established liberal parties also profited from the mass-mobilization of hitherto non-voters during the Weimar Republic. Rather, what the Danish-German issue in northern Schleswig illustrates is how ethno-nationalism, whether by deliberate choice or not, had come to permeate political life and orientations on all levels of society, regardless of party name.

Furthermore, at the heart of the problem was the fact that ethno-nationalism helped to enhance the inward-looking, and basically anti-modernistic view of the world, which most notably Tönnies (2001 [1887]) had found typical of pre-industrial communities. Insofar as nineteenth-century expressions of civic and political association in the German context, such as the 'Bürgervereine', originally served to link traditional and modern forms of societal organization, by the early twentieth century they had collapsed back into parochial traditionalism. When linked to ethno-nationalism, localism conceptualized in terms of 'Heimat' spelled political fragmentation. It became constitutive of German political culture that the federalistic underpinnings of the Wilhelmine state, when combined with a 'Blut und Boden' understanding of identity, by itself posed an obstacle to building a more inclusive political culture.

These features were enhanced during the turmoil of the Weimar Republic. With respect to liberalism, its ultimate failure lay in the fact that, although progressive, individualistic, and modernistic in principle, it was really steeped in romantic traditionalism. Compared to Swedish liberalism it failed to institute proper mechanisms for linking individual citizenry and collective agency, whether in the form of party, community, or nation. Thus understood, the German liberals never grasped the core of the idea of party and the potential it had for mastering the dynamics of mass politics. Against his background, liberalism, let alone liberal democracy, could not survive in a society in which, to follow Weitz (2009: 325), every issue, however miniscule, tended to be transformed into a political struggle to the death.

CHAPTER 5

Swedish and German political association compared

The problem revisited

Initially I posed the question of how nineteenth-century liberals in two European regions went about managing political association. From a certain point of view this issue might seem too singular to attract any serious attention, were it not for the wider ramifications of the problem.

Firstly, political association was without doubt one of the major challenges faced by modernizing societies on the threshold of democracy. Modes of organization and instruments for collective action, which we today take for granted, had to be invented when modern political movements formed. In the wake of the Napoleonic Wars, regimes across the whole of Europe faced the challenges of social upheaval, demands for constitutional reform, and the need for economic reform. All of this required new ways of conceptualizing the relationship between subject/citizen and ruler/state. Political parties filled the role of mediating agents, but only eventually. New forms of civic and political association had first to be tested in real-life politics. Therefore it was not merely an expression of wishful thinking that made Erik Gustaf Geijer hail voluntary association as emblematic of a new time and a new society in the 1840s. The kind of ubiquitous organizations he had in mind, and which have been depicted here in chapter 2, really were a societal innovation. 'Politics' – always a flammable topic – became a critical factor in that perspective. Early forms of civic and political association were certainly elitist. And 'politics' as such remained exclusive. Since the Renaissance it had, by definition, been closely related to and, in fact, more or less conflated with 'reasons of state' (cf. Viroli 1992); in our context Bismarck's reign in imperial Germany represents the clearest expression of such an conception. Quite naturally these circumstances made it difficult to establish parties as a legitimate form of association and as legitimate representatives of mass-based, social, and economic interests. The impression of parties being mere coteries rather than a viable solution for competition between interests and the selection of new governing elites (Gunther & Diamond 2001) lingered on throughout the nineteenth century.

Secondly, liberalism as such is of particular interest in regard to party systems. As diverse in composition as the opposition against *l'ancien regime* was in different countries, this feature was reflected in the making of 'Liberalism'. Yet it it crystallized into one of two major, radical alternatives for modern society, and into a driving force behind political modernization and democracy. From a Marxist point of view, as well as in various strands of postmodern philosophy, it is opportune to declare the demise of liberalism. Perhaps the critics of liberalism are even right on this matter. Liberalism may be but one of several possible strategies according to which mankind has tried to manage modernization and the tensions between the individual and the collective. But it is a very important one, and from a historical perspective a basic fact remains: regardless of the obvious drawbacks of 'economic individualism', Western society, and the manner in which we manage our polities, is to a considerable extent a result of 'political individualism'.

What concepts such as 'liberty' and 'individual freedom' may lack in clarity in everyday use, they make up for in terms of flexibility and applicability when put into practice in different social and cultural contexts. The two case-study regions researched in this book are excellent illustrations of this. And still, despite all obvious differences between Värmland and Schleswig-Holstein, there were also certain important similarities. Indeed, as my analysis demonstrates, liberalism, although technically speaking rational and anti-clerical, could quite easily merge with various expressions of religious values and activities on a grass-roots level. It is difficult to ascertain the extent to which the patterns of 'frisinne' in Värmland and 'linksliberalismus' in Schleswig-Holstein correspond to that typical of English popular liberalism in the era of Gladstone and Dickens. For instance, Biagini points out that nonconformism infused liberalism to the extent that it actually became an expression of 'applied Christianity' (Biagini 1992 [2004]: 31–41, quote at 34). However, evidence suggests this to be the case, particularly as far as Sweden as a whole and Värmland in particular are concerned (chapter 3).

Yet alignments such as these also had inbuilt tensions between different strands of individualism and different modes of associa- tion. The result was by all means a compromise if viewed from an organizational perspective on liberal party formation. With respect to the models proposed first by Maurice Duverger (1967 [1954]) and later Angelo Panebianco (1988), what the notion of 'organiza- tion by means of proxy' really conveys is the importance of ideas and ideology to party formation. Ideology as crystallized in early nineteenth-century forms of civic association was certainly a crucial factor in the original design of liberal parties, whether in Sweden or in Germany. In relation to emerging mass-politics by the end of the century, however, old and new forms of association clearly became locked in conflict with each other.

I have described, at some length, the tensions between the Liberal Party and its national umbrella organization in Sweden (i.e. 'Frisin- nade landsföreningen'), as well as the juxtaposition of 'Bewegung' and 'Partei' in the German context. This dimension of organizational dynamics embodied the struggle between middle-class elite politics by proxies, and more extensive grass-roots mobilization by means of mass-organizations and regular parties. These were options which, I argue, were of a strategic nature only secondarily but ideological primarily. Thus we also approach what was arguably one of the main reasons why liberalism ultimately failed in terms of an organized political movement and party. In line with Barrington Moore's clas- sic study (1967), however, the outcome with regard to democracy differed immensely, depending on the socio-economic setting of the process. Sweden and Germany are both critical cases in that respect.

Beginning with Sweden, the country displays a pattern of gradual and negotiated democratization. Liberalism provided an important link between early, popular radicalism and what later, in the inter- war period, became the nucleus of a modern welfarestate derived from a Social Democratic–Agrarian Party alignment in the 1930s; this line of argument has been forwarded most notably by Hurd (2000). Swedish liberalism compared to German liberalism was in that sense more inclusive, and prepared nineteenth-century society for more extensive grass-roots participation in politics. In a more specific sense the failure of liberalism, therefore, was due to it lacking the means – in ideological but also organizational terms – to maintain its initially extensive electoral support during the crucial years following the First World War. From that point of view it is interesting to look at some of the old arguments on the issue of the roots of the 'Swedish Model'. Most notably Therborn (1989) has suggested that two of the main reasons for the Swedish pattern of negotiated democratization under the social democratic aegis were the more benign nature of the state, and the inherent weakness and fragmentation of the middle classes. This, in turn, paved the way for the social democratic labour movement to conquer and subsequently dominate the political arena, and to gradually permeate the state bureaucracy and make it an instrument of welfare policies (see also Esping-Andersen 1990).

However, this interpretation holds up to closer scrutiny only insofar as we accept two important premises: firstly, that the liberal and conservative parties depended, if not solely then in any event heavily, on the support of what was a numerically weak middle-class electorate; and, secondly, that 'left' and 'right' were really the only two political orientations in nineteenth-century society. With respect to the first assumption, it simply lacks support in empirical evidence concerning the Liberal Party/'Frisinnade landsföreningen'. The average liberal voter in 1900 was, as I have shown in the previous chapters, rural and more often than not agrarian (see also Nilson 2010). As far as the peasants are concerned, it is difficult to posit them as unanimously 'left' or 'right', at least up to the First World War, viz. the formative stage of the modern Swedish party system. Regarding the second assumption it is, in brief, anachronistic from a historical point of view. Although most notably the tariffs debates in the 1880s promoted a left-right cleavage of the classic ('normal') kind, it is only at a later stage, beginning with the step-by-step extension of the right to vote from 1909 onwards, that a conception of political life in terms of 'left' and 'right' becomes entirely meaningful in analytical terms.

The liberals' claims to represent a non-biased, cross-class, middle-of-the-road politics might appear naïve in hindsight. It might also have lacked credibility among contemporary opponents and, increasingly, a majority of voters. The fact remains, however, that 'left' and 'right' as we perceive these orientations were only part of the picture. The role of the farmers as a core group among the liberal voters and, increasingly, the challenge of organized Agrarianism, provide apt illustrations of the problem. Yes, Agrarianism was certainly in many ways conservative in outlook but, no, not every facet of it can so easily be translated into a matter of left vs. right (Eriksson 2010). Because of the diverse composition of the liberal partisans, the prospects of alternative paths to political modernization were always there. That none of these alternative paths were successfully explored is another matter.

The post-1870 German case is more complicated to assess, not least because of the greater regional diversity in terms of political culture. What held true for Prussia did not necessary hold true for her more recently acquired provinces, let alone the south German states. Despite the shortcomings of the 'Sonderweg hypothesis', though, any standard assessment of German political modernization must still account for the specific nature of the state; for the domestic social and economic tensions in the Weimar era; for the almost hypnotic fear of 'Socialism' among the German elite and the middle classes; and, importantly, for the xenophobic and militant outlook of German nationalism. In particular Kurlander (2006a, 2006b) stresses that an overwhelming majority of the German liberals were ethnic nationalists by the time of the First World War. At the same time, however, there were strategically important exceptions to this pattern, as I have tried to demonstrate in chapter 4. Kurlander's succinct argument is nevertheless compelling. This is not least the case if we take stock of what traditionally was a core group of liberal voters in Schleswig-Holstein, the farmers. In a sense Kurlander's explanation touches upon that of Barrington Moore (1967) and Tilton (1975), i.e. that the German farmers never completely modernized in terms of values and beliefs. But if so, we need also to ask how and why the liberal mindset developed in this direction. How, more precisely, were societal and political value systems created and diffused, and how were political ideologies translated to the grass-roots level?

I would not hold that liberal ideology in itself, at least not left-liberalism, was generically infested by ethnic nationalism as this dimension increased in importance in the 1890s. Indeed, as late as 1898, for instance, the *Kieler Zeitung* had stressed that 'parochial anti-Semitism' and liberalism were opposites.[1] What should be noted was a gradual shift in this direction, much due to tactical necessity; this is, if anything, illustrated by the intricacies of liberal election campaigning during the period studied in this book. Rather, ideology was certainly important, but for more reasons than the dissemination of ethnic nationalism. What changed with the appearance of the 'Bund der Landwirte' and the 'Deutsch-sozialen Reformpartei' was the competition; more specifically, the number of available options to the electorate.

Continued left-liberal electoral success in the early twentieth century was therefore dependent on a combination of ideological adaptation to changed conditions and, importantly, the safety catch provided by the election system with its second ballots. This was crucial in a social environment characterized by peasant individualism and self-determination; features which could just as easily be incorporated with extreme, right-wing politics as with liberalism. This was particularly the case in a situation where organizational tenets of political action were lacking. Yet at the same time the liberals' emphasis on individuality seems to have been counterproductive precisely in establishing an extensive, centralized party organization. Although the 'Reformpartei' failed to make its position in the party system permanent, the inroads made into the electorate if anything demonstrated the drawbacks of liberal organization by proxy at large and left-liberal organization in particular. Put simply: the need for ideological adaptation as well as the dependency on the institutional underpinnings of the electoral system were triggered by the organizational weakness of the party apparatus. The latter, in turn, reflected the traditional liberal ambiguity towards civic and political association.

Although the organizational factor has been highlighted most recently by Thompson (2000), it is important to discuss the implications more comprehensively. Following Gunther and Diamond's (2001) blueprint of party functions, political parties also serve as instruments of 'societal representation' and 'social integration', not only electoral mobilization. Insofar as they succeed in doing this, even modern mass parties may well be considered as large-scale examples of social cooperation. Social cooperation, in turn, implies shared values and beliefs on the basis of which mutual trust may evolve (see chapter 1). Consequently, parties are also important instruments for the formation and dissemination of political values and beliefs in society. If proper institutional arrangements, which facilitate the building of trust and shared beliefs, fail to develop, so also do cooperation and the formation of, for example, democratic values. This, I believe, is the ultimate lesson to be learnt from liberal organization in the case of Schleswig-Holstein.

Making sense of history by means of comparison

The difference between left-liberal party organization in Schleswig-Holstein and that of 'Frisinnade landsföreningen' in Värmland is, in terms of principle, only a difference of degree when viewed in this perspective. In both cases proxies, not outright, mass-based organizations, patterned liberal mobilization, although Swedish proxies drew on much more extensive grass-roots networks. Differences such as these between the regions lead us on to the more general problem of making historical comparisons. Heinz-Gerhard Haupt is one of a long succession of scholars who stress that 'all historians compare' (Haupt 2007: 697). Indeed we do. And his claim that localities and regions may be more appropriate units of analysis than countries is also a reasonable one. Presumably the latter holds true not only in regard to the study of social practices and demographic patterns – two examples advanced by Haupt (2007: 711) – but also in relation to political organization and mobilization. This is so since modern party systems owe their origins as much to regional processes and conflicts as they do to national initiatives. The Netherlands and Germany are but two classic examples (Lipset & Rokkan 1967); Sweden a perhaps less obvious but still third illustration of this pattern. For instance, if nothing else the tariffs elections in the 1880s and the different regional attachments of protectionists and free traders demonstrate this. Yet this does of course still leave us with the question of *which* sub-national regions and localities to compare.

In this case two dissimilar regions have been analysed in the search for an explanation for one common feature, i.e. relatively speaking successful political mobilization brought about by emerging liberal parties. In social science terminology the approach is basically a 'most different systems design' (MDSD). Compared to comparative research informed by 'most similar systems design' (MSSD), it does not aim to mimimize the number of experimental variables (Przeworski & Teune 1970: 32). Rather, the principal task in … [MDSD] is to find relationships among variables that can survive being transported across a range of very different regions' (Peters 1998: 41). Note however, firstly, that 'regions' in the context of Peters do not necessarily imply sub-national regions but, more often, groups of countries and hence a type of macro-level analysis which is different from the kind of perspective I offer here. Secondly, I have refrained from using the above terminology until now largely because both strands of comparative research are more often than not associated with statistical probing and testing of hypotheses. Neither are possible in the present case, nor do I believe them appropriate considering the nature of the problem at hand. Nevertheless, the scientific logic underpinning MDSD and MSSD raises important issues with respect to the number of cases appropriate for qualitative analysis.

On the one hand, for instance, Peters warns against two-country studies since these impose limits as to how far the results of empirical observation may be stretched and, at the same time, make it difficult to control for extraneous variation. Indeed, from that perspective MDSD may be problematic since its logic is ultimately Popperian: the ambition is to falsify any number of possible explanations in the search for those factors which may explain an observed similarity. MDSD executed on a small number of cases would therefore seem more suitable for formulating hypotheses rather than for testing them (Peters 1998: 37–41, 58–69; see also Lijphart 1971). On the other hand, any in-depth approach as well as the need for extensive historical contextualization does, of course, limit the number of cases likely to be successfully managed. This is certainly true, although at the same time I find Peter's analogy to Clifford Gertz's famous method of 'thick description' (Peters 1998: 5– 6) slightly misleading. One need not be excessively post-structuralist in outlook to realize that the historian's task is never strictly descriptive. Nor can it provide a fully 'neutral' context to the cases being compared. Since historians cannot create their own primary data for experimental purposes, there is and always will be a tension between the need to rely on available primary sources, such as they are, and the equally important lack of trust in just about any claim made by these sources. Membership statistics from contemporary civic associations are a case in point (chapters 3 and 4).

Because of this, the possible number of cases for comparative purposes remains limited. 'Normally, it is not possible to integrate more than two or three realities in a research project' (Haupt 2007: 703). We then approach the reasons for including Värmland and Schleswig-Holstein in this particular study. To begin with, there is a large body of literature ostensibly indicating that both regions were atypical with respect to liberalism. Reiterating my initial argument, however, liberalism could just as easily become successful in rural environments as in urbanized and industrialized ones. Urbanization and industrialism were two of the outcomes of modernization, but these processes posed new challenges with political implications for rural societies, too. This certainly goes for Scandinavia and it holds true for parts of Germany as well, such as Schleswig-Holstein. In fact, writes Haupt, participants in the old *Sonderweg* debate all too carelessly let themselves become infused by 'an idealized vision of the British situation', and too easily overlooked German regional differentiation (Haupt 2007: 707). Rather, as any attempts at unearthing anything like 'average liberalism', or an 'average path' to political modernization are likely to fail, the historian's task must be to identify and explain variation in terms of this process. That political modernization is not necessarily sequential does not thereby rule out certain crucial commonalities between seemingly different countries and regions. This feature is amply illustrated by the cases of Värmland and Schleswig-Holstein.

In relation to the crucial variables researched here – strong liberal turnout in a basically rural environment –Värmland and Schleswig-Holstein therefore turn out to be quite similar to each other regarding the modus operandi in terms of organization. This is the case regardless of the orientation of liberal policies in the main in Sweden and Germany (one set of policies gradually being more oriented towards progressivism, the other becoming more closely bound up with the intricacies of economic liberalism, deregulation, and free trade). This also holds good regardless, for instance, of the position taken in relation to the respective electoral systems and their design. In the early 1890s, local liberals in Värmland pointed to the example of Germany and the system of direct elections based on the rule of absolute majority, as a means of engendering grass-roots participation and, consequently, the liberal turnout. Only gradually did proportionalism, as later promulgated by the 1909 election reforms, gain ground.[2] Absolute majority and the system of second ballots were, however, used by German liberals to effectively block unwanted grass-roots competition from the socialists.

Finally, considering the rural framework of liberalism and, indeed, of all political movements in these two regions, it is worthwhile noting the importance of geography. Party formation processes and political mobilization were, in one sense, all about distance. From this perspective rural regions, particularly in Scandinavia, become extreme from a historical point of view. Put simply, organizing political parties and mobilizing one's partisans is obviously easier in densely populated areas than in regions where much arduous and time-consuming travel is required. Albert Hänel's criss-crossing of Schleswig-Holstein during the 1884 elections is one example of this (chapter 4). Swedish campaign workers had to overcome worse obstacles than that.

Indeed, Värmland was far from being the worst of the boondocks. Conditions in the north were even more extreme: in connection to the 1911 elections one of the liberal campaigners in the province of Västerbotten covered 1,634 kilometers by train, by horse, and by bicycle (chapter 3, n. 63). The same distance travelled could have taken him down to Cracow, almost the whole way across to Iceland, or to the far side of Moscow, should he have so wished. People like him might have been particularly hard-nosed. We do not know. It is safe to say, though, that feats such as these make the successes of rural liberalism and its organization, haphazard as they many times were, all the more remarkable. It was, perhaps, precisely because of factors such as these that organization by means of proxy worked, at least up to a point, or – even – became a necessary means during the initial stages of party formation. Compared to a homogeneous and hierarchic mass-organization, which depended on continuous directions from the national executive, a political movement based on more or less autonomous bodies was more flexible during an age in which the technical means of communication were poorly developed. This might be somewhat of a paradox. For all its drawbacks – one of which facilitated the rise of political right-wing alternatives in Schleswig-Holstein – organization by means of proxy also served a purpose, when viewed in relation to the practical constraints on political association in turn-of-the-century Europe.

We have so far spoken of parties rather than party systems, the latter a more important analytical category from the point of view of political scientists. Still, even studies of single parties and political movements may be enlightening from a systems perspective. Thus, from a systemic perspective the main problem for contemporary liberals in both Sweden and Germany – that of managing emerging mass-politics – was a general feature of party systems development in countries across the Continent as well as in the US. Although the precise sequence of events as well as outcomes differed between Europe and the US, 'the development of the contemporary party systems … coincided with extensions of the franchise and the mobilization of a peripheral electorate' (Petrocik & Brown 1999: 43). This, in turn, unleashed the kind of challenges and crises faced by contemporary parties and factions when the expanding electorate gradually realigned according to the diverse patterns typical of our two regions. Self-evident as this observation might seem, it is nevertheless important for our historical understanding of party dynamics. In the words of Petrocik and Brown, 'electoral mobilization is not likely to be a major contributor to future party system changes among the developed democracies' (ibid.). In terms of causality, therefore, the eventual failure of organized liberalism in Sweden and Germany was as much a reflection of more general trends in Western political modernization as it was due to any specific historical 'necessity' inherent to Swedish and German liberalism. Ultimately the matter of 'sequentialism' versus 'non-sequentialism' does, of course, remain more complex than this. But at least with respect to the rise and fall of liberalism, these theoretical models fail to capture the intricacies of the story.

Notes

Introduction

1 'Det säger sig själft, att de nu föreslagna jämkningarna i metoden ingalunda kunna förebygga sådana oegentligheter, som hafva sin grund vare sig i obekantskap med valmetoden eller i illojala valmanövrer. Särskildt gäller detta den några gånger försökta kuppen att illojalt använda ett annat partis partibeteckning. Skulle den frihet, som den nuvarande valmetoden i detta hänseende lämnar, fortfarande missbrukas, och den politiska moralen icke tillräckligt reagera mot dylika tilltag, så återstår intet annat än att införa den offentliga kandidaturen med officiellt fastställda vallistor.' Albert Petersson, 'Om ändringar i lagen om val till Riksdagen med flera författningar', no. 5, 10. *Motioner väckta inom andra kammaren, 1–190. Bihang till riksdagens protokoll 1912.* The motion was brought in protest against the liberals and the social democrats, who had formed cartels under joint party labels in 15 constituencies during the election campaign. *SOS. Allmänna val. Riksdagsmannavalen åren 1909–1911,* 40.

2 1918–21, because constitutional reforms of this kind required confirmation by two consecutive parliaments. Women's right to vote was introduced parallel with democratization of the municipalities.

3 To make his point, Duverger referred to Hume's 'Essay on Parties'. The English, 1954, edition of Duverger reads: 'In his 'Essay on Parties' (1760) David Hume made the shrewd observation that the programme plays an essential part in the initial phase, when it serves to bring together scattered individuals, but later on organization comes to the fore, the "platform" becoming subordinate. Nothing could be truer.' More specifically, Hume published three essays on parties. These were 'Of Parties in General' [1741], 'Of the Parties of Great Britain' [1742], and 'Of the Coalition of Parties' [1760]. The closest match between Hume and Duverger in this respect is to be found in the 1741 essay, where Hume notes that 'Nothing is more usual than to see parties, which have begun upon a real difference, continue even after that difference is lost. When men are once inlisted on opposite sides, they contract an affection to the persons with whom they are united, and animosity against their antagonists; and these passions they often transmit to their posterity', Hume 1904 [1741], 56–57; Hume 1964 [1882], 129. This, however, has little to do with the organizational framework of parties.

4 Matters of translation, spelling and placenames are never easy to resolve when the topic involves more than one linguistic and historical setting. Here

Swedish and German quotes have been translated into English, but with the original text given in the notes. I have used the standard English place names, but otherwise Swedish and German names; hence for instance Bavaria rather than Bayern and Gothenburg rather than Göteborg, but Värmland, Schleswig-Holstein, Flensburg, Karlstad and so on.

5 The debate most notably on German liberalism, and on the issue of how and when liberal ideology changed in nature has been extensive. In later research, Eley 1980, and Blackbourn 1980, for instance, have stressed the 1890s as the crucial period, in addition to which they, like Langewiesche 2000 [1988], also provide a more nuanced picture of German liberalism. See more recently Palmowski 1999, and Gross 2004, for extensive historiographical reviews. By comparison, Swedish research on liberalism is far less extensive. Hurd 2000 and Nilson & Åberg 2010, are among the most recent contributions.

6 It should be pointed out that, like Sweden, Denmark and Norway may also be used as examples of 'rural liberalism'; see Thomas 1988. According to the rationale of the present study, however, Germany, rather than Denmark or Norway, is to be preferred for the purpose of comparison.

7 The approach therefore rests on a 'most different systems design' (MDSD); see for instance Przeworski & Teune 1970, and Denk 2002. However, I refrain from using this terminology mainly for two reasons. Firstly, my point of departure is not contingent on one particular theory of parties or party system formation. Secondly, considering the historical context, data does not allow systematic, let alone quantitative, testing of hypotheses in a manner consistent with MDSD models.

8 Archive material pertaining to liberal organization on the regional level is, with certain exceptions, usually scarce. (This might, indeed, be indicative of liberal attitudes towards formal organization.) Although regional-level party material exists in the public archives in the case of Värmland this is not the case for Schleswig-Holstein. Political activities and elections in Germany were, however, more closely monitored by the government compared to Sweden, and the official records kept, for instance in connection to the election campaigns, provide valuable information which to some extent makes up for the lack of party records. In both countries newspapers are also rich in information on political association and elections.

1. Parties – the roots of suspicion

1 The Swedish Social Democratic Party did however display a more decentralized pattern from the outset (the party was founded in 1889) similar to Austria. Soon enough, however, the party moved closer to the German model, and it began to adopt a more centralized structure in the 1890s. The final stages of this transition, though, were not completed until the inter-war period (Gidlund 1989, Schüllerqvist 1992).

2 Gustaf Albert Petersson in my introductory example was minister of justice in

the conservative cabinet of Admiral Arvid Lindman, 1906–11, and member of parliament 1912–17. See also the Introduction, endnotes, on the background to his complaints.

3 Protokoll, 29 July 1917, § 7. Norra Värmlands frisinnade valkretsförbund, Protokoll, 1, 1909–22. Folkrörelsernas arkiv för Värmland. Arkivcentrum Karlstad.

4 The essay in question is 'Of Parties in General' [1742], originally published in the second volume of Hume's essays. On the topic of Whigs and Tories, however, Hume believed that the formation of British parties was an inescapable part of political life, considering the specificities of British constitutional development. See 1904 [1741–42], 'Of the Parties of Great Britain'.

5 *Kieler Zeitung*, 10 February 1871.

6 Other relevant concepts, such as 'Gemeinschaft' and 'Gesellschaft' (see chapter 2) were also, and still are, extremely difficult to transfer between different historical, ideological, and linguistic settings. We may simply consider the manner in which the translations into English of Ferdinand Tönnies' concepts differ across time. For instance, the 1955 Routledge & Keegan Paul edition of *Gemeinschaft und Gesellschaft* is titled *Community and Association*, whereas the 2001 Cambridge University Press edition is titled *Community and Civil Society*. Other editions have the title *Community and Society*.

7 I am aware that this is not in line with common conceptions of civil society, such as in Keane's, analysis (1988). Historically speaking, however, 'civil' and 'political association' were often considered to be closely connected. Then again, the problem is not easily resolved. It is, among other things, contingent on how we define the 'state' and 'politics'; also it could be said about 'civil' and 'political' associations that they operate in the interface between 'society', or the 'individual', and the 'state'. See also Trägårdh 1999.

8 Staaff's principles on the matter were laid down in his posthumously published, comparative study of democracy as political system (Staaff 1917, I, 370–73).

9 Protokoll, 2 April 1934, § 11. Värmlands frisinnade valkretsförbund, Protokoll, A I:1, 1922–34. Folkrörelsernas arkiv för Värmland. Arkivcentrum Karlstad.

10 On public opinion towards Prussia during this period, see Reinhardt 1954.

11 'Im Serenissimus-Zustande politischer Unschuld.' Preuss later became the principal architect of the ill-fated Weimar constitution. Sentiments were heightened during the war, of course. Still, Preuss's statement should be seen in the context of the conflict between Prussian militarism and civic virtue in Wilhelmine Germany. Thus it has a bearing not only on the 'Sonderweg hypothesis' strictly speaking, but also on the traditional and strong role played by 'Historismus' as self-image in German society. See Raulet 2001; Clark 2006.

12 The notion of the 'popular movement' traditionally refers to the emergence of nonconformist religious movements from the 1860s onwards; organized teetotalism from the late 1870s onwards; the labour movement from the 1880s onwards; and the women's movement. Although the difference is not always obvious, the popular movements should be seen in contrast to earlier expres-

sions of voluntary association (c. 1815–70), which also included for instance temperance movements (non-teetotal) and worker's associations. The latter types of voluntary association were, however, as a rule more 'elitist' (in the sense of emerging as a result of middle-class organization 'from above') rather than grass roots movements proper. See also chapter 2 and 3. In addition it is worth noting that, as with teetotalism, the ideas as such did not originate in Sweden but, rather, in the US. Yet again, the movement – as was also the case with nonconformism – was blended with indigenous tradition and transformed accordingly. Obvious as this might seem, it is nevertheless emblematic of the criss-crossing of ideas in modernizing societies. Another case in point is, of course, the very idea of party and how it was managed in different societies.

13 Sources suggest that left-liberalism was occasionally considered a catalyst of socialism. As late as the 1912 general elections, the district commissioner ('Landrat') in Pinneberg, outside Hamburg, complained that both the social democratic *and* the left-liberal newspapers, had 'systematically fomented a sense of ill will' among the public which, in combination with the concerns caused by recent foot-and-mouth disease in the constituency, might tip the scales in favour of the social democratic candidate. ('Bei der weitverbreiteten, durch die sozialdemokratische und links-liberale Presse im Wahlkreise dauernd und systematisch genährten Mißstimmung.') District Commissioner in Pinneberg to the Oberpräsidentur, 4 November 1911. 6759. Reichstagswahl 1912. Oberpräsidium und Provinzialrat der Provinz Schleswig-Holstein. LAS.

14 'Only three people understood the Schleswig-Holstein Question. The first was Albert, the Prince Consort, and he is dead; the second was a German professor, and he is in an asylum; and the third person was myself – and I have forgotten it.'

15 71.9 per cent in Västerbotten, SOS. *Allmänna val. Riksdagsmannavalen åren 1909–1911*, Table 3.

16 *Beiträge zur historischen Statistik Schleswig-Holsteins*, 1967, Table V 1 b.

17 BiSOS. *Befolkningsstatistik 1910*, Table 1; *Beiträge zur historischen Statistik Schleswig-Holsteins*, 1967, Table I 7.

18 BiSOS. *Befolkningsstatistik 1910*, Table 1.

19 Except for the 'Bondeförbundet' this was the highest level of rural voting among the competing parties, SOS. *Allmänna val. Riksdagsmannavalen år 1921*, Table 5. Detailed data for the 1911 elections are not available in the published election statistics. Cartels and joint party labels were frequently used throughout the first decades of the twentieth century – a feature which was not sufficiently taken into account when the 1911 election results were compiled.

20 There was a total drop in population in the region of almost 8,000 people in the 1880–1910 period. BiSOS. *Befolkningsstatistik 1880*, Table 1, BiSOS. *Befolkningsstatistik 1910*, Table 1.

21 *Statistisk årsbok för Sverige 1920*, Table 104.

22 *Handlingar rörande prestmötet i Karlstad 1899*, 1899, 26.

23 The north-west includes Schleswig-Holstein, Hanover, Hamburg, Braunschweig, Oldenburg, Bremen, Lippe, Schaumburg-Lippe, and Lübeck (37.6 per cent employment in industry, whereas the national average was 43.0 per cent), *Sozialgeschichtliches Arbeitsbuch, III*, 1978, Table 8 d, 56.

24 *Beiträge zur historischen Statistik Schleswig-Holsteins*, 1967, Table VI.3; *Historischer Atlas Schleswig-Holstein 1867 bis 1945*, 2001, 38.

25 Between 1907 and 1925 the total population of the province actually dropped from 1,545,700 to 1,519,400. *Beiträge zur historischen Statistik Schleswig-Holsteins*, 1967, Table VI.2.

26 *Sozialgeschichtliches Arbeitsbuch, II*, 1978, Table 13, 47–49.

27 *Beiträge zur historischen Statistik Schleswig-Holsteins*, 1967, Table I 7.

2. Partisanship rising

1 The ambiguities of liberalism are succinctly put by Kahan 2003. Liberals were 'both the confident heirs of Voltaire and the frightened successors of Robespierre' (ibid. 1).

2 'Den friare statsförfattningen började sprida ljus och värma till vinklar och vrår ... Det goda och det ädla af det gamla hade ännu icke multnat, och det nya sköt friska skott.'

3 In 1917, to be precise. Following the result of the 1917 elections, the conservative government of Carl Swartz resigned in favour of a liberal–social democratic coalition.

4 Samuel Pufendorf, of Saxon origin, had a background as professor in Lund, Sweden, and as court historiographer in Stockholm, but he is perhaps most commonly remembered for performing the same function at the Prussian court during the last years of his life – he was appointed in 1691 and died in 1694. Certainly the stress put on the role of the state and the monarch was as such far from unique in the era of absolutism. Clark, however, suggests that Pufendorf's ideas struck a lasting chord in Prussia particularly, due to the upheavals during the Thirty Years War.

5 i.e. the *Encyklopaedie der Staatswissenschaft* (1834), edited by Karl von Rotteck and Carl Theodor Welcker, in which prominent controvertialists ventured to address the critical, political issues of the day, Sheehan 1978. On Rotteck and civic association, see also below.

6 'Sie helten true zu König und bestehender Staatsverfassung, standen aber den Beamten kritisch gegenüber.'

7 Named after Uwe Jens Lornsen, 1793–1838.

8 '... aller nationalgesinnten, kaiser- und reichstreuen Männer': national liberal appeal, ninth constituency, Oldenburg-Segeberg-Plön, 6 July 1873. 8342. Reichstagswahlen 1871/1874. Regierung zu Schleswig. LAS.

9 *Bidrag till Sveriges officiella statistik (BiSOS). Kungl. Maj:ts befallningshafvandes femårsberättelser*, Värmland, 1881–85, Sammandrag för åren 1881–85, 124–25.

10 When the first issue appeared the newspaper was called *Wermlands Tidning*. Only from 1851 did it appear under the name *Nya Wermlands-Tidningen*.

11 Under this name from 1879.

12 The poem was called 'Riksdassbönnras marsch' (sic) (March of the Peasant Deputies) and was later set to music by actress and composer Helfrid Lambert.

13 *Nya Wermlands-Posten*, 1 May and 8 September 1869. See also *Nya Wemlands-Posten*, 18 August 1869.

14 Protokoll, 7 April 1902, § 3; 16 May 1902, § 2. Protokoll verkställande utskottet, A 2:9, 1902–07. Frisinnade landsföreningen. RA.

15 Such as the discussions held when the party was reunited in 1934, see Protokoll, 22 February 1934, § 2. Vol. 2., Protokoll 1923–34. Karlstads Frisinnade Valmansförening, Folkrörelsernas arkiv för Värmland, Arkivcentrum Karlstad.

16 *Sveriges officiella statistik (SOS). Allmänna val. Riksdagsmannavalen år 1909–1911*, Table 3.

17 *Bidrag till Sveriges officiella statistik (BiSOS). Kungl. Maj:ts befallningshafvandes femårsberättelser*, Värmland, 1901–05, Sammandrag för åren 1901–05, Tables E and F. An estimated 56.4 per cent of all teetotallers in Visnum, Väse, and Ölme were affiliated to the Blue Ribbon and other non-IOGT lodges.

18 Föreningsrapporter till valkretsförbundet, Ölme 1922 and Väse Södra, 1924. Vol. 8, Inkomna handlingar från lokalavdelningar 1919–26. Östra Värmlands Frisinnade valkretsförbund, Folkrörelsernas arkiv för Värmland, Arkivcentrum Karlstad.

19 The Norwegian connections are emphasized by among others Byström 1963, whereas the clergy itself noted how the 'emissaries' of nonconformism entered the region both from Närke in the east and from Vänersborg in the southwest: *Handlingar rörande prestmötet i Carlstad 1869* (1870), 51.

20 *Karlstads-tidningen*, 2 April 1887; ibid. 9 April 1887.

21 *Nya Wermlands-Tidningen*, 8 August 1893; *Karlstads-tidningen*, 19 July 1893; 1 July 1896; ibid. 6 July 1896; ibid. 15 July 1908; ibid. 23 August 1911.

22 Minutes of constituent meeting, 6 March 1904, § 3. Vol. 1, protokoll, 1904–67. Folkpartiets lokalavdelning i Munkfors. Folkrörelsernas arkiv för Värmland, Arkivcentrum Karlstad.

23 Rapport från Frisinnade landsföreningens ombud J. E. Cervin, 16 June–15 August 1917. Vol. 1, Ombudsmannens handlingar, 1917–22. Värmlands frisinnade länskommitté. Folkrörelsernas arkiv för Värmland, Arkivcentrum Karlstad. After the elections, though, Cervin stressed in his evaluation that the campaigning in the north suffered from insufficient advertising of election rallies, and the candidates' failure to appear to address the public at these meetings. Also, in many cases local liberals had failed to join the national organization of the party (Några iakttagelser vid resa i Wärmlands Norra valkrets, 14 September 1917. Vol. 1., Ombudsmannens handlingar, 1917–22. Värmlands frisinnade länskommitté. Folkrörelsernas arkiv för Värmland, Arkivcentrum Karlstad).

24 The problem will be addressed in a doctoral dissertation on pietist awakenings in the Swedish context by Per von Wachenfeldt, Department of Historical Studies, University of Gothenburg.

25 A debate on the topic of 'What is Freedom?' ('Hvad är frihet?'), held by the IOGT lodge at Visnum, 1893, gives a typical illustration (Protokoll, 1 July 1893, § 7. Protokoll A I:3. IOGT Logen 1544 Björneborg, Visnum. Folkrörelsernas arkiv för Värmland, Arkivcentrum Karlstad).

26 In Holstein and Lauenburg censorship was reintroduced between 1819 and 1848. In Schleswig, each new edition of a newspaper had to be submitted to the police authorities for scrutiny. In Sweden freedom of speech as well as freedom of the press were constitutionally guaranteed rights, but in the latter case with certain important exceptions in the 1812–45 period. Hence, periodicals which were deemed injurious to public safety, or otherwise libellous, could be withdrawn from publication. This was the fate of the liberal newspaper *Aftonbladet* on a number of occasions during the 1830s. Yet, the limitations were circumvented by publishing the newspaper under slightly modified names: Thus, in 1839, the 'Twenty-first Aftonbladet' (*Det tjugondeförsta Aftonbladet*) was printed.

27 Such as in connection to the 1884 elections. See *Amtsblatt* (4), 26 January 1884, 62; *Amtsblatt* (50), 18 October 1884, 1049–50 *et passim*.

28 See, for instance, the government surveillance reports pertaining to articles published in the *Kieler Zeitung* and the *Kieler Correspondenz-Blatt*, from the district commissioners in Segeberg, 31 August 1872, Holm, 31 August 1872, and Rendsburg, 31 August 1872. 8523. Öffentliche Stimmung in der Provinz Schleswig-Holstein, 1872–1873. Regierung zu Schleswig. LAS. See also surveillance report concerning a national liberal meeting in Kiel, 13 February 1871. 6820. Gendarmerie 1871–1874. Oberpräsidium und Provinzialrat der Provinz Schleswig-Holstein. LAS.

29 In this respect there are, at least superficially, certain parallels to the Swedish local heritage movement. However, the political context of the 'Heimatkunst' movement and its various expressions, such as for instance the 'Bund Heimatschutz', founded in Dreseden, in 1904, made it unique.

30 'Ich will mit!'

31 '… der fortschrittliche, rein theoretisch-unpraktische Liberalismus, wie ihn der Herr Prof. Hänel aus der Fremde hier in unser Land eingeschleppt hat.' *Schleswiger Nachrichten*, 24 October 1884.

32 The names of the constituencies vary according to the primary source and in the literature. This can be confusing since, for instance, Plön was divided between the seventh constituency of Kiel-Rendsburg (which often is referred to as Kiel-Rendsburg-Plön) and the ninth constituency of Oldenburg-Segeberg-Plön. In order to avoid confusion I use the labels applied by Schultz Hansen 2003, 464, in this and following chapters.

33 Letter from General von Lindequist, 5 December 1911, on behalf of the 'Preussischer Landes-Kriegerverband', to von Bülow, Oberpresident in Schleswig-

Holstein. 6759. Reichstagswahl 1912. Oberpräsidium und Provinzialrat der Provinz Schleswig-Holstein. LAS. The letter specifies measures with respect both to the first and second ballot.

34 The system meant that the voters in the municipalities were divided into three classes depending on taxable income. Votes were assigned accordingly, leading to a situation in which the wealthy minority of each municipality was entitled to one-third of all votes. Also, analogous to Sweden, local self-government was long considered a basically non-political sphere. Only by the turn of the twentieth century, and due to pressure from influential liberals such as Josef Redlich and, most notably, Hugo Preuss, did local self-government become considered more on a par with the national level in terms of importance, Palmowski 1999. At the same time, however, the 'Städteordnung' of 1869 – by and large a product of liberal efforts, too – added a somewhat more democratic flavour to local government in Schleswig-Holstein, compared to other Prussian provinces. See, for instance, Pust 1975, 134–35.

35 Apart from Hänel, professors Peter Wilhelm Forchhammer, Victor Hensen, Gustav Karsten, and Wilhelm Seelig were also members of the executive committee.

36 *Itzehoer Nachrichten*, 28 February 1871; *Schleswiger Nachrichten*, 2 March 1871.

37 Constituent meeting 3 November 1883. Vol 1, Protokoll des Friedrichsberger Bürgervereins, 1883–97, 1. 31. Friedrichsberger Bürgerverein. Vereine und Verbände. LAS.

38 *Kieler Zeitung*, 7 January 1907.

39 *Itzehoer Nachrichten*, 6 January 1907; Nicolai-Kolb, 1991, 171.

40 *Flensburger Nachrichten*, 12 and 15 June 1898; *Itzehoer Nachrichten*, 30 December 1906.

41 In his analysis of Hamburg, Breuilly, 1994, 211–12, notes that dissenting Protestantism excercised any real influence on the formation of urban liberalism only momentarily, viz. in the 1840s. Insofar as Breuilly had pietism in mind it is however beyond doubt that this particular expression of nonconformism had more far-reaching consequences, which significantly extended the limits of 1840s' radicalism.

42 Gellert, vol. 1, 1777 [1770], 18–19, 139.

43 '… wåra plikters i akttagande emot Gud och människor': Gellert, vol. 2, 1777 [1770], 7. The quote is from Gellert's *Moralische Charaktere*, which was included as a separate section when the *Vorlesungen* was originally published in Leipzig. The Swedish edition follows the same structure.

44 '… deutsche, dänische, liberale, orthodoxe, religiöse, konfessionelle sowie vereinstaktische Gesichtspunkte und Interessen erkennen.'

3. Värmland – liberalism one step to the left

1 In the poem *Den gamla goda tiden* ('The good old days'), 1894.

2 *Handlingar rörande prestmötet i Karlstad 1899*, 1899, 25–42; *Handlingar rörande*

prästmötet i Karlstad 1911 (1911), 26–61 and in particular 27–31. See also
Martling, 1958, 391–410.

3 Protokoll, 7 March 1918, § 4. Vol. 1, Protokoll 1916–18. Frisinnade diskussionsklubben, Karlstad, Folkrörelsernas arkiv för Värmland, Arkivcentrum
Karlstad.

4 Protokoll, 7 March 1918, § 3. Vol. 1, Protokoll 1916–18. Frisinnade diskussionsklubben, Karlstad, Folkrörelsernas arkiv för Värmland, Arkivcentrum
Karlstad.

5 '… det gives ock plikter mot anförvanter, särskilt mot hustru och barn'. Protokoll,
7 March 1918, § 4. Vol. 1, Protokoll 1916–18. Frisinnade diskussionsklubben,
Karlstad, Folkrörelsernas arkiv för Värmland, Arkivcentrum Karlstad.

6 *Nya Wermlands-Tidningen*, 30 April 1887.

7 *Karlstads-tidningen*, 7 May 1887.

8 '… flere föreningar här i Karlstad, de frireligiöse, goodtemplarne och medlem-
marne af arbetare föreningen'. *Karlstads-tidningen*, 2 April 1887.

9 *Karlstads-tidningen*, 6 April and 9 April 1887.

10 '… omfattande erfarenhet i lifvets skilda värf … ett lugnt och värdigt sätt att
uppträda inför ett större auditorium, ett skarpt och genomträngande förstånd,
stor lätthet att uttrycka sig, mycken vana vid offentliga förhandlingar och,
först och sist att komma ihåg, en omutlig rättrådighet och en aldrig svigtande
karakterens styrka.' *Filipstads Stads- och Bergslags Tidning*, 31 March 1887.

11 Ibid.

12 '… de olika samhällsklasser, hvaraf frihandelspartiet består'. *Karlstads-tidningen*,
16 April 1887.

13 *Nya Wermlands-Tidningen*, 16 April 1887.

14 Election results as presented in *Karlstads-tidningen*, 27 April 1887.

15 In general terms, though, ideas of blood, race, and racial purity were, in Sweden
as elsewhere in Europe, part of the 'Zeitgeist' among liberals. For instance, at
a meeting of the Liberal Debating Society in Karlstad in 1917, the audience
was entertained with a talk on races and racial eugenics. Protokoll, 1 February
1917, § 3. Vol. 1, Protokoll 1916–18. Frisinnade diskussionsklubben, Karlstad,
Folkrörelsernas arkiv för Värmland, Arkivcentrum Karlstad.

16 *Nya Wermlands-Tidningen*, 30 April 1887.

17 *Karlstads-tidningen*, 8 October 1887.

18 On Norway as model country from a parlamentarian point of view in the local
press, see for instance *Karlstads-tidningen*, 22 and 29 October 1887. Yet, it
should be pointed out that examples pertaining to the issues of parliamentarism
and suffrage could emanate from very diverse contexts. Some years later an
article in *Karlstads-tidningen* of 19 July 1893 actually referred to conditions
in Wyoming on the matter of women's right to vote. There, according to the
newspaper, inclusion of the women 'had led to the result that the elections could
be carried out in a kind of order, and peace, and quiet that was unknown in
other member states of the Union'. ('[H]ar gifvit valen en karaktär af ordning
och lugn, som är okänd i unionens öfriga stater'.)

19 In Värmland, when the conservative press commented on the 1893 elections, it used the established concepts of protectionists and free traders in order to describe the competing candidates (*Nya Wermlands-Tidningen*), 12 August 1893.

20 *Karlstads-tidningen,* 22 March 1893.

21 Årsberättelse 1889, 19 April 1890. Vol. 1, Årsberättelser m.m., 1889–97. Värmlands rösträttsförening. Folkrörelsernas arkiv för Värmland, Arkivcentrum Karlstad.

22 '... en hedersplats bland deras kamrater i landets öfriga landskap'. Årsberättelse 1892, 31 May 1893. Värmlands rösträttsförening, vol 1, Årsberättelser m.m., 1889–97. Folkrörelsernas arkiv för Värmland. Arkivcentrum Karlstad.

23 The archives for each branch usually include a brief historical account. In yet other cases the minutes of the respective associations have been used to track down when this or that lodge started.

24 Årsberättelse 1889, 19 April 1890; Årsberättelse 1890, 20 June 1891. Vol. 1, Årsberättelser m.m., 1889–97. Värmlands rösträttsförening. Folkrörelsernas arkiv för Värmland, Arkivcentrum Karlstad.

25 On Olson's affiliations: Årsberättelse 1889, 19 April 1890. Vol. 1, Årsberättelser m.m., 1889–97. Värmlands rösträttsförening. Folkrörelsernas arkiv för Värmland, Arkivcentrum Karlstad; Protokoll, 18 February 1900, § 1. Protokoll AI: 1, 1893–1904. Ransäters Blåbandsförening. Folkrörelsernas arkiv för Värmland, Arkivcentrum Karlstad. See also Larsson, 1977, 212–15. On Andersson see Svärd, 1954, 39.

26 Protokoll, 18 February 1900, § 3. Protokoll AI: 1, 1893–1904. Ransäters Blåbandsförening. Folkrörelsernas arkiv för Värmland, Arkivcentrum Karlstad.

27 *Handlingar rörande prästmötet i Karlstad 1911* (1911), 28. See also the comments in *Karlstads-tidningen*, 23 and 26 August 1911.

28 Rönblom 1929, 67–70; *Karlstads-tidningen*, 22 March 1893.

29 Proceedings as referred to by *Karlstads-tidningen*, 22 March 1893. Emilie Rathou is presently the subject of a doctoral dissertation by Åsa Bengtsson, Department of History at Lund University. See also Bengtsson 2010.

30 Årsberättelse 1893, 28 May 1894. Värmlands rösträttsförening, vol 1, Årsberättelser m.m., 1889–97. Folkrörelsernas arkiv för Värmland. Arkivcentrum Karlstad.

31 Ibid.; Carlsson 1953, 154–55; Larsson 1977, 212–15; Ekberg 2006, 54.

32 Årsberättelse 1893, 28 May 1894. Värmlands rösträttsförening, vol 1, Årsberättelser m.m., 1889–97. Folkrörelsernas arkiv för Värmland. Arkivcentrum Karlstad.

33 *Karlstads-tidningen*, 19 August 1893.

34 'Ett inflytelserikt, i värklig mening liberalt parti' (*Karlstads-tidningen*, 4 July 1896).

35 By early July, according to *Karlstads-tidningen*, Göthberg had deferred joining the People's Party, since he was waiting for a less left-wing liberal party to appear. The consequences were obvious: only one week later he was manifestly in the process of making up his mind, since the newspaper then claimed that the most likely

would become (if not necessarily formally) the candidate of the conservatives in this constituency (*Karlstads-tidningen*, 6 July and 15 July 1896). However, some years later Göthberg was also among those who signed the invitation to organize 'Liberala samlingspartiet' in 1900 (Rönblom, 1929, 92).

36 Svärd 1954, 19–20, 39, 42; *Svenska folkrörelser*, I, 1936, 450.

37 Arbetarföreläsningarne 1904–05, Verksamhets- och kassaberättelser, G2: 1, 1887–90. Karlstads föreläsningsanstalt. Folkrörelsernas arkiv för Värmland. Arkivcentrum Karlstad.

38 Protokoll, 26 March 1893, § 11. Protokoll, AI: 1, 1892–95. IOGT-logen 1810 Enigheten, Arvika. Folkrörelsernas arkiv för Värmland, Arkivcentrum Karlstad.

39 Protokoll, 11 January 1904, § 7. Protokoll verkställande utskottet, A 2:9, 1902–07. Frisinnade landsföreningen. RA.

40 Protokoll, 16 May 1902, § 4 and 7 November 1902, § 5. Protokoll verkställande utskottet, A 2:9, 1902–07. Frisinnade landsföreningen. RA.

41 Politiska fysionomier, series. No date, but probably issued in conjunction with the 1902 elections (Cirkulär, B 2:34, 1899–1914. Frisinnade landsföreningen. RA).

42 Cirkulär, 31 December 1907. Korrespondens 1907–22. Värmlands frisinnade länskommitté. Folkrörelsernas arkiv för Värmland, Arkivcentrum Karlstad.

43 Protokoll, 30 June 1902, § 2. Protokoll verkställande utskottet, A 2:9, 1902–07. Frisinnade landsföreningen. RA.

44 Protokoll, 19 September 1909, § 2. Vol. 1, Protokoll 1908–16. Föreningen för kvinnans politiska rösträtt, Värmlands länsförbund. Folkrörelsernas arkiv för Värmland. Arkivcentrum Karlstad. Some years earlier, in 1903, Gerda Hellberg had also been elected chairwoman of the local Karlstad branch of the women's suffrage movement (Protokoll, 16 March 1903, § 5. Vol. 1, Protokoll 1903–07. Föreningen för kvinnans politiska rösträtt, Karlstad. Folkrörelsernas arkiv för Värmland, Arkivcentrum Karlstad).

45 Protokoll, 5 March 1919, § 2. Vol. 2, Protokoll 1919–23. Föreningen för kvinnans politiska rösträtt, Karlstad. Folkrörelsernas arkiv för Värmland, Arkivcentrum Karlstad.

46 Protokoll, Easter Monday, 1922, § 8. Protokoll, A1: 1, 1922–34. Värmlands frisinnade valkretsförbund. Folkrörelsernas arkiv för Värmland, Arkivcentrum Karlstad.

47 *Karlstads-tidningen*, 22 August 1908.

48 'Elofson bör kastas.' Utkast till frisinnade valrörelsen 1906, no date. Protokoll verkställande utskottet, A 2:10, 1907–11. Frisinnade landsföreningen. RA. Note that the material has been filed in the wrong volume. Presumably it belongs to the A 2:9 volume and the 1902–07 proceedings.

49 29 July 1917, Appendix § 7. Norra Värmlands frisinnade valkretsförbund, Protokoll, 1, 1909–22. Folkrörelsernas arkiv för Värmland. Arkivcentrum Karlstad. Rylander was the third name on the liberal slate in this particular constituency, but he had been a candidate twice before, in the 1908 and 1911 elections.

50 For instance, 17 out of 27 members in Huggenäs, western Värmland (1918); 23 out of 26 members in Östra Stavnäs, also western Värmland (1919). Föreningsrapporter till valkretsförbundet Huggenäs, 1918, and Östra Stavnäs, 1919. Vol. 7, Inkomna handlingar från lokalavdelningar 1918–21. Västra Värmlands frisinnade valkretsförbund. Folkrörelsernas arkiv för Värmland, Arkivcentrum Karlstad.

51 Föreningsrapporter till valkretsförbundet 1920. Vol. 7, Inkomna handlingar från lokalavdelningar 1918–21. Västra Värmlands frisinnade valkretsförbund. Folkrörelsernas arkiv för Värmland, Arkivcentrum Karlstad.

52 Föreningsrapporter till valkretsförbundet 1922. Vol. 8, Inkomna handlingar från lokalavdelningar 1919–26. Östra Värmlands frisinnade valkretsförbund. Folkrörelsernas arkiv för Värmland, Arkivcentrum Karlstad.

53 Föreningsrapporter till valkretsförbundet 1920. Vol. 7, Inkomna handlingar från lokalavdelningar 1918–21. Västra Värmlands frisinnade valkretsförbund; Föreningsrapporter till valkretsförbundet 1922. Vol. 8, Inkomna handlingar från lokalavdelningar 1919–26. Östra Värmlands frisinnade valkretsförbund. Folkrörelsernas arkiv för Värmland, Arkivcentrum Karlstad.

54 Ibid.

55 Föreningsrapporter till valkretsförbundet 1920. Vol. 7, Inkomna handlingar från lokalavdelningar 1918–21. Västra Värmlands frisinnade valkretsförbund; Föreningsrapporter till valkretsförbundet 1922. Vol. 8, Inkomna handlingar från lokalavdelningar 1919–26. Östra Värmlands frisinnade valkretsförbund. Folkrörelsernas arkiv för Värmland, Arkivcentrum Karlstad.

56 607,487 voters participated in the elections (Esaiasson 1990, 113). According to Rönblom, membership figures in the party had risen to 42,675 by 1910 (Rönblom 1929, 200). The liberal result in the elections was 40.2 per cent, Table 1, chapter 1.

57 Appendix to Protokoll, 16 October 1911. Protokoll verkställande utskottet, A 2:10, 1907–11. Frisinnade landsföreningen. RA.

58 SOS. Allmänna val. Riksdagsmannavalen åren 1909–1911, 41; Schiller 1967, Table 19, 170. This proportion was impressive not least considering the fact that the Social Democratic Party had, by that time, lost a substantial number of its members because of conflicts between the party and the trade unions, economic depression, and a devastating defeat in the 1909 general strike (Schiller 1967, 169–70).

59 Protokoll, 8 September 1923, § 2. Styrelseprotokoll, A II: 2, 1917–24. Munkfors missionsförsamling (Ransäters Brödraförsamling). Folkrörelsernas arkiv för Värmland, Arkivcentrum Karlstad.

60 Göthberg had even been put forward as a candidate for the executive committee, but was not elected (Protokoll, 22 February 1902, § 5. Protokoll landsmötet, A 1:1, 1902–10. Frisinnade landsföreningen. RA).

61 Appendix Aa, Protokoll, 29–30 May 1910, § 23. Protokoll landsmötet, A 1:1, 1902–10. Frisinnade landsföreningen. RA. Nothing of detail is mentioned of Värmland in this report however.

62 Upprop till bildandet af en Valfond för 1911 års riksdagsmannaval i Värmlands östra valkrets, January 1911. Vol. 1, Korrespondens 1907–22. Värmlands frisinnade länskommitté. Folkrörelsernas arkiv för Värmland, Arkivcentrum Karlstad.

63 By 1911, though, opinions was still divided on the matter of modern technology. It is interesting to note how *Karlstads-tidningen*, in hindsight, expressed some concern regarding the new campaigning techniques, i.e. the use of motor cars, including the manner in which these had been made a topic of ridicule and political caricature. At least in terms of political organization this suggests a stress on tradition rather than innovation, curiously so for a political movement which hailed itself as a vanguard of radicalism and modernization. Even so, the mechanization of campaigning was, on occasion, also curtailed by lacking infrastructure, since Swedish geography simply did not allow the use of motor cars in some parts of the country, had they even been available. In the elections to the Provincial Councils the previous year, campaigners faced a particularly difficult task in those districts were public transportation was poorly developed, such as in northern Sweden or, for that matter, Värmland. One of the most extreme cases then had been editor Gustav Rosén, who, according to the annual report of the party had travelled 860 kilometres by rail across the province of Västerbotten – and another 774 kilometres by horse and bicycle (*Karlstads-tidningen*, 28 September 1911; Ombudsmannens årsberättelse, Frisinnande landsföreningen 1910, 2. Protokoll landsmötet, AI: 2, 1911–12, § 26. Frisinnade landsföreningen, RA). Usage of motorboats, cars, motorcycles, and horse carts was proposed in 'Några anvisningar rörande Folkpartiets organisationsarbete', no date, January, 1935, 4. Bilaga, Protokoll verkställande utskottet, A 2: 16, 1934–35. Frisinnade landsföreningen, RA.

64 *SOS. Allmänna val. Riksdagsmannavalen åren 1909–1911*, Table 3.

65 Protokoll, 19 March 1911, § 8. Protokoll verkställande utskottet, A 2:10, 1907–11. Frisinnade landsföreningen. RA.

66 Protokoll, 25 May, § 1 and 17 June, § 1, 1911. Vol. 1, Protokoll 1910–73. Folkpartiets lokalavdelning i Ransäter; Protokoll, 30 April 1911, § 5; Vol. 1, Protokoll 1907–35. Folkpartiets lokalavdelning i Filipstad. Folkrörelsernas arkiv för Värmland, Arkivcentrum Karlstad.

67 Protokoll, 19 February, § 8, 17 June, § 3, 1911. Vol. 1, Protokoll 1904–67. Folkpartiets lokalavdelning i Munkfors. Folkrörelsernas arkiv för Värmland, Arkivcentrum Karlstad.

68 Examples are given in *Karlstads-tidningen*, 30 August, 2 September, and 4 September 1911.

69 Protokoll, 30 August 1911, § 6. Protokoll, AI: 7, 1911–14. IOGT-logen 1810 Enigheten, Arvika. Folkrörelsernas arkiv för Värmland, Arkivcentrum Karlstad.

70 Protokoll, 5 February 1911, § 4. Vol. 4, protokoll, 1906–21. Membership figure, ibid., Årsberättelse för 1910 (66 members). Högeruds Blåbandsförening. Folkrörelsernas arkiv för Värmland, Arkivcentrum Karlstad.

71 *Karlstads-tidningen*, 18 September 1911.

72 *SOS. Allmänna val. Riksdagsmannavalen åren 1909–1911*, Table 3; Esaiasson 1990, 113.

73 *Karlstads-tidningen*, 30 September 1911.

74 Protokoll, 14 December 1910, § 1. Protokoll verkställande utskottet, A 2:10, 1907–11. Frisinnade landsföreningen. RA.

75 *SOS. Allmänna val. Riksdagsmannavalen åren 1915–1917*, Table 4; *Riksdagsmannavalen åren 1921*, Table 5; *Riksdagsmannavalen åren 1922–1924*, Table 4.

76 *SOS. Allmänna val. Riksdagsmannavalen åren 1922–1924*, Table 4.

77 Letter from Johan Bergman to Mauritz Hellberg, 31 December 1917. Mauritz Hellbergs brevsamling. Folkrörelsernas arkiv för Värmland. Arkivcentrum Karlstad.

78 Lindh and Björling were both deputies at the first, national party convention of the 'frisinnade' in 1924.

79 'Den brutala inträssepolitiken mällan klasspartierna är befryndad med krigspolitiken mällan nationerna.' *Karlstads-tidningen*, 12 August 1921.

80 Protokoll, 13 August 1920, § 2. Vol. 1, Protokoll 1914–23. Karlstads Frisinnade Valmansförening. Folkrörelsernas arkiv för Värmland, Arkivcentrum Karlstad.

81 Proceedings of 'Värmlands Ansgariiförening', the regional organization of the Mission Covenant Church, as quoted in: Protokoll 7 March 1921, §§ 3–4. Protokoll, AI: 4, 1898–1926. Väse Missionsförsamling. Folkrörelsernas arkiv för Värmland, Arkivcentrum Karlstad.

82 Protokoll, 21 March 1920, § 5. Protokoll AI: 2, 1904–20. Ölme Blåbandsförening. Folkrörelsernas arkiv för Värmland, Arkivcentrum Karlstad.

83 Protokoll, 13 August 1921, § 6. Protokoll AI: 4, 1920–25. IOGT-logen 504 Heijkensköld, Älvsbacka. Folkrörelsernas arkiv för Värmland, Arkivcentrum Karlstad.

84 Protokoll, 3 September 1921, § 7. Protokoll AI: 12, 1918–24. IOGT-logen 1544 Björneborg, Visnum. Folkrörelsernas arkiv för Värmland, Arkivcentrum Karlstad. On Svensson: *Svenska folkrörelser*, I, 1936, 1041.

85 Letter from Adolf Carlsson to Fritz Björn, 6 June 1921. Vol. 7, Inkomna handlingar från lokalavdelningar 1918–21. Västra Värmlands frisinnade valkretsförbund. Folkrörelsernas arkiv för Värmland, Arkivcentrum Karlstad.

86 Data based on the case of post-communist Poland (N = 725) show that the level of trust in other people increased from less than 30 per cent among the cases to over 40 per cent if we distinguish between active and inactive membership. For specific types of organizations, such as those concerned with art, music, or education, the respective figures are much higher: 50 and 90 per cent respectively. This feature is similar to the pattern we might expect to find in Western Europe, although the distinction between active and inactive membership has often been overlooked in previous research.

87 Protokoll, 7 August 1921, § 6. Vol. 2, Protokoll arbetsutskottet 1918–22, Värmlands frisinnade länskommitté. Folkrörelsernas arkiv för Värmland, Arkivcentrum Karlstad

88 *SOS. Allmänna val. Riksdagsmannavalen år 1921*, Table 5.

89 *Karlstads-tidningen*, 20 September 1921.

90 Protokoll, 27 March 1923, § 6, supplement L. Protokoll landsmötet AI: 6, 1923–24. Frisinnade landsföreningen, RA.

91 Protokoll vid möte för konstituerande av nytt liberalt parti, 7 October 1923, § 5. Protokoll, A:1, 1923–24. Sveriges liberala parti. RA.

92 Only in May 1924 do the first records for Värmland appear, pertaining to Karlstad and Töcksfors 'Uppgift å personer, vilka enligt undertecknads kännedom eller förmodan äro att – efter heställning från Huvudbyrån – påräkna som direkt anslutna medlemmar', Töcksfors, 3 May, and Karlstad, 5 May 1923. Medlemslistor 1923–30, Register, D: 7, 1923–30. Sveriges liberala parti, RA.

93 *SOS. Allmänna val. Riksdagsmannavalen åren 1922–1924*, Table 4.

94 *SOS. Allmänna val. Riksdagsmannavalen åren 1929–1932*, Table 3.

95 Protokoll, 16 January 1934, § 8. Protokoll verkställande utskottet A2: 16, 1934–35. Frisinnade landsföreningen, RA.

96 Några anvisningar rörande Folkpartiets organisationsarbete, supplement, January 1935. Protokoll verkställande utskottet A2: 16, 1934–35. Frisinnade landsföreningen, RA.

4. Schleswig-Holstein – 'Linksliberalismus' one step to the right

1 However, the opinion on free trade among the farmers is difficult to pinpoint exactly. For instance, Thompson's claim is derived solely from a newspaper article in the *Kieler Zeitung* (Thompson 2000, 294, n. 63).

2 *Beiträge zur historischen Statistik Schleswig-Holsteins*, 1967, Table V 1 a.

3 *Kieler Zeitung*, 11 January 1871.

4 Ibid.

5 Surveillance report, Kiel, 13 February 1871. 6820. Gendarmerie 1871–1874. Oberpräsidium und Provinzialrat der Provinz Schleswig-Holstein. LAS.

6 'Die Arbeiter sind der Fels, auf den die Kirche der Gegenwart gebaut werden soll.' Social Democratic appeal, eighth constituency, Altona-Stormarn, 1871 elections. 8342. Reichstagswahlen 1871/1874. Regierung zu Schleswig. LAS.

7 The preparations for at least one such celebration are documented in the official reports from the area (District commissioner Wiedt, Rendsburg, to Regierungspräsident Bitter, 8 April 1872. 12579. Öffentliche Versammlungen und Vereine Kr. Rendsburg, Bd I, 1869–1902. Regierung zu Schleswig. LAS).

8 Social Democratic appeal, eighth constituency, Altona-Stormarn, 1871 elections. 8342. Reichstagswahlen 1871/1874. Regierung zu Schleswig. LAS.

9 *Itzehoer Nachrichten*, 25 February 1871; Summary of the election results, 3 March 1871. Both in 8342. Reichstagswahlen 1871/1874. Regierung zu Schleswig. LAS. On Johannsen, see also chapter 2 in this book.

10 *Itzehoer Nachrichten*, 28 February, 1871; *Schleswiger Nachrichten*, 2 March 1871.

11 'Die Kandidatur des Herrn Grafen Baudissin halten wir nach wie vor für vollständig verloren.' *Schleswiger Nachrichten*, 26 February 1871.

12 Summary of the election results, 7 March 1871. 8342. Reichstagswahlen 1871/1874. Regierung zu Schleswig. LAS.

13 *Itzehoer Nachrichten*, 25 February 1871.

14 *Itzehoer Nachrichten*, 2 March 1871.

15 The topic was dealt with at a lecture arranged in Kiel, in February, by the local 'Harmonie' cultural society *Kieler Zeitung*, 11 February 1871.

16 *Kieler Zeitung*, 10 and 19 February 1871.

17 *Kieler Zeitung*, 14 February 1871.

18 *Sozialgeschichtliches Arbeitsbuch, II*, 1978, Table 9a, 172–176.

19 Summary of the election results, 7 March 1871. 8342. Reichstagswahlen 1871/1874. Regierung zu Schleswig. LAS.

20 *Nordslesvigs Good Templar*, 23 January 1898.

21 Ibid.

22 *Bidrag till Sveriges officiella statistik (BiSOS). Kungl. Maj:ts befallningshafvandes femårsberättelser*, Värmland 1901–05, Sammandrag för åren 1901–05, Table F.

23 A possible exception is the connection made between teetotalism and the 'social issue', a problem which was discussed in a series of articles published in the mid 1890s. See *Nordslesvigs Good Templar*, 28 July and 11 August 1895.

24 *Mitteilungen aus der Arbeit des Schleswig-Holsteinischen Provinzial-Vereins zur Bekämpfung des Missbrauchs geistiger Getränke*, 1900, 12–40.

25 *Protokoll der Generalversammlung des Schleswig-Holsteinischen Provinzialvereins zur Bekämpfung des Mißbrauchs geistiger Getränke*, 1885, 5; *Mitteilungen aus der Arbeit des Schleswig-Holsteinischen Provinzial-Vereins zur Bekämpfung des Missbrauchs geistiger Getränke*, 1900, 11.

26 *Schleswig-Holstein und der der Alkohol 1925 (zugleich Jahresbericht...)*, 18–20, vol. 20, II, Jahresversammlungen. Also, the organization seems to have been reformed in 1916, when a new 'Provinzialverband' was instituted, possibly as a result of internal conflicts dating back to, at least, 1914 (Letter from Professor Gonser to Pastor Dr. Stubbe, Berlin, 21 July 1914. Vol. 36, Guttemplerjubiläum in Flensburg 1914, IV. Aus der Tätigkeit des Provinzialverbandes); Letter from Professor Gonser to Pastor Dr. Stubbe, Berlin 18 May 1916. Vol. 1, Organisation des Provinzialverbandes 1914–18, I. Organisation. 408. Provzialverband gegen den Alkoholismus. LAS.

27 As in the fourth Tondern-Husum-Eiderstedt constituency in the 1907 elections, where the 'Bund der Landwirte' decided to vote for the national liberal candidate Feddersen (8344. Reichstagswahlen 1878/1911. LAS).

28 These were made public in the *Kieler Zeitung*, 6 October 1884.

29 See for instance *Kieler Zeitung*, 13 September 1884.

30 *Schleswiger Nachrichten*, 21 and 24 October 1884.

31 '...einer Partei, die ja eine wirtschaftliche Theorie zur Grundlage, zur *ungesunden*

Grundlage, ihrer Parteibildung gemacht hat, und alle, welche als *praktische* Männer dieser Theorie nicht huldigen, als "illiberal", als "reaktionär" verschreit. *Schleswiger Nachrichten*, 21 October 1884.

32 *Kieler Zeitung*, 27 October 1884.

33 'Steuer auf Steuer, Schutzzoll auf Schutzzoll ... dann handelt sie in aller Konsquenz mit den Konservativen und der Feindschaft mit uns.' Ibid.

34 'Alle übrigen zivilisierten Länder zeigen uns, daß in der möglichsten Befreiung des Individuums von beschränkenden Fesseln eine wesentliche Bedingung der Zivilisation liegt.' *Kieler Zeitung*, 13 September 1884.

35 *Kieler Zeitung*, 23 October 1884.

36 *Historischer Atlas Schleswig-Holstein 1867 bis 1954*, 2001, 38.

37 *Kieler Zeitung*, 18 and 19 September 1884.

38 Summary of the 1884 election results. 17370. Wahlen zum Reichstage 1884/1887. Regierung zu Schleswig. LAS.

39 Meeting, 17 November 1883. Vol 1, Protokoll des Friedrichsberger Bürgervereins, 1883–97, 3. Friedrichsberger Bürgerverein. Vereine und Verbände. LAS.

40 Meeting, 25 October 1884. Vol 1, Protokoll des Friedrichsberger Bürgervereins, 1883–97, 20–21. Friedrichsberger Bürgerverein. Vereine und Verbände. LAS.

41 *Schleswiger Nachrichten*, 25 October 1884.

42 Meeting, 25 October 1884. Vol 1, Protokoll des Friedrichsberger Bürgervereins, 1883–97, 20–21. Friedrichsberger Bürgerverein. Vereine und Verbände. LAS.

43 *Schleswiger Nachrichten*, 9 October 1884, *Kieler Zeitung*, 6 October 1884.

44 Election results in *Schleswiger Nachrichten*, 30 October 1884.

45 '...er sei keine Puppe, wohl ein Landmann, indeß doch ein Mann.' As quoted in *Schleswiger Nachrichten*, 9 October 1884.

46 *Kieler Zeitung*, 17 September 1884.

47 'Die Kieler Zeitung hält fest an den alten Idealen Schleswig-Holsteins: Freiheit, nationales Recht unde öffentliche Wohlfahrt.' *Kieler Zeitung*, 14 September 1884.

48 See for instance *Kieler Zeitung*, 12 September 1884.

49 *Kieler Zeitung*, 27 September 1884.

50 *Kieler Zeitung*, 10 October 1884.

51 For example Hotel Stadt Hamburg (liberals, Eckernförde), *Kieler Zeitung*, 18 September 1884; Gastwirt Henning Müller ('Antifortschrittliche Vereinigung', Süderbrarup), *Flensburger Nachrichten* 30 September 1884; Köbke'schen Gasthofe (liberals, Klein-Waabs), *Schleswiger Nachrichten*, 24 October 1884.

52 Advertisment in *Kieler Zeitung*, 6 October 1884.

53 'Dieses Programm hat nichts zu thun mit Kapitalismus und Opposition um jeden Preis, nichts mit einem abstrakten Manchesterthum, nichts mit einem absoluten Freihandelsystem.' *Kieler Zeitung*, 10 October 1884.

54 *Sozialgeschichtliches Arbeitsbuch*, II, 1978, Table 9a, 172–76.

55 *Beiträge zur historischen Statistik Schleswig-Holsteins*, 1967, Table VI 3.

56 Summary of the election results, 1898. In 8344. Reichstagswahlen 1878/1911.

Regierung zu Schleswig; 809. Reichstagswahl 1898. Oberpräsidium und Provinzialrat der Provinz Schleswig-Holstein, LAS.

57 Summary of the election results. 809. Reichstagswahl 1898. Oberpräsidium und Provinzialrat der Provinz Schleswig-Holstein, LAS; *Kieler Zeitung*, 8 June and 14 June 1898. Later, in the 1912 elections, Reventlow did run as an official candidate for the 'Bund' in the constituency (Landrat in Flensburg to Oberpräsidium, 1 November 1911. 6759. Reichstagswahl 1912. Oberpräsidium und Provinzialrat der Provinz Schleswig-Holstein, LAS).

58 *Kieler Zeitung*, 8 June 1898.

59 '… provinsielle Antisemitismus', *Kieler Zeitung*, 13 June 1898.

60 *Kieler Zeitung*, 12 June 1898.

61 *Kieler Zeitung*, 8 June 1898.

62 *Sozialgeschichtliches Arbeitsbuch, II*, 1978, Table 9 a, 175; Ibs 2006, 153.

63 *Segeberger Kreis- und Tageblatt*, 12 January 1912.

64 'Zwischen dem nördlichen und südlichen Theile des zweiten Wahlkreises hat schon seit Jahren ein Gegensatz bestanden in sofern als im nördlichen Theil die Parteigegensätze innerhalb der deutschen Wählerschaft gar keine oder verschwindend geringe Bedeutung hatten, während im Süden dieselben Parteifragen, wie überall im Reich, die deutsche Wählerschaft spalten. Dies liegt daran, daß im Norden die nationale Frage vorwiegend die Aufmerksamkeit und das Interesse in Anspruch nimmt, während im südlichen Theil des Wahlkreises nationale Gegensätze nicht vorhanden aber doch bedeutend zurückgetreten sind, dagegen die wirtschaftspolitischen Gegensätze um so mehr Bedeutung haben.' *Kieler Zeitung*, 10 June 1898.

65 *Flensburger Nachrichten*, 10 January 1912.

66 *Kieler Zeitung*, 7 January 1907.

67 *Itzehoer Nachrichten*, 6 January 1907.

68 '…in ernstem Mühen neue Werte der Kultur zu schaffen versucht, statt in unfruchtbaren Neinsagen sich um die besten Früchte seiner Arbeit zu bringen.' *Itzehoer Nachrichten*, 30 December 1906.

69 'Einen Freisinnigen wähle ich nicht, dann bleibe ich lieber zu Hause.' *Kieler Zeitung*, 18 January 1912.

70 'Ein solcher Landmann erfüllt aber nicht seine Pflicht gegen daß Vaterland', ibid.

71 Ibid.

72 Landrat in Flensburg to Oberpräsidium, 1 November 1911. 6759. Reichstagswahl 1912. Oberpräsidium und Provinzialrat der Provinz Schleswig-Holstein, LAS.

73 '…ein ungewöhnlich frivoler Strike'. District commissioner in Rendsburg to Regierungspräsidentur, 15 June 1912. 12580. Öffentliche Versammlungen und Vereine Kr. Rendsburg, Bd II, 1903–1922. Regierung zu Schleswig. LAS.

74 *Kieler Zeitung*, 6 January 1919.

75 The district commissioner's reports reveal the extent of Nazi campaigning during the last years of the Weimar Republic. For instance, in March 1931 alone, five Nazi rallies were held in Eiderstedt, as well as five by the communists and

'Rote Gewerksschafts-Opposition'. A Nazi meeting at Tönning, on 20 March, succeeded in gathering 500 listeners (Nachweisung der in der Zeit vom 1.III. bis 31.III. 1931 in Kreise Eiderstedt stattgefundenen Versammlungen radikaler Organisationen, Tönning, 1 April, 1931. 22996. Versammlungstätigkeit der rechts- und linksradikalen Organisationen, Bd. II, 1931–32. LAS). A thorough analysis of this problem is presented in Frank Omland's article, 2006.

76 The constituency was represented by a social democratic deputy following the 1893, 1903, 1907 and 1912 elections.

77 *Kieler Zeitung*, 5 January 1919.

5. Swedish and German political association compared

1 *Kieler Zeitung*, 13 June 1898.

2 *Karlstads-tidningen*, 19 August 1893. In fact, some doubts regarding proportionalism were expressed by the members of the executive committee of the Liberal Party as late as to the introduction of the new method (Protokoll 22 May 1909, § 3 incl. Supplement. Protokoll verkställande utskottet, 1907–10, A 2:10. Frisinnade landsföreningen. RA).

Bibliography

Primary sources
Sweden

Riksarkivet, Stockholm (RA)
Frisinnade landsföreningen
    Protokoll verkställande utskottet
    Protokoll landsmötet
    Cirkulär

Sveriges liberala parti
    Protokoll
    Register

Arkivcentrum, Karlstad
Folkrörelsernas arkiv för Värmland
    Värmlands frisinnade länskommitté
        Protokoll arbetsutskottet
        Ombudsmannens handlingar
        Korrespondens

    Värmlands frisinnade valkretsförbund
        Protokoll

    Norra Värmlands frisinnade valkretsförbund
        Protokoll

    Östra Värmlands frisinnade valkretsförbund
        Inkomna handlingar från lokalavdelningar
        Korrespondens

    Västra Värmlands frisinnade valkretsförbund
        Inkomna handlingar från lokalavdelningar

    Folkpartiets lokalavdelning i Munkfors
        Protokoll

229

Karlstads Frisinnade Valmansförening
Protokoll

Frisinnade diskussionsklubben, Karlstad
Protokoll

Folkpartiets lokalavdelning i Filipstad
Protokoll

Folkpartiets lokalavdelning i Ransäter
Protokoll

Värmlands rösträttsförening
Årsberättelser

Föreningen för kvinnans politiska rösträtt, Värmlands länsförbund
Protokoll

Föreningen för kvinnans politiska rösträtt, Karlstad
Protokoll

Karlstads föreläsningsanstalt
Verksamhets- och kassaberättelser

Munkfors Missionsförsamling (Ransäters Brödraförsamling)
Styrelseprotokoll

Väse Missionsförsamling
Protokoll

IOGT-logen 1544 Björneborg, Visnum.
Protokoll

IOGT-logen 504 Heijkensköld, Älvsbacka
Protokoll

IOGT-logen 1810 Enigheten, Arvika
Protokoll

Högeruds Blåbandsförening
Protokoll

Ransäters Blåbandsförening
Protokoll

Ölme Blåbandsförening
  Protokoll

Mauritz Hellbergs brevsamling

Germany
Landesarchiv Schleswig-Holstein (LAS)
Oberpräsidium und Provinzialrat der Provinz Schleswig-Holstein
  809. Reichstagswahl 1898
  6759. Reichstagswahl 1912
  6820. Gendarmerie 1871–1874
Regierung zu Schleswig
  8342. Reichstagswahlen 1871/1874
  8344. Reichstagswahlen 1878/1911
  17370. Wahlen zum Reichstage 1884/1887
  8523. Öffentliche Stimmung in der Provinz Schleswig-Holstein, 1872–1873
  12579. Öffentliche Versammlungen und Vereine Kr. Rendsburg, Bd I,
    1869–1902
  12580. Öffentliche Versammlungen und Vereine Kr. Rendsburg, Bd II,
    1903–1922
  22996. Versammlungstätigkeit der rechts- und linksradikalen Organisa-
    tionen, Bd. II, 1931–32
Vereine und Verbände
  31. Friedrichsberger Bürgerverein
    Protokoll
  408. Provinzialverband gegen den Alkoholismus
    Organisation
      Organisation des Provinzialverbandes 1914–18
    Jahresversammlungen
      Aus der Tätigkeit des Provinzialverbandes
      Guttemplerjubiläum in Flensburg 1914

Newspapers
Sweden

Filipstads Stads- och Bergslags Tidning
Karlstads-tidningen
Nya Wermlands-Posten
Nya Wermlands-Tidningen

Germany

Flensburger Nachrichten
Itzehoer Nachrichten
Kieler Zeitung
Nordslesvigs Good Templar
Schleswiger Nachrichten
Segeberger Kreis- und Tageblatt

Statistical works and official publications
Sweden

Bidrag till Sveriges officiella statistik (BiSOS). *Befolkningsstatistik 1880.*
Bidrag till Sveriges officiella statistic (BiSOS). Kungl. Maj:ts befallningshafvandes femårsberättelser 1901–1905.
Bidrag till Sveriges officiella statistik (BiSOS). *Befolkningsstatistik 1910.*
Motioner väckta inom andra kammaren, 1–190. Bihang till riksdagens protokoll 1912.
Sveriges officiella statistik (SOS). *Allmänna val. Riksdagsmannavalen åren 1909–1911.*
Sveriges officiella statistik (SOS). *Allmänna val. Riksdagsmannavalen åren 1915–1917.*
Sveriges officiella statistik (SOS). *Allmänna val. Riksdagsmannavalen år 1921.*
Sveriges officiella statistik (SOS). *Allmänna val. Riksdagsmannavalen åren 1922–1924.*
Statistisk årsbok för Sverige 1920.
Handlingar rörande prestmötet i Carlstad den 24, 25 och 26 augusti 1869, I. Karlstad: C. Forssells Boktryckeri, 1870.
Handlingar rörande prestmötet i Karlstad den 22, 23 och 24 augusti 1899, I. Karlstad: Nya Wermlands-Tidningens AB, 1899.
Handlingar rörande prästmötet i Karlstad den 22, 23 och 24 augusti 1911, I. Karlstad: Nya Wermlands-Tidningens AB, 1911.

Germany

Amtsblatt der Königlichen Regierung zu Schleswig.
Protokoll der Generalversammlung des Schleswig-Holsteinischen Provinzialvereins zur Bekämpfung des Mißbrauchs geistiger Getränke. Kiel: Schmidt & Klannig, 1885.
Mitteilungen aus der Arbeit des Schleswig-Holsteinischen Provinzial-Vereins zur Bekämpfung des Missbrauchs geistiger Getränke. Vierzehnter Jahresbericht. Glücksburg: J. J. Augustin, 1900.
Beiträge zur historischen Statistik Schleswig-Holsteins. Kiel: Statistischen Landesamt Schleswig-Holstein, 1967.
Sozialgeschichtliches Arbeitsbuch, II. Materialen zur Statistik des Kaiserreichs 1870–1914. Ed. G. Horst, J. Kocka & G. Ritter, 2nd edn. Munich: Verlag C. H. Beck, 1978.
Sozialgeschichtliches Arbeitsbuch, III. Materialen zur Statistik des Deutschen Reiches

1914–1945. Ed. D. Petzina, W. Abelshauser & A. Faust. Munich: Verlag C. H. Beck, 1978.

Literature

Abelius, Hans. *Det självpåtagna uppdraget. En undersökning av medborgarprojektet kring tidningen Östgötha Correspondenten 1840–1870.* Gothenburg: Avhandlingar från Historiska institutionen i Göteborg 50, 2007.

Åberg, Ingrid. *Förening och politik. Folkrörelsernas politiska aktivitet i Gävle under 1880-talet.* Uppsala: Studia historica Upsaliensia 69, 1975.

Åberg, Martin. 'Kompromiss och medborgaransvar. Borgerligheten i svensk kommunalpolitik 1860–1945. En fallstudie av Göteborg.' *Historisk tidskrift,* 4 (1997): 692–723.

Åberg, Martin. 'Sverige och liberalismerna – en jämförande utblick.' In *Parti eller rörelse? Perspektiv på liberala organisationsstrategier 1880–1940,* T. Nilson & M. Åberg (eds.), 149–176. Lund: Sekel bokförlag, 2010.

Åberg, Martin & Sandberg, Mikael. *Social Capital and Democratisation. Roots of Trust in Post-Communist Poland and Ukraine.* Aldershot: Ashgate, 2003.

Aldrich, John H. *Why Parties? The Origin and Transformation of Political Parties in America.* Chicago: University of Chicago Press, 1995.

Anderson, Benedict. *Imagined Communities. Reflections on the Origin and Spread of Nationalism.* London: Verso, 1991 [1983].

Andrén, Mats. *Mellan deltagande och uteslutning. Det lokala medborgarskapets dilemma.* Hedemora: Gidlunds förlag, 2005.

Andrén, Mats. *Den europeiska blicken och det lokala självstyrets värden.* Hedemora: Gidlunds förlag, 2007.

Applegate, Celia. *A Nation of Provincials. The German Idea of Heimat.* Berkeley: University of California Press, 1990.

Back, Pär-Erik. *Sammanslutningarnas roll i politiken 1870–1910.* Lund: Studentlitteratur, 1967.

Baier, Roland. *Der deutsche Osten als soziale Frage. Eine Studie zur preussischen und deutsche Siedlungs- und Polenpolitik in den Ostprovinzen während des Kaiserreichs und der Weimarer Republik.* Cologne: Böhlau Verlag, 1980.

Bengtsson, Åsa. 'Nykta, frisinnade kvinnor.' In *Parti eller rörelse? Perspektiv på liberala organisationsstrategier 1880–1940,* T. Nilson & M. Åberg (eds.), 17–49. Lund: Sekel bokförlag, 2010.

Berggren, Henrik & Trägårdh, Lars. *Är svensken människa? Gemenskap och oberoende i det moderna Sverige.* Stockholm: Norstedts, 2006.

Berman, Sheri. 'How Democracies Emerge. Lessons from Europe.' *Journal of Democracy,* 18/1 (2007): 28–41.

Bernstein, George L. *Liberalism and Liberal Politics in Edwardian England.* Boston: Allen & Unwin, 1986.

Beyer, Hans. 'Das Ende der "Landespartei" und die "Itzehoer Nachrichten".' *Zeitschrift der Gesellschaft für Schleswig-Holsteinische Geschichte,* 93 (1968): 147–59.

Biagini, Eugenio F. *Liberty, Retrenchment and Reform. Popular Liberalism in the Age of Gladstone, 1860–1880*. Cambridge: Cambridge University Press, 2004 [1992].

Bjørn, Claus. *1848. Borgerkrig og revolution*. Copenhagen: Gyldendal, 1998.

Blackbourn, David. *Class, Religion, and Local Politics in Wilhelmine Germany: the Centre Party in Württemberg before 1914*. New Haven: Yale University Press, 1980.

Breuilly, John. *Labour and Liberalism in Nineteenth-Century Europe. Essays in Comparative History*. Manchester: Manchester University Press, 1994.

Byström, Runo. *Lysviks Missionsförsamling genom hundra år*. Kristinehamn: Lysviks Missionsförsamling, 1963.

Båtefalk, Lars. *Staten, samhället och superiet. Samhällsorganisatoriska principer och organisatorisk praktik kring dryckenskapsproblemet och nykterhetssträvandena i stat, borgerlig offentlighet och associationsväsende c:a 1770–1900*. Uppsala: Studia Historica Upsaliensia 195, 2000.

Carlsson, Sten. *Lantmannapolitiken och industrialismen. Partigrupperingar och opinionsförskjutningar i svensk politik 1890–1902*. Stockholm: Lantbruksförbundets Tidskriftsaktiebolag, 1953.

Carrothers, Thomas. 'How Democracies Emerge. The "Sequencing" Fallacy.' *Journal of Democracy*, 18/1 (2007): 12–27.

Christensen, Jan. *Bönder och herrar. Bondeståndet i 1840-talets liberala representationsdebatt. Exemplen Gustaf Hierta och J P Theorell*. Gothenburg: Avhandlingar från Historiska institutionen i Göteborg 16, 1997.

Christensen, Jan. *Liberalernas stad. Fattigvård och kulturdonationer i artonhundratalets Göteborg*. Gothenburg: Daidalos, 2009.

Claesson, Urban. 'Grundtvig, bonderörelse och folkkyrka.' In *Grundtvig – nyckeln till det danska?*, H. Sanders & O. Vind (eds.), 60–90. Stockholm: Centrum för Danmarksstudier vid Lunds universitet/Makadam förlag, 2003.

Clark, Christopher. *Iron Kingdom. The Rise and Fall of Prussia, 1600–1947*. Cambridge: Belknap Press, 2006.

Daalder, Hans. 'The Rise of Parties in Western Democracies.' In *Political Parties and Democracy*, L. Diamond & R. Gunther (eds.), 40–51. Baltimore: Johns Hopkins University Press, 2001.

Denk, Thomas. *Komparativ metod – förståelse genom jämförelse*. Lund: Studentlitteratur, 2002.

Diederich, Nils. 'Germany.' In *International Guide to Electoral Statistics, I. National Elections in Western Europe*, S. Rokkan & J. Meyriat (eds.), 128–62. The Hague/Paris: Mouton, 1969.

Dolšak, Nives & Ostrom, Elinor. 'The Challenges of the Commons.' In *The Commons in the New Millennium*, N. Dolšak & E. Ostrom (eds.), 3–34. Cambridge, Mass.: MIT Press, 2003.

Duverger, Maurice. *Political Parties. Their Organization and Activity in the Modern World*, 3rd edn. London: Methuen, 1967 [1954].

Eckstein, Harry. 'Lessons for the "Third Wave" from the First: An Essay on Democratization.' Paper presented at the Annual Meeting of the American Political Science Association, New York, 1–4 September, 1994.

Edebalk, Per Gunnar. 'Bismarck och de första socialförsäkringarna.' *Socialveten-skaplig tidskrift*, 4 (2003): 352–65.

Edquist, Samuel. *Nyktra svenskar. Godtemplarrörelsen och den nationella identiteten 1879–1918*. Uppsala: Studia historica Upsaliensia 200, 2001.

Eisfeld, Gerhard. *Die Entstehung der liberalen Parteien in Deutschland 1858–70. Studie zu den Organisationen und Programmen der Liberalen und Demokraten*. Hannover: Verlag für Literatur und Zeitgeschehen, 1969.

Ekberg, Joakim. 'Värmländska förstakammarval. Konflikter och offentlighet i det plutokratiska landstinget 1866–1894.' D-uppsats i Historia, Avdelningen för politiska och historiska studier. Karlstad: Karlstads universitet, 2006.

Eley, Geoff. *Reshaping the German Right. Radical Nationalism and Political Change after Bismarck*. New Haven: Yale University Press, 1980.

Eriksson, Fredrik. 'Bondeförbundet och liberalism 1914–1935.' In *Parti eller rörelse? Perspektiv på liberala organisationsstrategier 1880–1940*, T. Nilson & M. Åberg (eds.), 91–121. Lund: Sekel bokförlag, 2010.

Esaiasson, Peter. *Svenska valkampanjer 1866–1988*. Stockholm: Allmänna Förlaget, 1990.

Esping-Andersen, Gøsta. *The Three Worlds of Welfare Capitalism*. Cambridge: Polity Press, 1990.

Festschrift anlässlich des hundertjährigen Bestehens des Flensburger Arbeiter-Bauvereins eG 1878–1978. Flensburg, 1978.

Forsell, Anders. 'Emancipation och politik – en studie av tre värmländska arbetare-föreningar.' D-uppsats i Historia, Institutionen för samhällsvetenskap. Karlstad: Karlstads universitet, 2005.

Fraenkel, Hans. 'Deutsche und amerikanische Demokratie.' In *Deutscher Staat und deutsche Parteien. Beiträge zur deutschen Partei- und Ideengeschichte*, P. Wentzcke (ed.), 294–307. Berlin: R. Oldenbourg, 1922.

Frostlund, Jörgen. *Ett initiativ i tiden. Bergselementarskolan i Filipstad 1830–1860*. Karlstad: Institutionen för utbildningsvetenskap, Pedagogiskt arbete, 2005.

Furuskog, Jalmar. *De värmländska järnbruken. Kulturgeografiska studier över den värmländska järnhanteringen under dess olika utvecklingsskeden*. Filipstad: AB Bronellska Bokhandelns Tryckeri, 1924.

Gadd, Carl-Johan. *Det svenska jordbrukets historia*, iii: *Den agrara revolutionen 1700–1870*. Stockholm: Natur och Kultur/LTs förlag, 2000.

Gall, Lothar. 'Liberalismus und "bürgerliche Gesellschaft": Zur Charakter und Entwicklung der liberalen Bewegung in Deutschland.' *Historische Zeitschrift*, 220 (1975): 324–56.

Galston, William A. 'Pluralism and Social Unity.' In *John Rawls. Critical Assessments of Leading Political Philosophers, IV. "Political Liberalism" and "The Law of Peoples"*, Kukathas, Chandran (ed.), 113–128. London: Routledge, 2003 [1989].

Geijer, Erik Gustaf. 'Det europeiska samhällets begynnelser.' [Tal vid installationen av professorerna Olof Wingqvist och C. O. Delldén]. Uppsala: Leffler och Sebell, 1844.

Geijer, Erik Gustaf. *Vår tids inre samhällsförhållanden i synnerhet med afseende på fäderneslandet. Tre föreläsningar ur den hösten 1844 i Upsala föredragna historiska kurs.* Stockholm: P. A. Norstedt & Söner, 1845.

Gellert, Christian Fürchtegott. *Moraliska Föreläsningar, 1–2.* Stockholm, 1777 [1770].

Gidlund, Gullan. 'Folkrörelsepartiet och den politiska styrelsen. SAP:s organisationsutveckling.' In *Socialdemokratins samhälle. SAP och Sverige under 100 år,* K. Misgeld, K. Molin & K. Åmark (eds.), 282–310. Stockholm: Tiden, 1989.

Goodman, Paul. 'The First American Party System.' In *The American Party Systems. Stages of Political Development,* W. N. Chambers & W. D. Burnham (eds.), 56-89. London: Oxford University Press, 1967.

Grant, Oliver. *Migration and Inequality in Germany 1870–1913.* Oxford: Clarendon Press, 2005.

Gross, Michael B. *The War against Catholicism. Liberalism and the Anti-Catholic Imagination in Nineteenth-Century Germany.* Ann Arbor: University of Michigan Press, 2004.

Gunther, Richard & Diamond, Larry. 'Types and Functions of Parties.' In *Political Parties and Democracy,* L. Diamond & R. Gunther (eds.), 3–39. Baltimore: Johns Hopkins University Press, 2001.

Hahn-Bruckart, Thomas. 'Die Anfänge des Methodismus in Hamburg und Schleswig-Holstein.' *Schriften des Vereins für Scheswig-Holsteinische Kirchengeschichte,* 52 (2006): 221–249.

Hänel, Albert. *Das Kaiserthum. Rede zum Antritte des Rektorates der Christian-Albrechts-Universität in Kiel am 5. März 1892.* Kiel: Universitäts-Buchhandlung, 1892.

Hänel, Albert. *Der 18te Januar 1871. Rede bei der Erinnerungsfeier der Christian-Albrechts-Universität in Kiel am 18. Januar 1896.* Kiel: Universitäts-Buchhandlung, 1896.

Hansen, Peter Christian. *Eine Lebenswanderung. Vom Leben und Schaffen eines achtzigjährigen Schleswig-Holsteiners.* Flensburg: Schriften der Gesellschaft für Flensburger Stadtgeschichte 31, 1982 [1928, manuscript].

Hartmann, Michael et al. 'Der "Makel des Revolutionismus" und ein End emit schrecken (1815–1849).' In *Geschichte der Stadt Freiburg im Breisgau, III. Von der badischen Herrschaft bis zur Gegenwart,* Haumann, H. & Schadek, H. (eds.), 61–129. 2nd edn., Stuttgart: Theiss Verlag, 2001 [1992].

Haupt, Heinz-Gerhard. 'Comparative History – A Contested Method.' *Historisk tidskrift,* 127/4 (2007): 697–716.

Heberle, Rudolf. 'The Ecology of Political Parties: A Study of Elections in Rural Communities in Schleswig-Holstein, 1918–1932.' *American Sociological Review,* 9/5 (1944): 401–414.

Hedin, Marika. *Ett liberalt dilemma. Ernst Beckman, Emilia Broomé, G H von Kock och den sociala frågan 1880–1930.* Stockholm/Stehag: Brutus Östlings Bokförlag Symposion, 2002.

Hejselbjerg Paulsen, H. 'Pietisme og rationalisme.' In *Flensborgs bys historie, 2. Tiden efter 1720,* 36–44. Copenhagen: Hagerups forlag, 1955.

Heldt, Uwe. *125 Jahre Turn- und Sportbund Flensburg, I. Ein Beitrag zur Entwicklung von Turnen und Sport in Flensburg.* Flensburg: Kleine Reihe der Gesellschaft für Flensburger Stadtgeschichte 21:1, 1991.

Historischer Atlas Schleswig-Holstein 1867 bis 1954, I.E. Mommsen, E. Dege & U. Lange (eds.). Neumünster: Wachholtz Verlag, 2001.

Hume, David. *Essays. Moral, Political and Literary.* London: Grant Richards, 1904 [1741–42].

Hume, David. *A Treatise of Human Nature,* (ed. L. A. Selby-Bigge). Oxford: Clarendon Press, 1960 [1739–40].

Hume, David. *The Philosophical Works, vol. III,* (ed. T. Hill Green & T. Hodge Grose). Scientia Verlag: Aalen, 1964 [1882].

Hurd, Madeleine. *Public Spheres, Public Mores, and Democracy. Hamburg and Stockholm, 1870–1914.* Ann Arbor: University of Michigan Press, 2000.

Ibs, Jürgen Hartwig. *Politische Parteien und Selbstverwaltung in der Provinz Schleswig-Holstein bis zum Ersten Weltkrieg.* Neumünster: Wachholtz Verlag, 2006.

Inglehart, Ronald. *Modernization and Postmodernization: Cultural, Economic, and Political Change in 43 Societies.* Princeton: Princeton University Press, 1997.

Jakubowski-Tiessen, Manfred & Lehmann, Hartmut. 'Der Pietismus.' In *Orthodoxie und Pietismus. Schleswig-Holsteinische Kirchengeschichte, 4,* 269–384. Neumünster: Karl Wachholtz Verlag, 1984.

Jansson, Esbjörn. 'Sweden.' In *International Guide to Electoral Statistics, I. National Elections in Western Europe,* S. Rokkan & J. Meyriat (eds.), 281–308. The Hague/Paris: Mouton, 1969.

Jansson, Torkel. *Adertonhundratalets associationer. Forskning och problem kring ett språngfullt tomrum eller sammanslutningsprinciper och föreningsformer mellan två samhällsformationer c:a 1800–1870.* Uppsala: Almqvist & Wiksell International, 1985.

Jefferies, Matthew. 'Back to the Future? The "Heimatschutz" Movement in Wilhelmine Germany.' *History, 77/251* (1992): 411–20.

Johansson, Gösta. *Liberal splittring. Skilsmässa – och återförening 1917–1934.* Gothenburg, 1980.

Kahan, Alan S. *Aristocratic Liberalism. The Social and Political Thought of Jacob Burckhardt, John Stuart Mill, and Alexis de Tocqueville.* New York: Oxford University Press, 1992.

Kahan, Alan S. *Liberalism in Nineteenth-Century Europe. The Political Culture of Limited Suffrage.* Houndmills: Palgrave Macmillan, 2003.

Keane, John. *Democracy and Civil Society. On the Predicaments of European Socialism, the Prospects for Democracy, and the Problem of Controlling Social and Political Power.* London: Verso, 1988.

Kettler, David. 'History and Theory in Ferguson's Essay On the History of Civil Society: A Reconsideration.' *Political Theory, 5* (1977): 437–60.

Kiehl, Hans-Georg H. *Albert Hänel und der Linksliberalismus im Reichstagswahlkreis Kiel-Rendsburg-Plön 1867 bis 1884. Ein Beitrag zur politischen Parteiengeschichte Schleswig-Holsteins im 19. Jahrhundert.* Kiel: Christian-Albrechts-Universität zu Kiel, 1966.

Kihlberg, Leif. *Karl Staaff, I. Verdandist, advokat, politiker 1860–1905.* Stockholm: Albert Bonniers förlag, 1962.

Kocka, Jürgen. 'Commentary on Keane: "Eleven Theses on Markets and Civil Society".' *Journal of Civil Society,* 1 (2005): 35–37.

Kopitzsch, Franklin. 'Schleswig-Holstein im Gesamtstaat 1721–1830: Absolutismus, Aufklärung und Reform.' In *Geschichte Schleswig-Holsteins Von den Anfängen bis zur Gegenwart,* U. Lange (ed.), 281–332, 2nd edn. Neumünster: Wachholtz Verlag, 2003.

Koselleck, Reinhard. *Zeitschichten. Studien zur Historik.* Frankfurt am Main: Suhrkamp, 2000.

Kretzschmer, Knud. 'Dansk og tysk fra 1864 til den første verdenskrig.' In *Flensborgs bys historie, 2. Tiden efter 1720,* 253–299. Copenhagen: Hagerups forlag, 1955.

Kulczycki, John J. *School Strikes in Prussian Poland, 1901–1907: The Struggle over Bilingual Education.* Boulder: East European Monographs 82, 1981.

Kurlander, Eric. 'The Rise of Völkisch Nationalism and the Decline of German Liberalism: A Comparison of Schleswig-Holstein and Silesian Political Cultures 1912–1924.' *European Review of History,* 9/1 (2002a): 23–36.

Kurlander, Eric. 'Nationalism, Ethnic Preoccupation, and the Decline of German Liberalism: A Silesian Case Study, 1898–1933.' *The Historian,* 65/1 (2002b): 95–121.

Kurlander, Eric. 'Völkisch-Nationalism and Universalism on the Margins of the Reich: A Comparison of Majority and Minority Liberalism in Germany, 1898–1933.' In *Germany From the Margins,* M. Roseman, N. Gregor & N. Roemer (eds.), 84–103. Bloomington: Indiana University Press, 2006a.

Kurlander, Eric. *The Price of Exclusion. Ethnicity, National Identity, and the Decline of German Liberalism.* Oxford: Berghahn Books, 2006b.

Kvick, Gudrun. 'Folkrörelserna och andrakammarvalet 1902.' *Värmland förr och nu,* 75 (1977): 216–20.

Kåpe, Leif. 'Regioner i Värmland En studie av de värmländska kommunernas befolkningsutveckling och näringslivsstruktur.' D-uppsats i Ekonomisk historia, Institutionen för samhällsvetenskap. Karlstad: Karlstads universitet, 2005.

Langewiesche, Dieter. *Liberalism in Germany,* Houndmills: Macmillan, 2000 [1988].

Larsson, Tage. 'Ett märkligt riksdagsmannaval i Värmland.' *Värmland förr och nu,* 75 (1977): 212–15.

Lijphart, Arend. 'Comparative Politics and the Comparative Method.' *American Political Science Review,* 65 (1971): 682–93.

Lilljebjörn, Henrik. *Minnen från förra hälften af 1800-talet.* Stockholm: Wilhelm Billes Bokförlags AB, 1912 [1867–1874].

Lindström, Ulf & Wörlund, Ingemar. 'The Swedish Liberal Party: The Politics of Unholy Alliances.' In *Liberal Parties in Western Europe,* E. J. Kirchner (ed.), 252–77. Cambridge: Cambridge University Press, 1988.

Linz, Juan & Stepan, Alfred. *Problems of Democratic Transitions and Consolidation. Southern Europe, South America, and Post-Communist Europe.* Baltimore: Johns Hopkins University Press, 1996.

Lipset, Seymour Martin & Rokkan, Stein. 'Cleavage Structures, Party Systems and Voter Alignments.' In *Party Systems and Voter Alignments: Cross National Perspectives*, S. M. Lipset & S. Rokkan (eds.), 1–67. New York: Free Press, 1967.

Lorenzen-Schmidt, Klaus-Joachim. 'Auf dem Weg in die moderne Klassengesellschaft – Soziale Entwicklung 1830–1918.' In *Geschichte Schleswig-Holsteins Von den Anfängen bis zur Gegenwart*, U. Lange (ed.), 400–425, 2nd edn. Neumünster: Wachholtz Verlag, 2003.

Lundberg, Victor. *Folket, yxan och orättvisans rot. Betydelsebildning kring demokrati i den svenska rösträttsrörelsens diskursgemenskap, 1887–1902.* Umeå: Bokförlaget h:ström – Text & Kultur, 2007.

Lundkvist, Sven. *Folkrörelserna i det svenska samhället 1850–1920.* Uppsala: Studia historica Upsaliensia 85, 1977.

Mannström, Oscar. *Bilder och blad ur svenska nykterhetsrörelsens historia.* Stockholm: P. A. Norstedt & söners förlag, 1912.

Martling, Carl Henrik. *Nattvardskrisen i Karlstads stift under 1800-talets senare hälft.* Lund: Berlingska boktryckeriet, 1958.

Michels, Robert. *Organisationer och demokrati. En sociologisk studie av de oligarkiska tendenserna i vår tids demokrati.* Stockholm: Ratio, (1983 [1911]).

Moberg, Ove. *Karlstads historia, IV. Karlstad under fyra sekler. Sammanfattning av delarna I–III. Utvecklingen efter 1950.* Karlstad: Nermans Trycksaker, 1983.

Mommsen, Wolfgang J. *Imperial Germany 1867–1918. Politics, Culture, and Society in an Authoritarian State.* London: Arnold, 1995.

Moore, Barrington Jr. *Social Origins of Dictatorship and Democracy: Lord and Peasant in the Making of the Modern World.* London: Allen Lane, 1967.

Nicolai-Kolb, Britta. 'Itzehoe unter königlich-preußischer Regierung 1867–1918.' In *Itzehoe. Geschichte einer Stadt in Schleswig-Holstein, 2. Von 1814 bis zur Gegenwart*, 113–93. Itzehoe, 1991.

Nilson, Tomas. *Framgång och vår Herre. Industriellt företagande, social struktur och karriärmönster i två svenska städer: Borås och Örebro 1890–1920.* Gothenburg: Avhandlingar från historiska institutionen i Göteborg 41, 2004.

Nilson, Tomas. 'Liberalism och riksdagsval: en regional studie av Värmlands och Örebro län 1911–1932.' In *Parti eller rörelse? Perspektiv på liberala organisationsstrategier 1880–1940*, T. Nilson & M. Åberg (eds.), 123–47. Lund: Sekel bokförlag, 2010.

Nilsson, Göran B. 'Den samhällsbevarande representationsreformen.' *Scandia*, 35 (1969): 198–271.

Nilsson, Torbjörn. *Mellan arv och utopi. Moderata vägval under hundra år, 1904–2004.* Stockholm: Santérus Förlag, 2004.

Nilsson, Yngve. *Bygd och näringsliv i norra Värmland. En kulturgeografisk studie.* Lund: Carl Bloms Boktryckeri AB, 1950.

Norrlid, Ingemar. 'Kommunen som bolag? En studie i liberal rösträttspolitik före första världskriget.' *Scandia*, 36/1 (1970): 46–120.

Offermann, Toni. 'Preußischer Liberalismus zwischen Revolution und Reichsgründung im regionalen Vergleich. Berliner und Kölner Fortschrittsliberalismus in der Konfliktszeit.' In *Liberalismus im 19. Jahrhundert. Deutschland im europäischen Vergleich*, D. Langewiesche (ed.), 109–135. Göttingen: Vandenhoeck & Ruprecht, 1988.

Ohlsson, Per T. *100 år av tillväxt. Johan August Gripenstedt och den liberala revolutionen*. Stockholm: Brombergs, 1994.

Olausson, Peter. *Rikedom, makt och status i bondesamhället. Social och ekonomisk skiktning i västra Värmland från 1600-talet till 1800-talets mitt, I*. Karlstad: Karlstad University Studies 30, 2004.

Olausson, Peter. *Gillbergaknaparna. En studie i den svenske storbondens habitus ca 1750–1850*. Gothenburg: Avhandlingar från Historiska institutionen i Göteborg 51, 2007.

Omland, Frank. '"Jeder Deutsche stimmt mit Ja". Die erste Reichstagswahl und Volkabstimmung im Nationalsozialismus am 12. November 1933.' *Zeitschrift der Gesellschaft für Schleswig-Holsteinische Geschichte*, 131 (2006): 133–75.

Omland, Frank. '"Wie ihr wählt, so wirt regiert". Wahlen, Wählerherkunfte und Wählerwanderungen in Schleswig-Holstein 1919–1924.' *Zeitschrift der Gesellschaft für Schleswig-Holsteinische Geschichte*, 132 (2007): 133–76.

Oredsson, Sverker. *Järnvägarna och det allmänna. Svensk järnvägspolitik fram till 1890*. Lund: Bibliotheca historica Lundensis 24, 1969.

Örnklint, Bertil. *Brev till Gerda och andra från Mauritz Hellberg. Sammanställda av Bertil Örnklint*. Karlstad: Toms Bokförlag, 1993.

Ostrom, Elinor. *Governing the Commons. The Evolution of Institutions for Collective Action*. New York: Cambridge University Press, 1990.

Palmowski, Jan. *Urban Liberalism in Imperial Germany. Frankfurt am Main, 1866–1914*. Oxford: Oxford University Press, 1999.

Panebianco, Angelo. *Political Parties: Organization and Power*. Cambridge: Cambridge University Press, 1988.

Peters, Guy B. *Comparative Politics. Theory and Methods*. Houndmills: Macmillan, 1998.

Petersen, Jens Owe. *Schleswig-Holstein 1864–1867. Preußen als Hoffnungsträger und 'Totengräber' des Traums von einem selbständigen Schleswig-Holstein*. Kiel: Christian-Albrechts-Universität zu Kiel, 2000.

Petrocik, John R. & Brown, Thad A. 'Party System Structure and Electoral Realignments.' In *Comparative Political Parties and Party Elites. Essays in Honor of Samuel J. Eldersveld*, B. A. Yeşilada (ed.), 11–54. Ann Arbor: University of Michigan Press, 1999.

Petterson, Lars. *Frihet, jämlikhet, egendom och Bentham. Utvecklingslinjer i svensk folkundervisning mellan feodalism och kapitalism, 1809–1860*. Stockholm: Almqvist & Wiksell, 1992.

Polley, Rainer. 'Ferdinand Tönnies – Lebenserrinnerungen aus dem Jahre 1935 an Kindheit, Schulzeit, Studium und erste Dozententätigkeit (1855–1894).' *Zeitschrift der Gesellschaft für Schleswig-Holsteinische Geschichte*, 105 (1980): 187–227.

Preuss, Hugo. *Das detusche Volk und die Politik*. Jena: Eugen Diedrichs, 1916.

Przeworski, Adam & Teune, Henry. *The Logic of Comparative Social Inquiry*. New York: Wiley, 1970.

Pust, Dieter. *Politische Sozialgeschichte der Stadt Flensburg. Untersuchungen zur politischen Führungsschicht Flensburgs im 18. und 19. Jahrhundert*. Flensburg: Schriften der Gesellschaft für Flensburger Stadtgeschichte 23, 1975.

Putnam, Robert D. *Bowling Alone. The Collapse and Revival of American Community*. New York: Simon & Schuster, 2000.

Raulet, Gérard (ed.). *Historismus, Sonderweg und dritte Wege*. Frankfurt am Main: Peter Lang GmbH, 2001.

Regling, Heinz Volkmar. *Die Anfänge des Sozialismus in Schleswig-Holstein*. Neumünster: Karl Wachholtz Verlag, 1965.

Reinhardt, Georg. *Preußen im Spiegel der öffentlichen Meinung Schleswig-Holsteins 1866–1870*. Neumünster: Karl Wachholtz, 1954.

Roberts, James S. *Drink, Temperance and the Working Class in Nineteenth-Century Germany*. Boston: George Allen & Unwin, 1984.

Rönblom, Hans-Krister. *Frisinnade landsföreningen 1902–1927. Skildringar ur den liberala organisationsrörelsens historia i vårt land*. Stockholm: Saxon & Lindströms Förlags AB, 1929.

Sartori, Giovanni. *Parties and Party Systems. A Framework for Analysis*. Cambridge: Cambridge University Press, 1976.

Sartori, Giovanni. 'The Party Effects of Electoral Systems.' In *Political Parties and Democracy*, L. Diamond & R. Gunther (eds.), 90–105. Baltimore: Johns Hopkins University Press, 2001.

Schattschneider, E. Eric. *Party Government*. New York: American Government in Action Series, 1942.

Schiller, Bernt. *Storstrejken 1909. Förhistoria och orsaker*. Göteborg: Elanders Boktryckeri Aktiebolag, 1967.

Schmidt, Sönke. 'Die Reichstagswahl am 10.1.1874 im 9. schleswig-holsteinischen Wahlkreis (Oldenburg-Plön-Segeberg).' *Zeitschrift der Gesellschaft für Schleswig-Holsteinische Geschichte*, 110 (1985): 173–228.

Schultz Hansen, Hans. 'Demokratie oder Nationalismus – Politische Geschichte Schleswig-Holsteins 1830–1918.' In *Geschichte Schleswig-Holsteins Von den Anfängen bis zur Gegenwart*, U. Lange (ed.), 427–85, 2nd edn. Neumünster: Wachholtz Verlag, 2003.

Schüllerqvist, Bengt. *Från kosackval till kohandel. SAP:s väg till makten (1928–33)*. Stockholm: Tiden, 1992.

Sheehan, James S. *German Liberalism in the Nineteenth Century*. Chicago: University of Chicago Press, 1978.

Sievers, Kai Detlev. 'Peter Christian Hansen (1853–1935) – ein schleswig-holsteinisches Sozialpolitiker der Kaiserzeit.' *Zeitschrift der Gesellschaft für Schleswig-Holsteinische Geschichte*, 104 (1979): 231–52.

Smith, Gordon. 'Between left and right: the ambivalence of European liberalism.' In *Liberal Parties in Western Europe*, E. J. Kirchner (ed.), 16–28. Cambridge: Cambridge University Press, 1988.

Søllinge, Jette D. & Thomsen, Niels. *De danske aviser 1634–1989, II. 1848–1917.* Odense: Dagspressens Fond/Odense universitetsforlag, 1989.

Staaff, Karl. *Det demokratiska statsskicket. Jämförande politiska studier, I.* Stockholm: Wahlström & Widstrand, 1917.

Staaff, Karl. *Politiska tal samt några tal och inlägg vid skilda tillfällen, II.* Stockholm: Wahlström & Widstrand, 1918.

Stenlås, Niklas. 'Kampen om högern – uppbyggnaden av Allmänna valmansförbundet 1904–1922.' In *Anfall eller försvar? Högern i svensk politik under 1900-talet*, T. Nilsson (ed.), 49–82. Stockholm: Santérus Förlag, 2002.

Stolare, Martin. *Kultur & natur. Moderniseringskritiska rörelser i Sverige 1900-1920.* Gothenburg: Avhandlingar från Historiska institutionen i Göteborg 34, 2003.

Stråth, Bo (ed.). *Language and the Construction of Class Identities. The Struggle for Discursive Power in Social Organisation: Scandinavia and Germany after 1800. Report from the DISCO II Conference on Continuity and Discontinuity in the Scandinavian Democratisation Process in Kungälv 7–9 September 1989.* Gothenburg: Historiska institutionen, Göteborgs universitet, 1990a.

Stråth, Bo. 'Liberalismen och moderniseringen av Sverige.' In *Liberala perspektiv. Vision och verklighet i historia och politik. Till Jörgen Weibull sommaren 1990*, 231–250. Höganäs: Förlags AB Wiken, 1990b.

Stråth, Bo. *Union och demokrati. De förenade rikena Sverige och Norge 1814–1905.* Nora: Nya Doxa, 2005.

Suval, Stanley. *Electoral Politics in Wilhelmine Germany.* Chapel Hill: University of North Carolina Press, 1985.

Svenska folkrörelser, I. Nykterhetsrörelse, Politisk arbetarrörelse, Fackföreningsrörelse, Folkbildning, Kooperation. Stockholm: Esselte AB, 1936.

Svärd, Lydia. *Väckelserörelsernas folk i andra kammaren 1867–1911: frikyrkliga och lågkyrkliga insatser i svensk politik.* Stockholm: Svenska Missionsförbundets förlag, 1954.

Therborn, Göran. *Borgarklass och byråkrati i Sverige. Anteckningar om en solskenshistoria.* Lund: Arkiv förlag, 1989.

Therborn, Göran. 'Nation och klass, tur och skicklighet.' In *Den svenska modellen*, P. Thullberg & K. Östberg (eds.), 59–74. Lund: Studentlitteratur, 1994.

Thermænius, Edvard. *Sveriges politiska partier.* Stockholm: Hugo Gebers förlag, 1933.

Thomas, Alastair H. 'Liberalism in Denmark: agrarian, radical and still influential.' In *Liberal Parties in Western Europe*, E. J. Kirchner (ed.), 279–303. Cambridge: Cambridge University Press, 1988.

Thompson, Alastair P. *Left Liberals, the State, and Popular Politics in Wilhelmine Germany.* Oxford: Oxford University Press, 2000.

Tighe, Carl. *Gdańsk. National Identity in the Polish-German Borderlands.* London: Pluto Press, 1990.

Tilton, Timothy A. *Nazism, Neo-Nazism, and the Peasantry.* Bloomington: Indiana University Press, 1975.

Tocqueville, Alexis de. *Democracy in America*. New York: Modern Library, 1981 [1835–40].

Tocqueville, Alexis de. 'Relation of Civil to Political Associations.' In *Foundations of Social Capital*, E. Ostrom & T. K. Ahn (eds.), 12–17. Cheltenham: Edward Elgar, 2003 [1840].

Tönnies, Ferdinand. *Community and Civil Society*. Cambridge: Cambridge University Press, 2001 [1887].

Trägårdh, Lars. 'Det civila samhället som analytiskt begrepp och politisk slogan.' In *Civilsamhället*, E. Amnå (ed.), 13–59. Stockholm: Fritzes, 1999.

Vallinder, Torbjörn. 'Folkpartiets ideologiska och organisatoriska bakgrund 1866–1934.' In *Liberal ideologi och praktik 1934–1984*, 12–79. Stockholm: Folk & Samhälle, 1984.

Viroli, Maurizio. *From Politics to Reason of State. The Acquisition and Transformation of the Language of Politics 1250–1600*. Cambridge: Cambridge University Press, 1992.

Watt, Richard M. *The Kings Depart. The Tragedy of Germany: Versailles and the German Revolution*. New York: Simon & Schuster, 1968.

Weitling, Günter. 'Die Indre Mission und ihre Nachwirkungen in der Geschichte des Grenzlandes Nordschleswig.' *Schriften des Vereins für Schleswig-Holsteinische Kirchengeschichte* 45, (1992): 9–23.

Weitz, Eric D. *Weimartyskland – löfte och tragedi*. Stockholm: Dialogos Förlag, 2009.

Wolff, Stefan. *Disputed Territories. The Transnational Dynamics of Ethnic Conflict Settlement*. New York: Berghahn Books, 2003.

Wulf, Peter. 'Revolution, schwache Demokratie und Sieg in der "Nordmark" – Schleswig-Holstein in der Zeit der Weimarer Republik.' In *Geschichte Schleswig-Holsteins Von den Anfängen bis zur Gegenwart*, U. Lange (ed.), 545–84, 2nd edn. Neumünster: Wachholtz Verlag, 2003.

Index of names